PRAISE FOR RURAL ROOTS TO HARVARD

Rural Roots to Harvard is more than an autobiography; it is an inspirational handbook on the importance of hard work, dedication, and the courage to follow one's dreams. Jarnail Singh's journey from the fields of Punjab to the global stage of Harvard showcases the transformative power of education and his invincible spirit to overcome obstacles.

This book is a must-read for aspiring students, professionals, and anyone looking to be inspired by the remarkable life of a visionary who traversed the distance from a remote village in India to one of the world's most prestigious universities. It reminds us that with perseverance, support, and a relentless pursuit of our goals, the path to excellence is within reach for all of us.

—AMITABH KANT
India's G20 Sherpa and former CEO, NITI Aayog

I first met Jarnail Singh when he reported for attachment in the district in Manipur where I was the Deputy Commissioner (DC), and then more closely when he was posted as the sub-divisional officer (SDO) in my district. Since then, we have stayed in touch, and I have followed his rise in his career with much interest.

Jarnail has now written an autobiographical narrative chronicling his journey from a remote, small village school beneath a tree in Punjab to the hallowed precincts of Harvard University in the USA. It is a captivating read, brimming with inspiration for every aspiring young individual in India. His journey highlights the enduring message that regardless of how poorly placed one is and whichever remote corner of India one comes from, success is achievable through unwavering focus, hard work, and the determination to overcome life's obstacles with honesty and resilience. By seizing upon small opportunities and leveraging them effectively, greater opportunities are bound to come one's way.

Presented in simple language and an engaging style, his life story makes for very interesting reading. In fact, I found it gripping partly because I found many parallels with my own experiences, albeit under different circumstances. I'm sure others will also find echoes of their own journeys within his narrative. I wholeheartedly recommend this book to all readers, not only to young people aspiring for meaningful achievements and but also to young officers serving in the North-eastern region of India.

—S.S. SHARMA IAS (Retd)
Former Secretary (Sports), Government of India

After his first book, *My Tryst with Manipur,* former Chief Secretary of Manipur, Jarnail Singh's *Rural Roots to Harvard* offers a treat, especially for Manipuris who wish to travel back in time to understand remote Manipur. While Singh credits Manipur for his journey to Harvard University, it is equally noteworthy that he contributed to the state's governance as an Indian Administrative Service (IAS) officer. What he reveals in his chapters on Manipur is eye-opening for the present generation and sets on record some narratives of contemporary issues such as the disappearance of border pillars, which remains a matter of concern even today. Given the current developments, including the construction of a border fence along Indo-Myanmar border in the midst of the Myanmar conflict and Manipur crisis, one would look for someone like him to deal with them. I wish he could have been stationed in Chandel for a little longer than he was. As always, his books on Manipur could come in handy for both aspiring and seasoned IAS and Manipur Civil Service officers, whether they work in Manipur or in any Central administration responsible for the North-eastern region of India.

—YUMNAM RUPACHANDRA SINGH
Editor-in-Chief, Impact TV, Manipur

RURAL ROOTS

to

HARVARD

ALSO BY THE SAME AUTHOR

1. ***Project Appraisal, Risk Analysis and Risk Management Techniques***, (co-authored with Dr D.N.S. Dhakal), Konark Publishers, New Delhi, 2023
2. ***Manipur University: Restoring Normalcy***, Konark Publishers, New Delhi, 2022
3. ***With Four Prime Ministers: My PMO Journey***, Konark Publishers, New Delhi 2020
4. ***My Tryst with Manipur: A Memoir***, Konark Publishers, New Delhi, 2018

RURAL ROOTS *to* HARVARD

A JOURNEY OF LEARNING, CHALLENGES AND SUCCESS

JARNAIL SINGH

KONARK

Konark Publishers Pvt. Ltd
206, First Floor,
Peacock Lane, Shahpur Jat,
New Delhi 110 049
Phone: +91-11-41055065
e-mail: india@konarkpublishers.com, us@konarkpublishers.com
website: www.konarkpublishers.com

The photographs used in this book are from the author's personal collection unless otherwise stated.

ISBN: 978-81-963629-6-6

Edited by Dipali Singh

Title and subtitle by Vishnu Ramachandran

Cover Design by Syed Dilshad Ali

Cover and Inside Sketches by Meinam Irikhomba Meetei

Typeset by Saanvi Graphics, Noida

Printed and bound at Saurabh Printers Pvt. Ltd, Greater Noida

This book is affectionately dedicated to my maternal grandmother, the late Sardarni Nihal Kaur, as well as my parents, the late Sardar Dalip Singh and the late Sardarni Surjit Kaur, and my wife, Smt. Seraphina Singh, for providing unwavering support throughout my academic and professional journey.

Contents

PART III: MY CAREER AND STUDIES AT HARVARD

Preface

This book chronicles my academic journey, commencing in 1954 at a remote school in Punjab and culminating at Harvard University in 1988. It delves into my challenging yet carefree childhood, the obstacles I faced during my years as a student, and the important moments that shaped my life. I have also shared the stories of those who encouraged and supported me.

I was born into a family of illiterate parents a couple of years after India gained independence, in the remote village of Balian, nestled in the Malwa region of Punjab. The village school, where my educational journey began in 1954, lacked a proper building. Classes were conducted beneath a *jand* tree (*jand* being the Punjabi word for a type of evergreen thorny tree scientifically known as *Prosopis cineraria* or *Prosopis spicigera*). *Jand* trees thrive in drier regions of India, and have slender branches armed with conical thorns and light bluish-green foliage. During the rains, we would relocate to an abandoned mosque nearby.

After studying in my village school for about three months, I moved to Kanjla, my mother's village. I stayed with my maternal grandmother, who was more than 65 years old and lived alone. This phase of my childhood was both tough as well as adventurous. My grandmother had limited means, with an annual income equivalent to about 450 kg of grains. Even though I was just five years old, I kept her company in her old age and assisted her with household chores. It was at the Government High School in Kanjla where I excelled in studies and proudly achieved the first rank in Class X.

For my college education, I went to Sangrur and later joined Punjab Engineering College in Chandigarh, where I completed my undergraduate and postgraduate degrees in electrical engineering. My engineering studies boosted my confidence. While residing in one of the hostels in Chandigarh, I prepared for the Combined Competitive Examination (CCE) conducted by the Union Public Service Commission (UPSC). To my delight, I passed the examination and joined the Indian Administrative Service (IAS) in July 1974. I was allocated to the Manipur Tripura cadre and served in Manipur state for over 19 years. As a Sub-Divisional Officer (SDO) and later as a Deputy Commissioner (DC), I travelled extensively and visited nearly all villages within my jurisdiction.

As fate would have it, Mrs P.P. Trivedi, IAS, Adviser in the then Planning Commission, visited my district. She appreciated my work and later played an important role in nominating me in 1988 to pursue a Master in Public Administration (MPA) degree in 'Public Policy and Management' at the John F. Kennedy School of Government at Harvard University in the USA. I consider myself fortunate to have been in the right place at the right time and to have encountered individuals who supported me both in my studies and my career. After reflecting on my own career journey, I am convinced that if anyone works diligently and fulfils their assigned responsibilities with dedication, the Indian governance system will consistently recognise and reward their efforts.

During my time at Harvard University, I focused on acquiring skills in public policy analysis, policy formulation, and decision-making. These skills proved invaluable during my tenure as a joint secretary in the Prime Minister's Office (PMO), where I served for eight years (1996-2004). My Harvard education boosted my confidence, leading me to initiate numerous advancements in public administration. These initiatives earned me the 'Prime Minister's Award for Excellence in Public Administration for the Year 2007–08'. I also had the privilege of successfully holding significant positions during crisis situations, including serving as Chief Secretary of Manipur (2004-2008), Chief Executive Officer of Organising Committee Commonwealth Games 2010 Delhi, and Administrator/Vice-Chancellor of Manipur University (2018-2020). In this book, I have discussed the essential qualities of head and heart, as well as the critical skills of public policy analysis and decision-making, all of which are equally crucial for success in public service.

My specialisation and area of interest lie in project appraisal, risk analysis, and risk management. In 2012, I established my own company called 'Project Appraisal Consultants LLP' for consultancy and conducting capacity-building programmes related to project appraisal, risk analysis, and risk management. I have derived immense satisfaction from applying the skills I acquired at Harvard University in my IAS career and other roles I've undertaken. I take pride in sharing my knowledge in this field with professionals through capacity-building programmes.

More than my hard work and determination, I attribute my success in my career to the individuals who supported me at various stages of my education, from school to engineering college, and throughout my service in the IAS. Without their assistance, I might not have got the opportunity to attend Harvard University and achieve whatever I could in my professional career.

Jarnail Singh

Acknowledgements

I would like to begin by expressing my gratitude to the teachers at Kanjla School, where I studied till Class X. This school laid the foundation for my education, nurtured self-confidence, and instilled in me a strong desire for academic excellence. I thank Sardar Gurbachan Singh, my primary school teacher, who helped me in enhancing my handwriting – I came to realise the significance of this skill both in my subsequent studies and during my career in the Indian Administrative Service (IAS). I am indebted to Shri Durga Parshad, the headmaster of the school at that time, who cycled about 25 km on a scorching day in June 1964 to visit my village and counsel my parents about sending me to a city college for higher studies. I express my sincere appreciation to all neighbours in Kanjla village who supported me and my grandmother. I specially thank Kirpal Singh, who served as my guide, mentor, and source of unwavering support throughout my school and college years.

My gratitude extends to my professors and fellow students at Punjab Engineering College, Chandigarh, where I spent six years, earning my BSc and MSc in Engineering and honing my self-confidence. My special thanks to Professor Gurnam Singh and Mr Rajinder Manhas, whose invaluable support sustained me during the challenging period of 1972-74 when I was preparing for the CCE to enter the IAS. I am deeply grateful to Professors K.K. Suri and M.S. Ghumman of Punjab Engineering College, Chandigarh, for encouraging me to pursue a career in the civil services. I acknowledge the tremendous help and support of Dr Ram Lal Goel from Rajindra Medical College, Patiala, who graciously hosted me during my competitive examinations in Patiala.

I express my gratitude to my senior and junior colleagues, as well as the public with whom I collaborated during my early years of service in the IAS in Manipur. I also thank the office staff of SDO Tadubi, DC Chandel, and DC Ukhrul in Manipur as well as the villagers, who accompanied me on extensive foot journeys through the interior areas of Senapati, Chandel and Ukhrul districts. I also appreciate the fairness shown to me by the political leaders in Manipur during my long service in the state.

In a significant turn of events, Mrs P.P. Trivedi, IAS, the Adviser in the then Planning Commission, visited Ukhrul district in Manipur in 1980-81, where I was working as Deputy Commissioner (DC). In 1987-88, when I applied for the Master's in Public Administration programme at Harvard University under Edward S. Mason Program, Mrs Trivedi was the Secretary of the Department of Personnel and Training in the Government of India. Her recollection of her visits to Ukhrul and my work there influenced her to provide me with the opportunity to attend Harvard University, for which I am profoundly indebted to her.

I am immensely grateful to my wife, Seraphina Singh, who not only endured my extended absences during my frequent journeys to the remote hill areas of Manipur but also motivated me to excel in my professional work. The comfort and happiness at home enabled me to wholeheartedly commit to my professional duties.

I am grateful to Meinam Irikhomba Meetei, Assistant Professor in the Department of Fine Arts at Manipur University, for creating the sketches used in the cover design and inside the book.

Last but not the least, I extend my gratitude to K.P.R. Nair and the dedicated editorial team at Konark for their outstanding efforts in bringing this book to fruition.

Acronyms

ADM	Additional District Magistrate
AFSPA	Armed Forces (Special Powers) Act
ATI	Administrative Training Institute
BBMB	Bhakra Beas Management Board
BHEL	Bharat Heavy Electricals Limited
BPs	boundary pillars
BSc (Hons)	Bachelor of Science Honours
BSF	Border Security Force
CBI	Central Bureau of Investigation
CCE	Combined Competitive Examination
CEO	Chief Executive Officer
CMC	Christian Medical College
CrPC	Criminal Procedure Code
CRPF	Central Reserve Police Force
DAV	Dayanand Anglo-Vedic
DC	Deputy Commissioner
DC	Direct Current

DOP&T	Department of Personnel and Training
DySP	Deputy Superintendent of Police
EE	Executive Engineer
GFR	General Financial Rules
HDVC	High-voltage direct current
HIID	Harvard Institute for International Development
HV	high voltage
IAS	Indian Administrative Service
IB	Intelligence Bureau
IIT	Indian Institute of Technology
KV	kilo volt
LBSNAA	Lal Bahadur Shastri National Academy of Administration
LLP	Limited Liability Partnership
MB	Measurement Book
MBBS	Bachelor of Medicine and Bachelor of Surgery
MD	Doctor of Medicine
MIT	Massachusetts Institute of Technology
ML	Marks Late
MLA	Member of Legislative Assembly
MoS	Minister of State
MPA	Master in Public Administration
MR	Manipur Rifles
MSR	Manipur Schedule of Rates

MTech	Master of Technology
MU	Manipur University
MW	megawatts
NCC	National Cadet Corps
NNC	Naga National Council
NPTC	National Power Transmission Corporation Ltd
PCM	Physics, Chemistry and Mathematics
PEC	Punjab Engineering College
PEPSU	Patiala and East Punjab States Union
PET	Physical Education Teacher
PIAM	Project Investment Appraisal and Management
PIL	Public Interest Litigation
PMO	Prime Minister's Office
Powergrid	Power Grid Corporation of India Limited
PPSC	Punjab Public Service Commission
PSEB	Punjab State Electricity Board
PSIDC	Punjab State Industrial Development Corporation Ltd
PWD	Public Works Department
PWD (B&R)	Public Works Department (Buildings and Roads)
RAC	Rajasthan Armed Constabulary
RSS	Rashtriya Swayamsevak Sangh
SDC	Sub-Deputy Collector
SDE	Sub-Divisional Engineer

SDO	Sub-Divisional Officer
SE	Superintending Engineer
SGPC	Shiromani Gurdwara Parbandhak Committee
SOG	Special Operations Group
SP	Superintendent of Police
TA	Teaching Assistant
TIET	Thapar Institute of Engineering and Technology
TNL	Tangkhul Naga Long
UBI	United Bank of India
UG	underground
UNDP	United Nations Development Programme
UPSC	Union Public Service Commission

PART I

GROWING UP IN PUNJAB

CHAPTER 1

Life in Village

I belong to a village called Balian, situated in the Sangrur district of Punjab. Among the tales frequently recounted by the elderly, there is one that traces the origin of our village back to around AD 1750. According to this story, my ancestor had migrated from a distant region, somewhere in present-day Pakistan. He constructed a modest hut, planted a bush, and began to establish a settlement at its current location. An interesting facet of this story is that the village derived its name 'Balian' from the fact that the founder wore earrings (Balian translates to 'earrings' in the Punjabi language).

The founder had three sons: Chhajoo, Laada, and Chandu, along with one stepson, Klaske. The descendants of Chhajoo and Laada lived in the areas named after them—'Chhajoo Patti' and 'Laada Patti,' respectively ('Patti' in Punjabi means a locality). The descendants of Chandu and Klaske were fewer in number and also lived in the village. My family belongs to Chhajoo's lineage and inhabited Chhajoo Patti. Later on, with migration from neighbouring villages, more 'Pattis' were established.

The majority of the village's residents are Jat Sikhs, primarily engaged in agriculture. Other inhabitants belong to various castes with distinct professions—cobblers, goldsmiths, carpenters, masons, *teli*s (*teli*s used oxen-/donkey-driven machines called *kohlu*s to crush mustard seeds for extracting mustard oil, and also operated Persian wheels to draw water from village wells for both humans and animals), tailors, shopkeepers and ironsmiths, among others. The Mazbhi Sikhs, constituting about 20 per cent of the village's population, supported the Jat Sikhs in agricultural and related activities.

In the 1940s, development was scarce in the villages of this region. Before 1947, Balian village was under the jurisdiction of the Jind State. From 1948 to 1956, it was part of PEPSU (Patiala and East Punjab States Union), which later merged with Punjab in 1956. Basic amenities like electricity, water supply and proper roads were nonexistent. Villagers had to manually fetch water from wells for both personal use and their domestic animals. Agriculture primarily relied on rainfall, with only certain areas benefitting from canal water for irrigation. Some farmers had installed Persian wheels driven by oxen and camels.

In 1948, the government began setting up schools in some villages. There were very few educated persons in rural areas, and in my own village, no one had been to school. The rural people depended on traditional Ayurvedic doctors, as there were no healthcare facilities. Farmers' income levels were meagre as they could grow only one crop in a year. To sell surplus grain, the farmers had to take their produce to urban centres, which were about 15 to 25 km away, using bullock carts. The highest-ranking government officials villagers often met were *patwari*s (the lowest level revenue officials responsible for land measurement and record-keeping), police constables, and school teachers. Given the low literacy rate, there was limited awareness among rural residents about the advantages of higher education. Most farmers wanted their children to follow their footsteps and do agriculture. While some aspiring villagers wished their children to become *patwari*s or police constables after getting education, the idea of their children becoming engineers, doctors, or high-ranking government officials was largely unimaginable.

Between 1865 and 1870, Bahaal Singh, a descendant of Chhajoo, was blessed with three sons: Budh Singh, Ran Singh, who later became a *sadhu* (ascetic) and Ghan Singh. Ghan Singh, the youngest, joined the army and received parcels of land as rewards from the then British government in India. He became influential and wealthy, and also commanded respect in the village. Budh Singh, a farmer, had two sons, Alwail Singh and Mihan Singh. Alwail Singh became the head of the family and, due to his amiable nature and effective communication skills, often assisted Ghan Singh in managing domestic matters. He married Shyam Kaur from Khadial village, and took charge of cultivating Ghan Singh's government-allocated land. Both families of Budh Singh and Ghan Singh lived in a *haveli*, a large house.

Travails of My Grandparents

Alwail Singh faced difficulties when the families of Budh Singh and Ghan Singh decided to divide their properties. Budh Singh had already passed away, and Ghan Singh adopted a cunning strategy to keep most of the property for himself. Initially, Alwail Singh was asked to leave the *haveli* along with his wife Shyam Kaur, and he was given a small piece of residential land measuring about 800 square feet, which had only two mud-walled rooms covered by a flimsy roof of thatched grass.

After some time, Mihan Singh, Alwail Singh's younger brother, was also asked to leave the *haveli* and join Alwail Singh. Ghan Singh's decision to deal with each brother separately suited him, as Alwail Singh and Mihan Singh could not unite their efforts to exert combined pressure on him and negotiate for a fair share of the *haveli's* ownership. This haveli had been built through the combined labour and earnings of the entire family.

My grandparents were Alwail Singh and Shyam Kaur. My grandmother possessed golden ornaments received during her marriage, which she had secured in her *sandukh* (a big wooden box) given by her parents to keep her clothes and jewellery. However, when asked to leave the *haveli* by Ghan Singh, she left without her ornaments. Being a proud woman, she never returned to claim her belongings, choosing instead to build her own future through hard work. My grandfather was not aggressive enough to demand his share of the family property, which resulted in my grandparents being left in a difficult position without receiving what was rightfully theirs.

My grandmother expressed her dissatisfaction at being given a small thatched hut. In response, Ghan Singh gave my grandfather another piece of land measuring about 4200 square feet and having two mud rooms. However, Ghan Singh ungraciously declared that he would reclaim half of this land. This angered my grandmother, prompting her to fight for her rights. One day, following Ghan Singh's instructions, the village *patwari* tried to demarcate the 4200-square-foot homestead land between my grandfather and Ghan Singh. Despite recognising the injustice, he could not openly refuse Ghan Singh due to his stature in the village. However, he discreetly advised my grandmother to protest strongly when he came for the land demarcation.

Despite my grandfather's reluctance to quarrel, my grandmother staunchly opposed the division of the homestead land. Like a fierce tigress, she stood her ground on the plot, wielding a sword and threatening the *patwari* and his team with violence if they dared to set foot on the land. On seeing my grandmother's determined stance with her sword drawn, the *patwari* discarded the measuring equipment and fled. So did Ghan Singh, who was following the *patwari*! After this incident, the *patwari* refused to demarcate the plot, and Ghan Singh also developed cold feet. That is how my family retained ownership of the house and even expanded it by two more rooms. Hats off to my brave grandmother, who fearlessly faced challenges head-on!

My grandfather and parents often regaled me with tales of my grandmother's extraordinary bravery. One memorable story centred around her skirmish with the then Raja of Sangrur during a horseback hunting expedition. While coming from her native village Khadial to Balian on a horseback, my grandmother was accompanied by my grandfather who was walking behind. Bags filled with clothes and provisions hung from either side of the horse's belly. In the absence of roads back then, villagers travelled freely on paths through the fields, a norm of the time.

Coincidentally, my grandmother and the Raja of Sangrur happened to cross each other on a narrow path. Unfortunately, during crossing, their horses brushed against each other, jostling her belongings and nearly causing them to fall. Unaware that the person on the other horse was the Raja of Sangrur, my grandmother reacted in frustration and shouted at him in Punjabi, exclaiming, 'Couldn't you see that my horse was about to pass? You should have kept your *khhachar* (pony) away to prevent it from colliding with mine.'

The Raja, being a courteous individual, stopped his horse and apologised. Despite my grandfather's concerns about the well-armed escorts accompanying the Raja, nothing untoward happened. This incident underscored my grandmother's determination, pride, and fearlessness—qualities she displayed when Ghan Singh unjustly deprived my grandfather of his rightful share of the family land. Due to this injustice, my grandmother never set foot in the *haveli* from which she and my grandfather were thrown out one cold night.

Alwail Singh and Shyam Kaur had four children: a daughter and three sons. The eldest was the daughter, followed by Amar Singh, Chattar Singh, and Dalip Singh in that sequence. Amar Singh, an accomplished athlete and shooter, had joined the army at a very young age. However, in the early 1940s, after a few years of military service, he decided to desert the army, absconding with his rifle—a grave violation of military regulations, as desertion with a weapon is a serious offence. Subsequently, he joined a group of men engaged in dacoities. He began drinking and adamantly refused to return to the army. Although Amar Singh rarely visited our family home in the village, he often met some of his friends in Balian. The police had issued an arrest warrant against him, and consistently pressurised my grandfather to hand over Amar Singh to the law enforcement authorities.

Amar Singh always carried his .303 rifle, which, in those days, was a powerful weapon. With it, he carried out dacoities in various locations around the area, causing notable disturbances in law and order. The police formed search parties to track him down, but they had to proceed with caution as he was an ace shooter. In a bid to apprehend him, and preferably kill him, the police devised a plan and bribed some of his associates to aid in his capture.

One fateful day, Sarwan Singh, an associate of Amar Singh, enticed him into a drinking session. After ensuring that Amar Singh was sufficiently intoxicated, Sarwan Singh advised him to dismantle his rifle and carry it in that state when he went back to the village. Simultaneously, Sarwan Singh had alerted the police of Amar Singh's imminent arrival on the outskirts of the village. As the sun began to set, Amar Singh reached the village's *halti,* only to be confronted by the police. In the ensuing confrontation, the police challenged him and fatally shot him in the head. He was killed on the spot. His death was a shock to our family, particularly my grandmother. His descent into alcoholism and straying away from the army had already taken an emotional toll on our family, and his untimely death further deepened our grief.

Later, during my school days in the late 1950s, some persons used to refer to me as the nephew of the infamous dacoit, Amar Singh. My grandmother would often recount stories to us about Amar Singh's accomplishments as an athlete in the army and how his association with bad influences led him down the path of alcohol consumption and criminal activities. She frequently condemned Sarwan Singh for his involvement in leading Amar Singh astray and orchestrating his demise through deceit. She consistently held a wish for Sarwan Singh to experience a similar destiny, and as fate would have it, he was shot dead by his own younger brother in his field. After Sarwan Singh's death, my grandmother would often remark that justice had been served.

My Birth

My father was Dalip Singh, the youngest son of Alwail Singh. My mother, Surjit Kaur, was the daughter of Bakhtaur Singh and Nihal Kaur from Kanjla village, and she happened to be in Kanjla at the time of my birth. Back in those days, there were only one or two hospitals in each district of Punjab. Deliveries were conducted by midwives in the villages. Although they were experienced, they lacked formal training and could not handle advanced equipment or complicated deliveries. Fortunately, Fattan Kaur, a renowned midwife of Kanjla, assisted my mother during my birth.

My parents did not document the exact date of my birth because there was no system in place for registration of births and deaths in Punjab's villages in those times. My mother recalled that I was born four days before Diwali and two years after violence had erupted between Hindus/Sikhs and Muslims during the Partition of India. This meant that I was born in 1949, just ahead of Diwali. However, when I was enrolled in the school in Kanjla, my date of birth was recorded as 14 September 1949.

My grandfather named me Eikam Singh due to an additional toe on my left foot. He also considered 21 a lucky number and believed that I brought blessings to the family. However, my maternal aunt, Labh Kaur, later changed my name to Jarnail Singh—the literal translation of the English word 'General' in Punjabi is 'Jarnail'. It may be worth mentioning here that during that era, Jat Sikhs in Punjab were fond of naming their children after military ranks. Hence, names like 'Karnail Singh' which is the Punjabi translation of 'Colonel', 'Kaptan' Singh where 'Kaptan' is the Punjabi translation of 'Captain' and 'Major' Singh were quite common. My younger brother was named Karnail Singh.

Even though I come from a family of Jat Sikhs, my family members were devout followers of Swami Ishwarananda. He had a small temple and orchard called *Kutian* (a group of small huts), situated about one kilometre from the village. My father visited *Kutian* regularly to help in construction of the temple complex and tend to the trees there. Through his association with Swami Ishwarananda, my father learnt many *sloka*s, as well as absorbed the narratives of the *Mahabharata* and the *Ramayana*, shared by the Swami with his disciples every day. The Swami himself hailed from Haridwar, where his sect's main congregation was based.

When I was a few months old, my parents took me to Swami Ishwarananda to seek his blessings. He immersed his front toe in sweetened water and chanted some *mantras*. This ritual, known as '*charan ghol*', involved pouring the blessed water in my mouth. He emphasised that, like all his followers, I should uphold five core practices: abstaining from intoxicants such as liquor, refraining from consuming meat and eggs, avoiding tobacco and speaking the truth always. The Swami believed that adhering to these principles would shape me into an important person, bringing laurels to the family. I do not know whether it was the Swami's blessings or some other influence, I have followed these five practices throughout my life. Both my parents and grandfather used to attribute my success in life to Swami Ishwarananda, who strongly believed in the purity of life, dedication and hard work.

Swami Ishwarananda would often embark on foot pilgrimages to Haridwar, Prayagraj (Allahabad) and Kashiji (Varanasi), accompanied by my grandfather on these long and risky journeys spanning over two months. Whenever I asked my grandfather why they chose to walk instead of taking the train, he explained that it gave them greater spiritual satisfaction. He would often narrate stories of the '*deras*' where they would rest for the nights during these long journeys.

In his diary, he meticulously documented the names of all the *deras* and villages where they halted during the travels. Among these entries, he also described a dense forest that pilgrims would typically avoid for the fear of encountering wild animals, particularly wolves and leopards. Instead of passing through the forest, they would take a circuitous route which was safe but longer. However, there was one occasion when they decided to take the shorter route through the thick forest, on the suggestion of a well-built and confident *sadhu* who assured them of his capability to fend off wild animals with his machete. My grandfather's diary essentially served as a written roadmap outlining the route from our village to Kashiji and Prayagraj.

Recollections of My Early Childhood

I do not know from what age one begins to remember/recollect events of their childhood later in life. Elders often narrate incidents of one's early years, including both intelligent and mischievous actions. Personally, I recall some incidents from my early childhood, including some places and people involved in those incidents. I believe my memories started to become clearer around the age of four.

I remember playing with my younger brother, Karnail Singh, in front of the main door of our house and watching stray dogs in the street. I had a sense of responsibility to protect my younger brother Karnail from these dogs. Whenever they approached us, I would scare him by saying they might bite and persuaded him to come inside the house.

Once, Swami Ishwarananda advised our family to take all children to Naina Devi, a holy shrine situated atop a hill near Anandpur Sahib, now in the state of Himachal Pradesh. My grandparents were devout worshippers of Goddess Naina Devi and made annual pilgrimages to the temple in July or August. In those days, transportation arrangements were not as efficient as today, so the journey to Naina Devi typically spanned three to four days.

In 1953, when I was about four years old, our family went on a pilgrimage to Naina Devi. Unfortunately, before reaching Anandpur Sahib, a sudden flash flood inundated the Sirsa rivulet, leaving our bus stranded in the midst of gushing water. The women and children were safely evacuated to the bank, but the male members of our group, including my grandfather, started to pull the bus out of the rivulet using ropes. As I sat on the bank of the Sirsa rivulet, watching my grandfather standing waist-deep in the water, I started crying and begged him not to stay there, fearing he might drown. My mother often recounted this incident, and I have a faint memory of sitting in my mother's lap on one side of the Sirsa rivulet, weeping and shouting, '*Baba, pani andar na jao, dub jawenga. Baba pani andar na jao, dub jawenga.'* (Grandfather, do not go in the water; you will drown). Fortunately, the pilgrims managed to pull the bus, and the journey resumed.

While travelling from Anandpur Sahib to Kaulan's Pond, where the ascent to the temple began, I remember seeing distant lights in the midst of surrounding darkness. During that journey, my grandfather gave me biscuits, and I still vividly recall their taste, rather like the Britannia biscuits I used to enjoy at the Rajpura bus stand between 1966 and 1973, when I commuted to the Punjab Engineering College in Chandigarh from my village. Upon reaching the hilltop, I sat on my grandfather's shoulders as he handed me some one-paisa coins to give to the beggars who followed us on the way to the Naina Devi shrine. He also gave me a one-rupee coin. I continued to offer one-paisa coins to the beggars, but at one point, as my father later told me, one beggar persistently followed us. Frustrated, I gave him my one-rupee coin, saying, *'Lay ikk rupia, pichha chhad.'* (Take one rupee and do not follow us now.)

I recall the day when my family went to harvest onions from one of our agricultural lands—a one-acre field irrigated by a Persian wheel known as 'Pondewala Khuh'. I played in the field, throughout the day, chasing butterflies and running around. As evening approached and a portion of the crop was harvested, my family members packed the onions and left for our house. It wasn't until they arrived home that they realised I was missing. My father rushed back to the field, where I was still playing, unaware of their absence. I recall hearing my father shouting for me. He took me home, and during the journey, he mentioned that my grandmother had made *khichdi* for dinner. I still remember running barefoot, tightly holding his hand near the village *halti*. I had imagined that *khichdi* would be something delicious, but when I ate it, I did not like it. To this day, I still have an aversion to *khichdi*. I wonder how I was quite happy playing in the dark onion field and did not cry when I was left alone. Perhaps my dislike for *khichdi* developed as a belated reaction to that incident.

We had another agricultural field located about 1.5 km away from the village, towards Swami Ishwarananda's *Kutian.* One day, my cousin Charan Kaur, affectionately known as Charno, and I insisted on accompanying our parents to the field. We were taken along for some distance, but every time they tried to send us back, we cried and stubbornly persisted in following them. After all attempts to send us back to the village failed, our parents devised a clever ruse as they did not want the responsibility of babysitting us. Spotting a herd of goats coming towards us, our parents shouted that they were wolves! Fearing for our safety, we ran back home to escape what we believed was an impeding attack. That's how our parents managed to get rid of us.

My mother used to wash my hair once a week with sour curd, an act I hated. During these hair washes, my mother would vigorously rub my scalp, and at times, the sour curd would sting my eyes. Like many other houses in the village, we lacked a proper drainage system, and all wastewater was collected in a small chamber, emptied once a day using buckets.

One fateful day, in the midst of my hair wash, my mother went inside to bring more water. Sensing an opportunity to escape, I tried to run away, but fell headfirst into the water chamber, with legs up. I could have drowned if my mother had not come quickly and pulled me out. After that incident, I never tried to run away during the dreaded hair wash.

In those days in Punjab, a cluster of jewellery called *saggi phull* was popular. It was worn on the head and consisted of three cone-shaped inverted golden cups, adorned with sparkling and multi-coloured glass pieces. As I was the eldest child in the family, my maternal grandmother had a gold-plated *saggi phull* specially made for me. It was quite unconventional for a boy to wear such jewellery, but my mother used to attach it to my head for ceremonial functions like weddings. It was a cumbersome process to fasten and remove it. As I grew older, my mother decided to have the goldsmith in our village extract the gold from the *saggi phull* so that it could be used elsewhere.

In the early 1950s, it was customary for young men in Punjab villages to wear earrings and a specially crafted gold necklace called *kantha*. My father also wore golden earrings with a peacock design. Following this tradition, my parents pierced my ears, assuming that I would wear custom-made earrings in the future. Small silver earrings were inserted in my ears, and the ear piercings were somewhat painful. However, in 1964 when I moved to Government Ranbir College in Sangrur, I discarded the earrings. Even after more than 70 years, the scars from the piercings are still there, though the holes themselves have closed up.

In 1954, my parents enrolled me in the newly opened school in Balian. At that time, the village school lacked a proper building and functioned under two *jand* trees, as well as in an unused room of the mosque. Following the Partition, the Muslim population in the village had migrated to Pakistan. Most days, we sat on our spread-out gunny bags beneath one of the *jand* trees to study. These trees were covered with thorns that frequently fell to the ground, pricking our bare feet.

The school teacher had affixed a red mail box to the trunk of the second *jand* tree for people to drop off their letters. *Jand* trees typically thrive in arid desert regions and have small leaves that provide no shade. Additionally, these trees produce beans that attract large brown ants, and their bites can be quite painful. Therefore, sitting beneath these trees was an uncomfortable experience.

The school lacked a hand pump for drinking water, relying solely on a small Persian wheel to lift water from the well. Once, my friend named Gohda and I went to drink water, but we were too young to push the Persian wheel's handle, even with our combined strength. As I stood by the side, Gohda tried to reach into the well to touch the water in the Persian wheel bucket. Unfortunately, he lost his balance and fell into the well with a loud noise. I shouted for help, and fortunately, some senior students rushed to the scene and pulled Gohda out to safety.

One day, my mother gave me a new schoolbag and also a new gunny bag to use as a mat. During school hours, it started raining and we took shelter in the mosque room. The heavy rain and thunder scared me. When the school ended in the evening, a group of students who were eyeing my schoolbag advised that leaving it in the mosque would protect it from the damage by lightning. Believing them, I left the bag behind. However, I didn't go home out of fear of my mother's scolding. I sat on a wooden platform at the junction of three streets, about 30 metres short of our house. Neighbours who saw me sitting there late into the evening informed my mother, who came to take me home.

The next day, when my father accompanied me to school to retrieve my new schoolbag, it was nowhere to be found. It appeared that those students had taken it after I had foolishly left it behind. After I grew older, whenever I saw that wooden platform, it served as a reminder of that sad evening of 1954.

One late evening, our family members gathered for dinner in the courtyard. My father climbed the staircase, and I followed him. However, he had to attend to an urgent matter, so he descended quickly, assuming I could do the same. However, I stood at the top of the stairs, crying and calling for my father to carry me down. Since he did not respond immediately, I shouted abuses at him while remaining on the staircase. My grandfather, Alwail Singh, who was also dining in the courtyard, heard my rude language and became angry. He climbed the stairs and slapped me hard on my cheek. My cries grew even louder. My mother hurried up the stairs and brought me down. The force of my grandfather's slap left a lasting memory; I have never forgotten it. After the incident, my mother was so angry with him that she did not speak to anyone for many days.

In 1954, our joint family owned about seven acres of agricultural land. However, due to our growing needs, we had to rent additional agricultural land for cultivation. One such piece of land was about one acre plot in size, located roughly 4 km away from the village. This fertile land was irrigated by a Persian wheel. My father and uncle would head to the field and start ploughing it about one hour before sunrise. My mother or my aunt, Dhan

Kaur, would bring them their morning meal, along with a pitcher full of *lassi* (buttermilk), around 9 a.m. to the field.

One day, as my father was ploughing this distant field, I accompanied my mother on foot. I still have vivid memories of walking alongside her on the sandy path. We walked for about 1.5 km, along the Kotla Branch canal before venturing onto a path towards our field through bushes, some of which bore berries. We crossed our Tahlianwala field and continued along a narrow path bordering adjacent fields, eventually entering a forest. There, I could see fruits hanging from branches. With my mother's permission, I plucked one and tasted it. It tasted like a cucumber but was the size of a *bhindi* (lady's finger) and not particularly sweet or bitter. My mother told me that it was called *kakkar* in Punjabi and could be eaten with salt.

Walking barefoot in the forest, I got pricked by thorny plants and bushes. After roughly 10 minutes, we emerged from the forest and saw my father ploughing with my uncle. I could also see peacocks gracefully roaming and eating insects in the freshly ploughed field. On the way, I saw many peacocks taking flights from the tall *Shisham* trees and landing on the large trees near the Kotla Branch canal.

My family had constructed an outhouse for domestic animals and to store agricultural tools. One evening, while I went with my father to the outhouse, my grandfather asked me whether I could lift four bricks at once. He tempted me with the promise of one rupee if I succeeded. I carefully arranged four bricks, stacking them one above the other, and attempted to lift them. Tears welled up as I lost my balance and had to quickly drop the bricks to the ground. Unfortunately, one brick hit me on my right foot, causing it to bleed. This injury troubled me for about one month. In the evening, when my grandfather came home, my grandmother scolded him for expecting a child less than five years to lift four bricks at once. To this day, the scar on my right foot serves as a reminder of that incident.

CHAPTER 2

A Turning Point

My mother had contracted smallpox during her childhood, but fortunately, she survived. As fate would have it, my younger brother Karnail also got this contagious disease. I vividly remember him, lying on a cot in one corner of our house, crying. Due to the risk of infection, my parents did not allow me to go near him. Sadly, Karnail did not recover from smallpox and passed away. I still recall my grandfather carrying his lifeless body in his arms near the village *halti*. I walked alongside my father, unaware of the situation. I was later informed that they were taking Karnail's body for burial.

Sikhs usually practice cremation, but in my brother's case, I was told that he would be buried near the Goonga Dera, a deserted place across the village pond. It was surrounded by bushes, and on one side, there was a mound of earth that appeared to be the remains of a building.

My maternal grandmother, Nihal Kaur, lived alone in Kanjla village, which was about 11 km from Balian. She came to our village along with a few relatives to mourn my younger brother's death and stayed overnight. The next morning, she left for Kanjla on foot, accompanied by fellow mourners, as there was no other means of transport available at that time. I joined my mother in seeing off my grandmother and other relatives. We had walked about 100 metres and crossed the village pond when my mother initially wanted me to return with her. However, I insisted on accompanying my grandmother to Kanjla. So, my mother and grandmother agreed to walk about 100 metres further, hoping that I change my mind. This continued until we were near *Kutian*.

After some discussions between my mother and grandmother, they decided that I could accompany my grandmother to Kanjla. The plan was for my father to bring me back to Balian after a few days. I was delighted with this arrangement and walked from Balian to Kanjla with my grandmother. I was partly carried by relatives and partly walked barefoot. This journey from Balian to Kanjla marked a turning point in my life.

Living in My Grandmother's Village

My parents were concerned that I might feel homesick in Kanjla within a few days and would want to return to Balian. However, I enjoyed staying with my grandmother, and, in turn, she appreciated my company since she was living alone. After about one week, my grandfather came to fetch me, but I refused to go with him. Instead, I started attending the school in Kanjla, which was located near our house. This was unlike Balian, where the school was far away, and I had to walk through narrow lanes with intimidating stray dogs. In Kanjla, I had half a dozen friends in the neighbourhood who also attended the same school. Recognising my desire to stay in Kanjla, my grandmother enrolled me in school and purchased a new bag, slate, and other study materials. I found staying with grandmother in Kanjla much more comfortable than in Balian. Among the many things she did for me, she never forgot to buy fruits and biscuits for me from street hawkers every day.

In the 1800s, most of the houses in the villages of this area (later known as PEPSU) were constructed using *kacha* mud bricks. The roofs of these mud houses were made with dried reeds and bamboo grass, plastered with clay mixed with wheat chaff to bind it. To ensure that the clay had adhesive properties, villagers extracted clay from the bottoms of the dried ponds. These mud houses offered comfort in both winter and summer, as the insulating qualities of the mud walls and roofs served well in the absence of electricity. Moreover, the raw materials needed for maintaining the mud houses were readily available locally. However, repairing the walls and roofs was challenging, and some mud houses would collapse during heavy rains due to the varying strength of the materials used. The masons who constructed these mud houses had not received any formal training but learnt the art of construction from their forefathers.

In the early 1900s, brick kilns were established, and some families began using baked bricks to build their houses. Almost all families who could afford it added rooms constructed with baked bricks to their existing mud houses. Consequently, during the period from 1920 to 1950, all brick houses had baked brick rooms standing alongside the older mud structures. Villagers did not demolish their mud houses but kept them for storing materials like wheat chaff or for housing cattle.

My grandmother's house in Kanjla was also a combination of mud and brick construction. The spacious rear room had minimal lighting, with only one window near the door that opened into our courtyard. The other three walls had no windows or doors. At the back of this large mud room, there was a roughly 10-inch hole in the roof, covered with an inverted iron or clay bowl, known as a *mogha* in Punjabi. This *mogha* had raised sides to prevent rainwater from leaking into the room. Whenever my grandmother needed more light in the room, she would ask me to remove the *mogha* cover, allowing her to carry out tasks like fetching wheat chaff from the room for our buffalo.

This dark room was the most important space in the house, and both of us would sleep there during winter. My grandmother's *sandukh* was placed in the centre of this room, along the half-wall that divided the area into two sections. She kept her money and other valuable belongings in an *almirah* inside the rear room. One-third of the rear room was used for storing wheat chaff, and there was an old iron trunk with a broken lid where I kept my school books and stationery. Our quilts and spare bedsheets were stacked on one bed, and various household items were scattered in different corners of the room. Just near the entrance of the room, my grandmother had placed about a dozen pitchers to store pulses, salt, jaggery, tea leaves and other edibles.

My grandmother was around 65 years old and had been living alone for a few years before I moved to Kanjla. She used a five-foot-long stick made of mulberry tree wood for support while walking. She was the poorest person in the locality, owning only 2.5 acres of agricultural land that yielded a meagre annual income. She had to cover all her household expenses for the year with this income and had no funds for even minor house repairs.

Out of her six children, she tragically lost three sons and one daughter at a very young age, leaving only my mother, Surjit Kaur, and her younger sister, Labh Kaur, in the family. My grandfather, Bakhtaur Singh, succumbed to leg cancer. I have vague memories of my grandfather suffering from leg sores and talking to himself throughout the night. He would often stay awake, wandering aimlessly outside during the midnight hours. Unfortunately, due to the lack of access to adequate medical treatment and pain-relieving medicine in the village, he had no choice but to endure his suffering until he eventually passed away.

During the 1950s, there was no source of electricity in Punjab except for isolated diesel engines used by district-level government functionaries. Work on the Bhakra Dam project started in 1948, and electricity reached Kanjla village only in 1959. We relied on crude kerosene lamps with flickering flames for lighting, which was not suitable for night-time study.

By the 1950s, villagers had started installing hand pumps to draw groundwater for domestic use. My grandmother also got one so that we could store water in covered earthen pitchers. Water stayed cool in these pitchers, and my grandmother used them to keep milk fresh and prevent it from souring.

My Memorable School

The school in Kanjla was established in 1949 as a primary school, housed in a brick building located opposite the common village well (*halti*). When I joined school in 1954-55, there were already five classes senior to mine and two regular teachers: Gurbachan Singh and Surjit Kaur. As the number of classes increased, more teachers joined, and the school was upgraded to Class VIII.

Teaching in those years was not highly competitive, and one teacher would often manage two to three lower-level classes simultaneously. The main focus in Class I was on memorising numbers up to 100 and practising Punjabi writing on a wooden board called *phatti* with erasable black ink. Our school day began with a morning assembly, where we recited a religious hymn from the Sikh scriptures. Over time, the national anthem, 'Jana Gana Mana', was added. The class monitor assisted the teacher in maintaining discipline and ensuring that daily assignments were completed. After finishing our class assignments, we got them checked at the end of the school day. In the last period, our teacher had us line up and count up to 100 aloud. When the final bell rang, we sprinted back to our homes.

During the 1954-55 academic year, there were approximately 100 students in the school. As the number of students increased, the Kanjla village panchayat relocated the school to the Gurdwara, where it continued until mid-1958.

In the early 1900s, various localities in the villages had their own *haltis*, which were operated using animal or human power. In Kanjla, a *halti* was possibly constructed in the early 1930s in the *Vadda Vehda* (big locality) where my grandmother lived. A raised platform was constructed by the villagers to keep the water safe from contamination. Cows, buffaloes, and oxen would come from the fields to drink water at the long water tank at the *halti*. During its construction in 1930s, a decree had been inscribed on the main wall of the water tank by the village elders: '*Kapda douna, aurat auni, mais namauhni mana hai. Chati ikk rupiah*' (Washing clothes, the coming of women and bathing buffalo are prohibited. Fine one rupee). This *halti* had facilities for bathing of men, but did not provide for women, who were barred from entering.

My grandmother's yearly earnings amounted to approximately 450 kg of grains, and she had to use it carefully throughout the year. She would stack bags of grain near the front pillar in the rear room with a small bag on top. She would use a bowl to scoop out the required amount from the top bag whenever she needed to buy vegetables, fruits, and other items from street hawkers. In those days, most hawkers and shopkeepers operated on a barter system, accepting food grains instead of currency coins.

We had a buffalo and a calf, which my parents had given to my grandmother. From the moment I started living with my grandmother, I began assisting her with household chores, such as filling pitchers and buckets with water from the hand pump. In the initial years, when I was about five to six years old, my grandmother used to carry about 10 kg of wheat on her head in a small bag to the grinding machine, which was about 750 metres away, to get the grain pounded into *atta* (flour). I would accompany her to the grinding machine.

During the scorching summer months of May and June, most of our neighbours would sleep on their rooftops. However, some men chose to sleep in the streets to protect their homes from thieves. We didn't have anyone to safeguard our most precious possession, our buffalo. In summers, our buffalo and calf were tethered in the courtyard outside our house. Sleeping on the rooftop like our neighbours would have made it relatively easy for a thief to enter the courtyard, which was connected to the street, and steal the buffalo during the night. Furthermore, since my grandmother was too frail to carry the *charpai*s (cots) to the roof, and I was too young to help, our best option was to sleep in the narrow, mosquito-infested street. The streets would become pitch dark and silent by 9 p.m., making it a bit scary to sleep outside. While some people also slept in the street, about 50 yards away from us near the main village entrance, the barks of the stray dogs would signal if they heard any sound or saw intruders. The village *chowkidar* patrolled the area, hitting the ground with a large stick and advising vigilance at night. To feel safe, I would wrap myself in a sheet, even in the sweltering summer heat.

In the winter of 1955-56, one day, we were warming ourselves near a fire burning at our neighbour Ajaib Singh's doorstep. Unfortunately, I was sitting with my face towards the fire but my back towards the street. The street was narrow, and our next-door neighbour's helper was trying to lead his camel to the field. The camel was reluctant to move, and as the helper attempted to pull it forward, it suddenly leaped and moved sideways instead of walking along the street. I felt an excruciating pain as it kicked me in the side. I fell with my face up while the camel stamped its right rear foot on my chest. I briefly lost consciousness, but luckily, there were no other injuries, and I survived. It was a perilous incident, but I was fortunate that the kicks were not severe.

Our neighbours were predominantly involved in agriculture, occupied throughout the year. They would rise early in the morning, prepare tea and meals for their labourers, and attend to their domestic animals, which included oxen and buffaloes. However, only our immediate neighbour Mengal Singh, an unmarried elderly man of about 65, residing alone in a *kacha* house, and our family were not engaged in agricultural activities.

A middle-aged person named Marha, commonly referred to as Mian, worked as a helper for another neighbour, Gurdial Singh. Marha, a Muslim who chose not to migrate to Pakistan during the Partition, opted to remain in Kanjla. He was a frail person with a wrinkled face. He resided with Gurdial Singh's family in their outhouse and worked diligently for them. My grandmother would often recount that Marha had survived the 1947 riots, a period of intense conflict between Muslims and Sikhs/Hindus, by hiding for a month. He sought refuge in Gurdial Singh's room, which was meant for storing husk. Gurdial Singh's family played a crucial role in saving him from almost certain death, and as a result, he continued to stay with them.

In the evenings, whenever I visited my neighbour, I would often meet Marha. He was a cheerful person who had accepted his circumstances. In 1959, Marha left Kanjla permanently and settled in Malerkotla. I still remember the day of his departure. Gurdial Singh had arranged a cart to transport his belongings from Kanjla to Malerkotla, and as he bid farewell to Kanjla, Marha had tears in his eyes.

In winters, we would tie our buffalo inside the house and bolt the door from inside. However, since it was relatively easy for anyone to scale a 10-foot wall and enter our courtyard, my grandmother feared thieves might harm both of us and steal the buffalo. That is why we both slept in our rear room. During my early childhood, I was of no help to my grandmother as I was too young to confront a thief. Moreover, since all families slept inside their houses during winter, no one would hear even if we shouted for help. Keeping this in mind, my grandmother was very cautious at night. Her sole possession was the buffalo; she had no gold ornaments left, as they had all been sold to finance the weddings of her two daughters.

On one harsh winter night when we were sleeping, there was a loud thud-like noise in our courtyard. She suspected that someone had jumped from the stairs into our courtyard. Luckily, our rear room door was locked from inside. After hearing the sound, she whispered that she could hear someone walking in our courtyard. Then, she said in a loud voice, '*Jarnail, bahar dekh vehde wich kaun ha*i (Jarnail, check who is outside in the courtyard).' I was frightened and clutched my quilt more tightly. But it seemed the intruder heard her voice and, fearing that there was a male adult inside the house, immediately fled towards the staircase and leaped over the wall. After a while, we could hear the sound of running footsteps in the deserted street and a few dogs barking. This incident left us shaken. Following that incident, my cousin

Mohinder Singh started sleeping in our house during the winter, which provided reassurance.

In contrast to my experience in Balian, I found many friends of my age in my neighbourhood in Kanjla. Among them were Jagga Singh, Amarjit Singh, Pritam Kaur, Murat Kaur, and Kirpal Kaur. Additionally, I had older companions like Kirpal Singh and Harnek Singh, who were always willing to offer guidance with homework, be it in reading or writing. Despite facing financial challenges, I was able to bear them and enjoy my time with my friends. The affection and care from my grandmother ensured that I never missed my parents and the life I had in Balian. I quickly adapted to life in Kanjla with my grandmother.

Living with My Grandmother

The neighbours empathised with my grandmother. Whenever I played outside, I could hear people referring to me as the grandson of Nihal Kaur 'Burhi', the widow of Bakhtaur Singh. *Burhi* means 'old lady' in Punjabi. Since she neither had adequate money nor enough food grains to buy vegetables every day, she would often prepare four to five chapatis for both of us and then instruct me to bring cooked pulses (called *dal* in Punjabi) or vegetables in a small bowl from one of our neighbours. Sometimes my grandmother would prepare *chutney* by grinding onions, chillies, and salt to add flavour to our meals. Life was tough for us, but I never realised it at that time. Whenever I went to a neighbour's house to ask for *dal* or vegetables, no one ever refused me. They all gave it to me with a smile, always willing to help.

My grandmother suffered from migraine attacks. I would often see her either working or lying down with a cloth tied around her head to soothe the pain. She frequently asked me to get medicine for her headaches. The shop owner, Lal Chand, would give me Anacin, an analgesic that provided her some relief. Whenever my grandmother needed medicine, I would hurry to Lal Chand's shop with a small bowl of food grains. He accepted the grains and gave me Anacin powder wrapped in paper. It seemed her frequent consumption of Anacin damaged her stomach lining, leading to the development of a stomach ulcer that later progressed into stomach cancer in 1961, the cause of her eventual demise.

Most of the families in the village kept domestic animals like buffaloes, calves and oxen. A few also had camels. Buffaloes provided milk, while oxen and camels were essential for agricultural work in the fields, including ploughing, land levelling, harvesting wheat, and pulling carts to transport grains and animal fodder. These animals required daily feeding and cleaning of their living areas to prevent disease. Our only source of milk was our buffalo. Every day, I pumped water from the hand pump for the buffalo and calf. This task was relatively easy. One of the daily chores my grandmother did, in addition to preparing meals for both of us, was cleaning the house and collecting the dung from the buffalo and calf in a heap for disposal. Due to her advanced age, carrying buffalo dung on her head and disposing it of outside the village *darwaja* (entrance) became difficult for my grandmother. So, it became my responsibility to carry the dung in an iron bowl every morning and dump it outside the *darwaja*. Since only women typically disposed of dung, my friends used to tease me, saying that I was doing a girl's task. I used to feel shy and embarrassed, but we had no alternative. Even today, I feel awkward when I remember how I carried buffalo dung on my head in a big iron bowl!

Sarson ka saag is one of the most important dishes prepared during the winter months in Punjab. Tender mustard leaves are plucked from mustard fields, and since it is popular, farmers allowed other villagers to take these leaves from their fields. Quite often, I accompanied my grandmother to gather mustard leaves, and no one ever stopped us. However, one day we faced an embarrassing situation when we went to pluck mustard leaves from our own field, located about 1.5 km from our house on the eastern side of the village. Upon reaching our field, we found that the mustard leaves were too small and unsuitable for plucking. My grandmother then decided that we should go further east along the road beyond 'Gutu Di Khuhi', a well-known landmark on the road leading to Ladda.

Walking slowly, we reached the boundary between Kanjla and Khillarian, a neighbouring village. Since we had never ventured into these fields before, my grandmother did not realise that we had crossed into Khillarian's territory. While my grandmother waited, I ran about 150 metres further to the east, climbed a small sand dune, and discovered a beautiful field with perfect mustard leaves. Excited, I called out to my grandmother to join me, but I heard her sternly say, 'Come back at once!' Surprised, I hurried back to her. Upon reaching the top of the sand dune, I saw an elderly man holding a large *khunda* (a six-foot bamboo stick with curved end for better hand grip), standing near my grandmother and scolding her for damaging his mustard crop. The old man threatened both of us with the *khunda* and instructed us not to pluck a single mustard leaf from his field. We were frightened and began walking back to our village, exhausted but relieved that we had escaped a possible beating.

A couple of times a week, I accompanied my grandmother to our field in Dakhaanawala to gather green fodder for our buffalo. Green fodder, especially sorghum, was quite beneficial for increasing the milk production of animals, particularly buffaloes. Our Dakhaanawala field was about 2 km from our house. The path to our field was uneven and in the early morning, before sunrise, it was quite desolate. On the left side of our field, there was a jungle where jackals and foxes roamed. There were thick bushes scattered around, and from a distance, I could spot some dark figures sitting on a log of wood. Every time I passed that spot, I felt scared, thinking they were ghosts. I had heard stories that an old lady was murdered there many years ago, and villagers often shared tales of ghosts searching for her killers in that area. Whenever I crossed that spot, I ran at full speed without looking at it. Because of my fear of ghosts, I was always hesitant about going to the Dakhaanawala field with my grandmother, especially in the early morning when there was no one in the fields.

My grandmother also owned a field towards Changal village, measuring about half an acre. This field consisted of sandy soil and was not suitable for growing crops like wheat or maize. Only sorghum or *guvara* was cultivated here, which we used as fodder for our buffalo. Since this area was less fertile, and farming here relied heavily on rainwater, very few people could be seen working in the fields on this side of the village.

One hot afternoon, I accompanied my grandmother to our Changal field. She had tied a sickle with a rope and carried it on her head. Both of us were walking on a narrow path between fields, and my grandmother kept telling me stories to distract me from my fear. On both sides of the path, there were sorghum and *guvara* fields. Suddenly, as we neared our field, mayhem struck. A wild cat pounced on my grandmother, landing right on her head! Fortunately, as my grandmother was carrying the sickle on her head, the cat's mouth got stuck in it. My grandmother screamed in fear, but the cat fell to the ground. Instead of becoming a predator, the cat became the prey and began running away with the sickle stuck in its mouth. Luckily, it eventually managed to free itself, and the sickle fell off after some distance. We got scared and decided to return home without harvesting or collecting any green fodder from our field. After that incident, my grandmother never went to the Changal field.

Our monthly requirement of *atta* was about 10 to 15 kg. When I reached the age of around eight years, I took on the responsibility of carrying about 10 kg of wheat grains on my head to the *chakki* (grinding machine). Generally, the machine operator waited for a sufficient number of customers before starting the *chakki*. Although my load for grinding was the smallest, this monthly task was crucial for our meals. While all the families in our neighbourhood sent adults to grind flour, I was the only boy under 10 years old doing this chore.

We spent a considerable amount of time playing near the *halti*. While the adults sat on its boundary walls, chatting as they waited for their turns to bathe, we children had fun riding the wooden plank which rotated the Persian wheel. After pulling the plank up midway, one of us would unlock the hinge near the central gear wheels, causing the plank to rotate back under the weight of the water-filled buckets on the Persian wheel. One day, while we were riding the plank, I had to unlock the hinge from the central gear wheels. Something went wrong, and my thumb got caught between two gear wheels. A shock of pain surged through me, and blood started oozing out, which frightened me even more. My right thumb was severely crushed, and the nail was flattened.

Clutching my thumb and crying loudly, I ran towards my house. It seemed somebody had already informed my grandmother about the injury. My aunt Labh Kaur, who was in Kanjla that day, came running to me. She cleaned and bandaged my wound, and my grandmother applied a black, gum-like ointment on my thumb. My grandfather had used the same ointment on his afflicted leg about 10 years ago, and it still proved effective. My hand hurt, and I found it difficult to do my school homework. After about 15 days, I was able to use my right hand again, but my thumb's nail had been damaged. Looking back, I feel lucky to have escaped with a small injury. It could have been much worse if my hand had become trapped in the pulleys. In the mid-1950s, there were hardly any facilities in villages to treat such injuries.

In 1956, the Punjab government approved the establishment of a small dispensary for animals in Kanjla. The Kanjla village panchayat decided to locate it in the old school building opposite the *halti*. A veterinarian was also posted at the dispensary to care for the animals. After school, we used to play near the new animal dispensary. One day, when a large amount of sand was dumped in front of the *halti*, we children began playing in the sand. I found a large pea in the sand and placed it against my nostril, intending to blow it away. Unfortunately, as I inhaled, the pea got lodged into my nostril. I tried to remove it but couldn't. I got scared, and ran to my house, shouting for my grandmother. She tried to take the pea out from my nostril but couldn't. She then took me to the animal dispensary and sought help from the veterinarian. He brought a small tool, and although it was painful, he managed to remove the pea from my nostril.

Matiana was a small religious place on the outskirts of the village, consisting of two separate rooms. Villagers worshipped a pyramid-shaped mound of earth, approximately five feet in diameter and five feet high, in the *pakka* room. They generally visited on Tuesdays, the day of Bajrangbali, Lord Hanuman, to light lamps. Sweetened bread was also specially prepared and distributed in the shrine. My grandmother and I used to visit there quite often. Near this religious place was a *kacha* thatched room where *sadhu*s, who frequented the village, could stay. They received alms from the villagers and then moved on.

Matiana was owned by a family headed by Parmananda, who also practised Ayurveda. Once, a sadhu came to Matiana and stayed for a few months. He had a peculiar habit of never standing still at one place; he always kept moving. Even when he went to collect alms, his movements would not cease. People believed that he had been blessed by some supernatural power that gave him boundless energy. One evening, I along with my neighbourhood friends went to meet the *sadhu* after playing hockey. He regaled us with stories about Lord Hanuman, and we listened attentively. The night was dark and cold, and we sat comfortably around the burning fire, with time slipping away unnoticed.

My grandmother was waiting for me at home. We generally ate dinner around sunset and prepared to retire for the night. However, that day, we lost track of time. While we were engrossed in the *sadhu's* stories at Matiana, we heard distant shouts. I stepped out of the hut, into the complete darkness and bitter cold. There was no light anywhere. It was then that I realised my grandmother was calling my name and asking where I was. She had already crossed the village's peripheral *kacha* road (called *phirni*) and had come within about 100 metres of Matiana. In response to her calls, I shouted back that I was on my way. I ran at full speed to reach her in the dark night. When I reached her, she scolded me, saying, '*Agar tu eih kuchh karna hai, tan apne pind vagja. Mere kol na rah. Main tainu nahin lab sakdi ratan nu.* (If you want to do such things, then stay in your own village. Do not stay with me. I cannot search for you at night.)'

I understood that she was worried about my safety, and this responsibility rested on her shoulders. It was challenging for an elderly lady to search for me at night. Most families had already locked their doors, turned off their lights, and gone to bed. That day, I promised her that I would never go out at night without informing her. Moreover, my grandmother had to lock the house and then search for me, as there was no one else who could look after it in her absence.

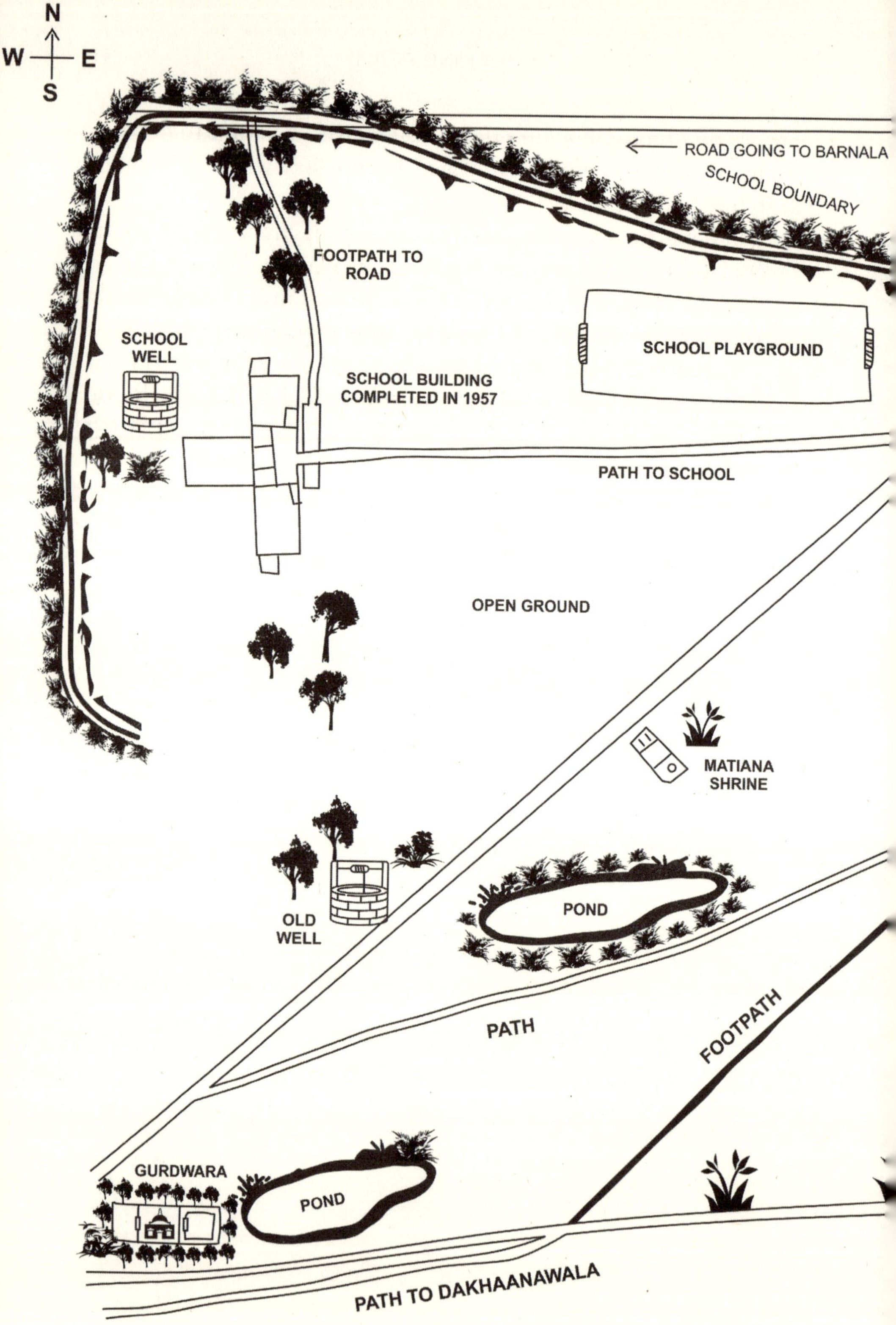
N
W
E
S
ROAD GOING TO BARNALA
SCHOOL BOUNDARY
FOOTPATH TO ROAD
SCHOOL WELL
SCHOOL BUILDING COMPLETED IN 1957
SCHOOL PLAYGROUND
PATH TO SCHOOL
OPEN GROUND
MATIANA SHRINE
OLD WELL
POND
PATH
FOOTPATH
GURDWARA
POND
PATH TO DAKHAANAWALA

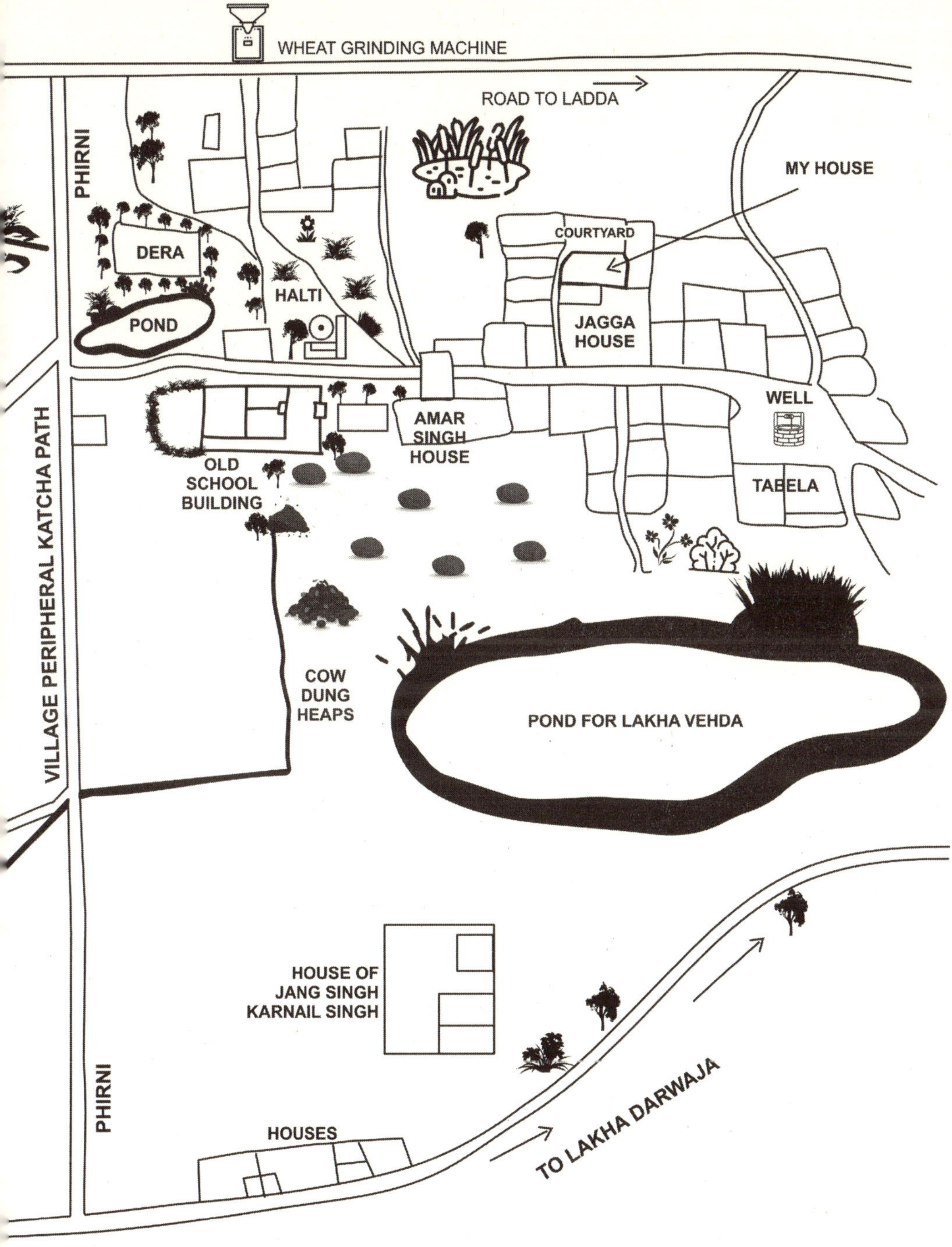

MAP OF RELEVANT AREA OF KANJLA VILLAGE

MAP-NOT TO SCALE

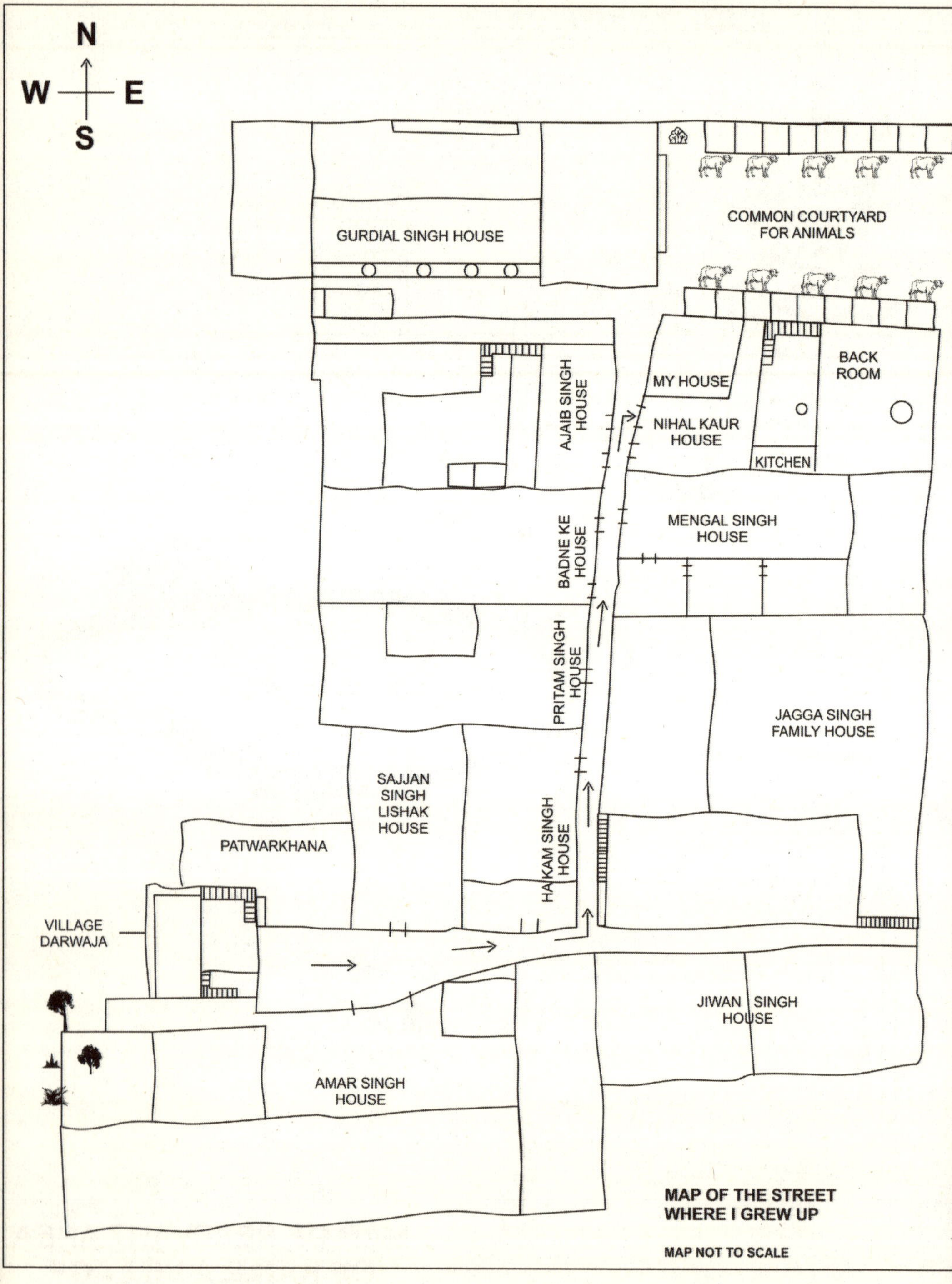

MAP OF THE STREET WHERE I GREW UP

MAP NOT TO SCALE

CHAPTER 3

Excelling in School

The school in Kanjla commenced in 1949-50 in a brick building near the village *halti* and was later shifted to a Gurdwara in 1955. At the same time, construction began on a new school building on approximately 75 acres of land allocated by the village panchayat. In the Gurdwara, the students were accommodated on the southern side of the front courtyard.

Our classes were held on the rooftop, in the Gurdwara corridors, and on raised platforms in the courtyard. Since the lunch break was for one hour only, I would sprint at full speed, covering about one kilometre to reach my house in seven to 10 minutes. My grandmother would have my food prepared, and I would quickly eat before rushing back for the class. I fondly recall my friend Jagga Singh running alongside me. The image of us running and panting on a raised *kacha* path from the *phirni* towards the village *darwaja* remains vivid in my memory.

A vendor named Raghui used to make ice cream in our village and would come to the school during recess to sell it. I would daily request my grandmother to give me a two-paisa coin so that I could buy ice cream. We would stand along the southern side of the *kacha* track, eagerly awaiting Raghui's arrival on his bicycle when classes ended. Raghui used to give us ice cream in cups made of unbreakable material—neither steel, glass, nor porcelain, but a sturdy substance resembling hard plastic. He would wash the used cups and spoons at a nearby hand-pump, readying them for reuse. Reflecting back, I now realise the kindness and generosity of my grandmother, always giving me those two-paisa coins despite limited financial means. The taste of Raghui's ice cream still lingers in my memory.

During our time in the Gurdwara, additional teachers were assigned as the number of classes increased to six. The appointment of a Physical Education Teacher (PET) elevated outdoor activities by introducing daily exercises, races, and procuring sports equipment for hockey, volleyball and other outdoor games. Hindi and other subject teachers were also added. A fellow student, who was the PET's daughter, stood out for her aggressiveness, often engaging in quarrels.

A tamarind tree, situated near the raised plinth where classes were held, became a favourite spot for our playtime activities. We also enjoyed the tamarind fruit while playing there. On one occasion, a classmate picked the same tamarind that drew the attention of the PET's daughter. This action angered the girl, leading to her throwing dust at our classmate, pulling his hair, and slapping his face. The poor boy was visibly frightened, especially as the girl's elder sister, in a senior class, supported her. After about 10 minutes, when the situation calmed down, we tried to comfort our badly roughed-up classmate, whose hair was full of dust and cheeks were red from the slapping. Unfortunately, the girl and her elder sister, who had assaulted our classmate, were spared from consequences, as they were the daughters of the PET. Such unfair incidents were not uncommon in schools during those days.

Every day, our teacher emphasised the importance of neat and beautiful handwriting, along with memorising multiplication tables. In the afternoons, the teacher would gather us in the courtyard, and make us loudly recite multiplication tables for hours. I often took the lead role in both reciting tables and counting numbers. For our writing practice, we used the *phatti* (wooden board). After the teacher's corrections, we would wash the *phatti* to erase the writing, then apply a layer of sticky off-white clay and let it dry. After drying, we marked lines on one side for writing Punjabi and on the other side for numbers and multiplication tables. The *phatti*, along with a slate, was part of our school kit, and we used both for writing and solving arithmetic questions. Teachers instructed us to write on it daily, providing the necessary materials. We would return home, clean, plaster, and dry the *phatti*, then complete our homework on it. Teachers evaluated our work the next day, and following this routine kept us occupied both in the school and at home. Failure to complete homework resulted in reprimands and physical punishments from the teachers.

My teacher, Gurbachan Singh, was strict about handwriting. If anyone's handwriting fell short, he would instruct them to extend their hands, then strike their knuckles with a stick. On a day when my handwriting did not meet the standard, I faced the same punishment, which was quite painful. After that, I began to pay special attention to my handwriting, treating each letter as if I was designing it. Through consistent practice, I saw improvement in my handwriting. This habit endured, and during my tenure in the Indian Administrative Service (IAS) and my time at Harvard University in 1988-89, my handwriting garnered special appreciation. Whenever people praised my handwriting later in life, I always acknowledged the influence of Gurbachan Singh during my school days. He laid the foundation for my artistic handwriting, and the credit goes to him.

I excelled in school, and both my classmates and neighbours began referring to me as the best student in the class. My exceptional mastery of multiplication tables astonished everyone, leading my teachers to anticipate future success for me. Surjit Kaur, my Class III teacher, would often describe me as a genius. In her absence, she entrusted me with teaching and directing students to recite numbers. I was made the class monitor. Surjit Kaur even visited my house once to meet my grandmother, and told her that I was on a much higher level than other students. Her words not only encouraged me but also brought joy to my grandmother.

A day before the holidays, the class teachers announced the results of their respective classes. In Class III, our class teacher Surjit Kaur declared that I had secured the first position in the examination. As I stood up, everyone applauded. Excitedly, I ran home to share the news with my grandmother. To celebrate my achievement, she prepared *halwa* (a dessert made of wheat flour, sugar and ghee) and also bought a ball for me to play in the street.

In 1955, during the construction of the new school building in Kanjla village, the *sarpanch* (head of the village panchayat), Aala Singh, and Puran Singh, a panchayat member, played pivotal roles. I have seldom encountered someone as devoted as Aala Singh, who oversaw the construction work selflessly. The school had ample land for future expansion, development and playgrounds. Later, the panchayat and school administration constructed a mud boundary around the school.

Uncle Inder Singh took me to Dhuri to buy books for Class IV. The school had been upgraded up to Class X and was now known as Government High School. Kirpal Singh, my neighbour, who was five classes senior to me, had set an impressive precedent. He stood first in his class, gaining recognition in the village. Inspired by his success, I was determined to do as well as him, if not better, prompting me to insist on purchasing additional books.

Around this time, a new teacher named Nityanand Gupta joined the school. He was a frequent smoker, and when he traversed the village streets on his way to the school, we could see him puffing away. Playfully, the villagers coined a nickname *Railgadi* (railway train) due to his smoking habit. A few more new teachers joined the school, who focused on teaching senior classes.

Nityanand Gupta was also particular about handwriting. In instances where our handwriting fell short of his expectations, he would use a wet stick to strike our knuckles. After standing first in Class III, I was determined not to let another student claim the top spot. Many of my classmates were striving to catch up, and I realised that any lapse on my part could give them a chance to grab the first position. One notable competitor was Mohan Lal Sharma. So I was determined to always be thorough in studies and do all my homework daily. I also resolved not to miss a single class, and my punctuality became a consistent practice. My grandmother supported me, never asking me to skip any classes.

Every day after school, I would come home and organise my inkpot, exercise books, *phatti* and schoolbag containing books on a *pihrhi* (a wooden stool with woven surface for sitting) placed on the water drain next to my neighbour Ajaib Singh's wall. I would then shout for my grandmother, '*Nani, meri chah eathey lai ke aa. Main padh riha aan.* (Grandmother, bring my tea here. I am studying.)' She was old but very considerate. Moving around was difficult for her, so she would shout back, '*Tu dade magoniah ki DC banega? Meriya latan nahin chaldian. Apne pind bag ja.* (Will you become a DC [Deputy Commissioner]? My legs are not working properly. Go back to your village!)' She would grumble and rebuke me, but she would always bring tea for me in the street, albeit grudgingly.

By this time, all the neighbours had told my grandmother that I would study well and bring name and fame to the family. Being illiterate, she had no knowledge about career options after studies. She only knew that a DC is a powerful person and would often ask me if I would become a DC after studies. Little did she know that I would attain high-ranking positions, including working in places like the Prime Minister's Office (PMO), which only a few from the elite achieve. She could have never thought that I would pursue studies at Harvard University in the USA, the top-ranked university in the world, which is a dream for the most.

By the time I entered Class IV, the school had shifted to its newly constructed building. Remarkably, I never missed a single day of school in Class IV, a great accomplishment given that many students were occasionally absent due to household responsibilities. My determination to secure the first rank persisted. When the Class IV results were announced, I had stood first in that class too! This consistent success fuelled my motivation to always aim for the highest rank. I do not know if my grandmother took pride in my academic achievements, as she seldom expressed it. It is possible that she never imagined my later ascent in the Indian bureaucracy. Perhaps, she was preoccupied with family issues, her own health, financial challenges and advancing age.

In the primary school, a single teacher handled all our subjects, with Surjit Kaur and Gurbachan Singh taking charge of most classes. Gurbachan Singh, who also managed post office duties and prepared Ayurveda medicines for the villagers, had a unique teaching approach. His informal style included requesting students to fetch buttermilk (*lassi*) for him, and he had no reservations about assigning tasks like massaging his legs while in class. Dressed in pyjama-kurta and a turban like a village farmer, Gurbachan Singh stood out from other teachers. Occasionally, he would instruct us to wash his turban near the handpump. As soon as he took off his turban, he would throw it towards us, and we would jump to catch it and wash it. This informal arrangement continued until Class IV when we transitioned to having four to five teachers, each teaching a different subject.

When I was in Class V, about 15 students from Kanjli village enrolled at Kanjla Government High School. There were already about 30 students in our class. Our class teacher found that the academic standard of the students who had come from Kanjli village was lower, so he created a separate section for them rather than merging the classes. As these students had difficulty in reading books and solving mathematics problems, my teacher assigned me to teach these students for about two hours every day. This unexpected assignment not only aided the Kanjli students but also proved beneficial for my own studies.

In Class V, we had to learn Hindi alongside Punjabi. I worked hard, expecting that I would get the first rank in the class during the final examinations. However, when the results were declared, Pritam Singh, who often sought my help with his homework, claimed the first position, and I secured the second rank. When I returned home, my grandmother repeatedly asked whether I was first in the class. I evaded the truth and falsely claimed that the first and second positions would be declared later. Not securing the first rank left me in shock. After this setback, I resolved to study even harder.

Motivations to Study Harder

In Kanjla, the villagers considered passing the Class X (also called Matriculation) examination very difficult, primarily because it was conducted by Panjab University. In 1959, when the first batch of the school appeared for the matriculation examination, there was a lot of tension. The examination took place at Mastuana, situated along the Sangrur–Barnala road), accommodating several schools. Special invigilators were assigned by Panjab University. When the results were declared, Kirpal Singh from Kanjla Government High School achieved high marks, securing a high rank in the university merit list. This outstanding performance brought immense joy to Kanjla and the neighbouring villages, prompting students from far-off villages to enrol in our school.

In 1959, I was promoted to Class VI. Around the same time, a PET named Gurnam Singh initiated training sessions for hockey, volleyball and kabaddi, aiming to prepare the Kanjla school team for participation in district-level tournaments held annually at Sangrur or the sub-divisional headquarters. Although I was too young to actively participate, I regularly attended hockey practices in the evening, assisting players by retrieving the ball when it went out of bounds. Sometimes, when there was a shortage of players, I seized the opportunity to fill in. Whenever a player went to the hand-pump to drink water, I got brief chance to play. These days were filled with excitement and enjoyment.

I would always count the points in the volleyball matches. I used to sit below the pole on which the volleyball net was strung. To make sure that the net was tight enough, one brick was kept on top of the pole to add tension in the top string. One day when I was sitting by the side of the pole and counting the points, the ball hit the net with a lot of force. With the impact, the string bobbled a bit and then the brick became loose and slipped down. I was sitting right below the brick so it hit me on the centre of my head. I was not wearing a turban as I had just finished playing hockey, but luckily, the brick just struck the top of my hair knot. It absorbed the impact and saved me from a head injury.

When we were promoted to Class VI, a number of students from neighbouring villages—Hasanpur, Pedni, Bugray, Kila Hakima, Batuhe, Dhandiwal, Mullowal, Kumbharwal and Punnawal—joined our school. This solidified Kanjla school's status as an educational hub for the area. Inspired by Kirpal Singh's top-ranking performance in the Panjab University matriculation examination in 1959, where he scored 673 marks out of 850, I aimed to emulate his success and pledged to intensify my studies. The increased strength of students toughened competition in Class VI. Two new subjects, drawing and English, were introduced. We had also transitioned from writing on slates and *phattis* to using exercise notebooks.

During the summer vacation of 1959, while I was in Balian, my father shared stories about the operator of the government-owned irrigation tube-well of our Patianwala field. This operator frequently spoke about his younger brother, Sukhdev Singh, who had joined Class VI at Kanjla school. According to my father, the operator expressed great confidence in Sukhdev's intelligence, predicting that he would stand first in Class VI. Although I had never met the tube-well operator, my father's accounts of his dedication to coaching his brother for academic success left a lasting impression on me.

The teaching approach in Class VI was a change from lower classes, with specialised teachers instructing various subjects. I was appointed monitor of Class VI, a recognition of my capabilities. During attendance, I stood by the teacher, providing information about students who were present or on leave. I had purchased a drawing board, learning geometry and creating sketches of diverse objects. The teacher commended my clean geometry work and top-grade sketches. The results of the final examination were announced in the assembly, declaring me the first position holder with 454 marks, closely followed by Sukhdev in second place. Rushing home after the assembly, I shared the news with my grandmother, who was gradually realising my academic success.

In Class VII, I had tough competitors. During the summer break of 1960 in Balian, my father discussed his interactions with the tube-well operator. At this point, the operator had realised that Sukhdev had a formidable competitor in me. It seemed Sukhdev had told him that I outperformed him in nearly all subjects, but I remained diligent and continued my hard work. With minimal household chores in Kanjla, I had ample time for studies. My father brought additional books, which I revised thoroughly. Despite occasional illnesses, I attended school regularly, never missing a day. All these efforts paid off, and once again, I stood first in Class VII final examination, scoring 565 out of 700 marks, with Sukhdev closely trailing behind!

Class VIII started at a fast pace. As the final examination for Class VIII, then called 'The Middle Standard Examination', was to be conducted by the Education Department, Punjab Government, the class teachers were determined to cover the entire syllabus. The Kanjla school had no control over the setting of question papers and the final evaluation of marks. This was the reason why students became serious about their studies, with many opting for tuitions in mathematics and other difficult subjects. I did not go for any tuition, but persevered with doing my homework.

For the examination we had to stay in Mastuana. All the boys were allotted a large hall. Since there were no beds, we had to sleep on the floor, which we cushioned with paddy husk. We made our own arrangements for our meals. Kartar Singh, the uncle of my friend Jagga Singh, who was also my neighbour, brought our food every day to Mastuana, which was about 4 km from Kanjla. Since the examinations lasted about 10 days, food was required only for this duration. Whenever Kartar Singh was late, we would go up to the roof and look longingly towards the Kanjla road. Even though he was a slow walker, he brought our food regularly.

One day, Harbhajan Singh, our class teacher, was teaching us geography on the roof to prepare us for the next day's examination. We were all listening attentively. Just then, a smartly dressed man came up the stairs and stood at a distance, listening to the lecture. He stared at us as if he was searching for someone. It seemed he was related to one of the students, but we did not know who it was. When there was a pause in the lecture, he came to our class teacher and asked him who Jarnail Singh was. My teacher pointed his finger at me and asked me to stand up, saying, 'This is Jarnail Singh, the best student in the class.' Then the person introduced himself as the elder brother of Sukhdev Singh from Hasanpur. That was the first time I had seen him. He was the operator of the tube-well near our Patianwala field. Apparently, he wanted to see me because he was impressed by my academic credentials.

My grandmother had stomach cancer and died in October 1961. The Middle Standard Examination started on 2 February 1962. After the examinations were over, it became apparent that about five months of disturbance due to my grandmother's sickness and death had adversely affected my performance. I had not done well in the mathematics and drawing papers. In fact, I made mistakes in the mathematics paper, my favourite subject. During the first five minutes, I was confused and, as a result, could not attempt all the questions. While I had initially expected to score more than 98 per cent, after the exam, I considered it lucky if I could get even 70 per cent. This was a big slide for me. Similarly, in the drawing examination, in my haste, I did not read a seven-mark question carefully and solved it differently. If I had read the question correctly, I would have definitely drawn the required sketch better.

When the Middle Standard Examination results were declared, Mohan Lal Sharma secured the top position in the school, while I was placed second. Mohan was a brilliant and hard-working student. I missed the first position by only five marks. I accepted my second position gracefully and pledged to work hard to secure the first position in Class IX. The setback of securing the second position fuelled my determination to intensify my efforts.

CHAPTER 4

Other Reminisces of Living with My Grandmother

From 1957 to 1962, Punjab experienced severe monsoon rains. Due to the topography of the land, which slopes from the north-east to the south-west in the river basins of Punjab, rainwater during floods flowed to villages in the south-west. In the absence of drains in villages and fields, rainwater would accumulate in various areas, leading to blockages. Continuous rainfall for a week or more resulted in flooding in villages, with stagnant rainwater persisting for 15 to 30 days. The western side of Kanjla village, being a low-lying area, was particularly susceptible. During heavy rains, the village would be submerged, with water depths ranging from one foot to three feet. Residents had to wade through the water from the *darwaja*, the village gate. Domestic animals were kept confined in houses, and animal dung was disposed of by throwing it in the water outside the main *darwaja*. Quite often, one could see schools of ants and other insects floating in water, and snakes seeking higher ground or perches to survive.

The stagnant water surrounding the villages posed a health risk. Since farmers grew cotton and maize in those days, heavy rains and standing water would damage these crops. With persistent heavy monsoons until 1963, farmers changed the cropping patterns and began growing paddy, which could survive in water, instead of maize and cotton. For the first time, villagers from Kanjla brought paddy seedlings from Bangawali, a village near Sangrur, where some progressive farmers had already shifted to paddy cultivation in 1962-63. As the floods continued for about 10 years, the Punjab government initiated the construction of drainage channels. Two drainage channels, one on the eastern side and the second on the western side, were built in Kanjla village to drain out the rainwater. Completed around 1964, these drains brought relief to the villagers, particularly the local farmers.

During the monsoon, my grandmother faced a tough time. The roof of our house was *kacha*, made from weeds and plastered with mud on the top. Over time, sparrows and rats had made holes in the roof, allowing rainwater to seep into the house during the rainy season. Our neighbours had cemented or tiled their rooftops or applied fresh layers of mud annually before the rains to prevent leaks. However, the mud coating required labour, such as scooping out mud from the village pond, mixing it with water and wheat chaff and then applying it. My grandmother, being elderly and economically constrained, couldn't undertake such repairs. Consequently, leakages became an additional concern for her.

Whenever our roof leaked, my grandmother would tell me to shield myself with a jute gunny bag and climb onto the roof to seal the leaks with mud and broken bricks. In the midst of heavy rain, occasional lightning and thunder, I felt scared to go up to the roof. However, with no option, I had to proceed, even though patching the holes often involved a trial-and-error approach. Even now, after I have grown old, this fear has remained in my mind.

One day, when my grandmother needed to collect chaff from the rear room for the buffalo, I accompanied her. I was following her when she suddenly stopped, her face gripped with fear. She pointed to two snakes, each about three feet long, slithering towards the chaff. We rushed out of the room. This incident revealed the presence of snakes in the room where we slept during winter. The room, enveloped in complete darkness, housed many pitchers, tins, quilts on the beds and chaff, creating hiding spots for snakes. One day, my grandmother even summoned a snake charmer to capture the snakes. The snake charmer entered the room and played his *been* (wind instrument), but no snake came out. He left empty-handed but not before commenting that the snakes did not want to leave the room as they were souls of deceased family members. He advised us to feed them and not kill them, but his words only scared us more.

My grandmother kept coins in a small bowl in the *almirah* in the rear room. Sometimes, she would give me half an *anna* or one *anna* to buy sweets. One day, when she opened the *almirah*, she showed me a piece knitted by my aunt Labh Kaur. I told her that I could not see the design in the dark and asked her to let me take the bowl to the courtyard so that I could see it better. In the courtyard, however, my greed overtook me. I saw a one-rupee coin in the bowl and quickly pocketed it. I was sure my grandmother never thought that I would take money from the bowl without her permission. After a while, I ran to the shop in the locality with one rupee in my pocket. That day, Shardha, the elderly shopkeeper was there. I bought some sweets for two *annas* (there were 16 *annas* in one rupee). He returned two *annas*, but did not have the remaining 12 *annas*. He asked me to collect them in the evening, but unfortunately, when I went there in the evening, his son refused to give the balance. Despite numerous attempts, I could not recover my 12 *annas*. I felt deceived. Perhaps, it was a punishment for stealing from my trusting grandmother, who looked after me so well in spite of her problems and old age. I always felt guilty about this incident.

The Village Fair

An event that the villagers looked forward to was the fair at Mastuana, which was celebrated to commemorate the birth anniversary of Sant Attar Singh, the founder of Mastuana. For three days, many religious singers would gather to perform devotional songs, drawing hundreds of villagers for prayer and reflection. Shopkeepers set up stalls offering a variety of food and toys. Since my grandmother did not have much money, she would give me only two *annas*, but it was not enough to buy any toy. Fortunately, in my neighbourhood lived Mrs Chand Kaur, a good friend of my grandmother and around the same age. She spoke Punjabi with a Haryanvi accent and was the grandmother of another brilliant student, Sajjan Singh Lishak, who had stood first in Class X in Kanjla and later became a professor at Punjabi University. Mrs Kaur would always give me around 10 *annas* during each fair. She was aware of my grandmother's financial constraints, and her kindness allowed me to take my cousin Bachno and my sister Guddi to the fair in Kanjla, where we could enjoy snacks.

Since I could not afford expensive toys, I contended myself with buying balloons or whistles. During one Mastuana fair, I set my eyes on a turning wheel with a handle attached to it. This wheel, when pushed forward, would ring a bell fixed to it. It was priced at about one rupee, which I did not have. Disappointed, I left the fair for Kanjla, which was about an hour's walk. As I took a shortcut through the fields to reach Kanjla, I unexpectedly stumbled upon the desired toy lying on the path. Delighted, I picked it up, but my happiness was short-lived. I had walked only about 50 metres when I met a lady who was walking back in search of that toy. It belonged to her child, who had dropped it while walking. She took it back, leaving me to return home in a sombre mood.

An Inconvenient Visitor

My aunt Labh Kaur was married to Labh Singh in Kakarwal village, near Dhuri. Whenever Labh Singh visited Kanjla, he would purchase liquor on the way and arrive home late, fully intoxicated. This routine posed a challenge for my grandmother, who had to manage his late-night arrival and cook fresh vegetable curry for him. Cooking at such late hours was difficult for her, and I would often hear her grumbling. Generally, after dinner, Labh Singh would walk back to Kakarwal. While my grandmother could not stop him, she worried about his safety, considering his family's significant landholdings and the fact that he wore many gold ornaments. To address the situation, she would ask me to enlist the help of either Joginder Singh or Mohinder Singh, my cousins. They often found him passed out on the way to Kakarwal and had to bring him back. Labh Singh's impromptu visits became a recurring nuisance for my old grandmother. Despite being an adult, he seemed oblivious to the inconvenience and embarrassment he was causing my grandmother. She bore his inconsiderate behaviour silently, as she had no alternative solution to rectify the situation.

Notable Events in Kanjla

Many of my friends were learning to ride bicycles. Whenever my father or my uncle Labh Singh came to Kanjla, I would take their bicycles near the *halti* and practice riding. Labh Singh's bicycle was new and more enjoyable to ride. Moreover, he was quite lenient and didn't mind if I accidentally damaged his bicycle.

Around the age of 10, after spending my summer vacation in Balian, my grandfather accompanied me back to Kanjla. Since we needed milk, my parents decided to send one buffalo with a calf to Kanjla with us. After covering about one kilometre, we would take breaks to ensure the calf didn't become exhausted. This slowed down our journey. After we crossed Kila Hakima, our progress became even slower as the calf would sit down quite often. By the time we crossed Kanjli, the sun had already set. It was a moonlit night and we continued walking. When we reached near the cremation grounds of Kanjla, the calf fell down and refused to get up. Despite waiting patiently, it showed no signs of getting back on its feet. We stood there, pondering our next steps. We were still about one kilometre away from our house.

Since I was too young, I could neither go home alone to seek help nor could I stay alone with the calf in that isolated place. I was scared of the location, as it was close to the cremation grounds and I had heard stories of ghosts dancing at night. After thinking for some time, my grandfather decided that both of us should go home with the buffalo and leave the calf behind. It took us approximately half an hour to reach home with the buffalo.

Upon our arrival, my grandmother asked Mohinder Singh to retrieve the calf. Surprisingly, when Mohinder reached the school, the calf had already covered half the distance towards our house. It seemed as if she could sense her mother's (the buffalo's) whereabouts and was following her. After about half an hour, Mohinder brought the calf home.

My aunt Labh Kaur frequently visited and stayed with my grandmother. She was frail and had a poor appetite. Even though her in-laws were well off, they did not prioritise healthy eating. My aunt would get seizures at odd hours, prompting my grandmother to send me to seek help from the neighbours. I would hurry to them at unusual times, and they always tried to help. Frustrated with the lack of improvement, my grandmother approached various *tantrics* and *sadhus* who recommended rituals to dispel the ghosts that possessed my aunt. Some *sadhus* even made medallions for her to wear around her neck as a protective measure. However, nothing worked and she continued to remain in the same condition. Several doctors prescribed medications to prevent seizures, and one such medicine was Vitamin B Complex, leaving our almirah with a lasting scent of it.

Living on the left side of our house was our neighbour Mengal Singh, who was around 65 years old. Despite possessing a reasonably large landholding, he remained unmarried and lived alone in a fully mud-built house. He seldom interacted with anyone in the neighbourhood. Large quantities of wood were dumped in his courtyard and it seemed no one had ever cleaned his courtyard, which looked like an ideal hiding place for rats and possibly snakes. He had a substantial income, at least three to four times greater than my grandmother's, but he had not installed a handpump. I frequently observed him bringing water in a small pitcher. He had fixed a wooden staircase to climb up and stay in the first-floor *chaubara*, constructed of mud, having about 150-square-foot terrace for sleeping during the summer. Mengal Singh would pray loudly from there daily, uttering holy words. Whenever I met him, he was always in an angry mood, never smiling or laughing. His relatives from Badney Ke were to inherit his landed property after his death, so he used to get his food and other requirements from them. Even though he lived adjacent to our house, I had never entered his house. I was curious to see his *chaubara* but did not have the courage to ask him.

My classmate Darbara Singh resided in *Dayala Vehda*. Unfortunately, he had lost his mother, and his father had remarried. One day, he accompanied me to the annual district-level games in Sangrur city. On our way back, as we approached a railroad crossing gate, we heard the approaching train. Excited at the prospect of seeing a train at close range for the first time, we positioned ourselves near the tracks. In those days, steam locomotives were used for railway trains all over India.

As the train neared the crossing, the railway driver blared the horn as a warning. The sight of the approaching steam locomotive was both thrilling and frightening. As the train drew near, panic set in, and we hastily retreated from the railway gate. While I ran directly onto the road, Darbara veered towards the roadside ditches. In the process, his foot got entangled in the hooks of the railway gate. He fell down and struggled to free his foot. Although there was no danger of the train running over him, he shouted and cried in fear. Within a few seconds, the train passed, and I returned to help him disentangle. Even now, when I recall that scene, I can't help but laugh as I visualise Darbara first approaching the locomotive bravely, only to suddenly panic and run away.

One day, while waiting for my turn at the wheat-grinding machine, Darbara joined me after tending to his small kitchen garden located nearby. Spotting me, he invited me over to see his garden. It was small, but a lot of vegetables were growing there. He plucked some beans and gave them to me. That evening, my grandmother used those beans, along with onions and chillies, to make chutney. Later on, one day, I was shocked when fellow students from his area informed us at school that Darbara had died on the previous evening. Many suspected foul play, possibly poisoning, though no one could confirm. Despite being healthy, he unexpectedly died after consuming milk following his dinner.

I had never seen Dussehra celebrations or the burning of the effigy of Ravana, although I had read about the historical significance of Dussehra and Diwali. In cities like Dhuri and Sangrur, the effigy of Ravana was burned on Dussehra, but this tradition was not observed in villages. Since the effigies were burnt just after sunset, there was no way I could go to a city alone and return to Kanjla in the night.

On one Dussehra, my uncle Labh Singh came to visit us. As he was preparing to leave, I requested if he could take me to Dhuri, which was about 2 km away from his village, so I could partake in the Dussehra celebrations. He readily agreed. We reached Dhuri before sunset and sat in a position from where we could clearly see the burning of the effigies of Ravana, Kumbhkarna and Meghnath. The three effigies were set on fire one by one after sunset, accompanied by lots of fireworks. After about half an hour, it was over.

Our buffalo needed to be taken out for grazing every day. Since I was focused on my studies and my grandmother was old, we made an arrangement with a herder who took care of the grazing animals from morning to evening. My daily responsibility was to take the buffalo and leave it with the herder. Even though it looked like a simple task, it required a one-kilometre walk with the buffalo, which often engaged in fights with other cattle along the way. I would always wonder how the herder managed to oversee about 200 animals.

The herder would sit on one side of the grazing field, while his assistants were spread out in various locations. In the evening, he guided the animals back to the village from *darwaja*, and allowed them to find their own ways back to their respective owners' houses. He never came to drop our buffalo at our house. Instead, he left it approximately 50 metres away, and without fail, it always found its way back on its own. The buffalo's remarkable sense of direction never ceased to amaze me throughout the six years I observed this routine.

In 1957, electricity became available in Kanjla. My grandmother did not have adequate money to install the necessary wiring for lighting, so I continued to use kerosene lamps for studying at night.

Many Jat Sikhs in Punjab hold strong beliefs in *sadhus* and specific sacred places, especially those where their elders were cremated. In Kanjla, many villagers, including my grandmother, prayed at a small *samadhi* in Khillarian village, approximately 6 km away. It was believed that those who paid obeisance to the goddess at the *samadhi* would be protected from illness.

Part of this ritual involved making an offering, which included placing a handful of soil from a nearby pond near the mound before sunrise. Additionally, fried sweet wheat snacks were to be distributed to the people present there. My grandmother prepared the snacks for me, which she carefully packed in a cloth. Due to her health, she asked me to join a group of about 50 people, mostly ladies, going to Khillarian. It was a dark night, so four young men also accompanied us on our journey to Khillarian.

Around 3 a.m., we set out from our houses in a procession towards Khillarian village. After covering about 3 km, we started walking along a path through the fields. Suddenly, a group of armed men surrounded us, demanding that the ladies hand over their gold ornaments. The two young men at the front of our group confronted them, calling out to the other two to quickly join with weapons. Being at the front, I heard the commotion from the rear, with the young men shouting and running forward with weapons. Fearing a deadly clash, the robbers hastily fled the scene. The remainder of our journey proceeded without any further untoward events, and we reached Khillarian to pay obeisance at the *samadhi* before sunrise. We returned before lunch.

Tongas for Transport

In Kanjla, two men, Bhag Singh and Harnam Singh, operated horse carts, known as *tongas*, between Kanjla and Dhuri city. They usually parked their *tongas* in front of the main *darwaja* of *Lakha Vehda* (a locality). Even though a bus had started plying once a day from Balian to Dhuri via Kanjla, some villagers favoured *tonga*s, as they could be picked up directly from their houses, and they could easily transport loads of jaggery, animal fodder, sugar and other items directly to their doorsteps from the city.

Seeking help from my parents in Balian for a trip to Dhuri for books and stationery shopping posed challenges. Since my grandmother couldn't accompany me, I occasionally went with Bhag Singh in his *tonga*. He was an elderly man and quite considerate. I still remember one particular trip to Dhuri in the scorching month of May in his *tonga*. After picking up passengers along the way, we reached Dhuri, where I bought books and stationery. Unfortunately, I had to wait for about five hours in a *dharamshala* (public rest house) until Bhag Singh came back in the evening to take me back. Surviving just on water from a handpump, I refrained from leaving the *dharamshala* to ensure I didn't miss his return. It was an unpleasant experience, but I had no other alternative to reach Dhuri for my essential purchases.

One day, while sitting on the *halti* boundary wall, we saw Bhag Singh riding his horse into the village pond near the *halti*. Usually, buffaloes entered the pond from the western side while coming back from the fields, swimming out from the eastern side. As Bhag Singh entered the pond, we observed the horse hesitating but moving forward under Bhag Singh's direction. However, when the horse reached deeper water, it suddenly fell, taking Bhag Singh down with it. After a few seconds, Bhag Singh managed to stand up, but the horse struggled to rise. The water churned as the horse kicked frantically. Bewildered, we watched for about five minutes until the horse eventually became still. Sadly, the horse had drowned. Ropes were brought, and its carcass was retrieved from the pond. This horse was the Bhag Singh's only asset, crucial for his livelihood, but it all came to an end in just a few minutes. Later on, I learnt that Bhag Singh had made a fatal error by entering the pond while riding the horse. Due to his weight, the horse's legs got trapped in the sticky mud of the pond's floor, causing it to lose balance and fall, never to rise again.

Managing Life in Village

In the 1950s, the most common thefts in villages involved domestic animals, household items and gold. As mentioned earlier, since we were quite helpless, my grandmother requested my cousin, Mohinder Singh, to sleep during the night in our house. Every evening, he would arrive after dinner, and in the early morning around 5 a.m., he would head to plough his fields. Mohinder would often tell me stories. He was a handsome young man. Despite facing two tragedies in life—the loss of his two successive wives—I always found him cheerful and smiling.

From 1955 to 1962, I frequently experienced stomach aches caused by acidity. With no doctor in the village, we lacked guidance on how to address it. Whenever the stomach ache occurred, my grandmother would summon an elderly man called Buggar Singh to massage my stomach. Being a farm worker, his hands were rough, and despite using mustard oil, his massage sometimes caused discomfort to my skin. He followed a systematic approach, pressing my stomach from top to bottom, claiming to expel abdominal gas. This process, repeated a few times, provided relief after about 20 to 30 minutes. Buggar Singh, a uneducated and landless person, had no knowledge of human organs; had learnt this technique from a village elder. When I could not get his help, I applied his technique, which often alleviated or eliminated the stomach ache. In Kanjla village, Buggar Singh was famous for helping people with stomach troubles. Surprisingly, his uniform treatment approach proved effective in relieving pain.

We had a manually operated fodder-cutting machine, but neither my grandmother nor I had the strength to turn its wheel. As such, the machine was lying unused. Mohinder would bring chopped fodder for our buffalo, which my grandmother combined with wheat chaff to feed the animals. In 1957-58, when I was in Class IV, my grandmother decided to sell this idle asset and get some money to rent a fodder field for our buffalo. Our neighbour Amar Singh brought a client from the neighbouring Changal village who agreed to purchase our fodder-cutting machine for Rs 40. Out of this amount, Rs 20 went towards renting a small field near the village for growing fodder, while the remaining Rs 20 was used to purchase various household necessities. Reflecting on this now, I recognise the depth of my grandmother's poverty, a reality I never felt when I was staying with her, as she consistently ensured that I lacked nothing.

One source of our family income was the sale of milk to a vendor. In those days, milk was sold based on quantity alone, as there were no sophisticated methods as used today to measure fat content and set rates. We sold about two litres of milk each day, reserving around one litre for our household needs. The proceeds from these sales were used to buy essential items like potatoes, tea leaves, salt, onions, pulses, sugar and more. Unlike my aunt Labh Kaur, my grandmother never diluted the milk with water. Labh Kaur, on the other hand, employed a cunning method by keeping about one litre of water in the bucket and then milking the buffalo into it, effectively blending water with milk. Despite the milk vendor standing about 10 metres away, he never noticed. I did not say anything to anyone, as it was contributing to our family income. I knew my grandmother would not endorse dishonesty.

During my childhood in Kanjla, I had no worries and spent most of my time either playing with friends or engrossed in my studies. Of course, I did assist my old grandmother with household chores, but that did not impact my playtime or academic pursuits. Unfortunately, poverty and loneliness in my grandmother's life had taken a toll on her health. At that time, I was the only person available to offer support, but I was too young to fully grasp the responsibilities of managing a house. I could not share the pain and worries that burdened my grandmother, though she would often murmur about the unpleasant incidents of her life. In hindsight, I was amazed at her resilience—managing the household, handling finances, and caring for a buffalo single-handedly in her old age.

Reflecting on those times, I can now sense the sympathy our neighbours felt for her—a helpless and poor woman relying on the support and goodwill of neighbours and relatives to lead a reasonably comfortable life.

Bania Vehda, situated on the other side of Kanjla village, was home to a cluster of shops that catered to the essential needs of the villagers and were commonly referred to as a bazaar. A couple of moneylenders operated within this bazaar as well. Every couple of months, my grandmother would go to this bazaar, either to purchase mustard cakes for our buffalo or to borrow some money.

To reach the bazaar, she had to walk through the neighbouring areas of *Lakha Vehda* and *Bania Vehda*. Adhering to the customs of those days, my grandmother would dress in a white kurta, complemented by a white *ghaghara* and a white *chuni*. Armed with her mulberry walking stick, she would set off for the bazaar after cautioning me not to venture out of the house until her return. Interestingly, her dress for these trips to the bazaar, through the streets of other *Vehdas*, used to be different from what she wore within our locality. Anticipation would fill me as I eagerly awaited her visits to the bazaar, knowing that she would invariably bring back a toy or some treats for me.

My grandmother used to store pickles in a brown china clay jar. In those days, the villagers preferred china clay jars or baked earthen utensils to preserve pickles made from mangoes, chillies, ginger, lemons, lotus roots and *amla*s (gooseberries). Quite often, my grandmother would send me to the fields to bring some *delas* for making pickle. *Delas* (also called *Ker*) are green, berry-like fruits that grow on leafless, thorny bushes in dry or arid areas. I could easily find plenty of them near the cremation grounds in Kanjla, behind the school. Due to my grandmother's health and financial constraints, our meals often consisted of pickle and onions, as she found it challenging to prepare fresh vegetables or *dal* daily.

When my grandmother purchased a china clay jar from a street hawker to store pickle, she also acquired a brown china clay bowl that could hold about half a litre of water. This bowl was fragile but it became a cherished novelty for me. I developed a strong liking for this bowl and always drank tea or milk from it, rather than from those made of brass and copper alloy. The reason was that I could comfortably hold it even when filled with hot tea. Every day, my grandmother would give me tea in that bowl. Even today, I remember the brown spots inside the bowl which I used to see while drinking tea. My grandmother would clean it with ash daily and place it on the brick shelf near other utensils. She never allowed anyone else to use it, so it was exclusively mine for about five years. That unique sweet smell while sipping tea makes me nostalgic even today. Unfortunately, I don't recall how I lost that bowl, an item that was so dear to me.

In the winter months, *ber* or berries are easily available in the fields of Punjab. These grow on thorny trees and are a treat to eat. I would often go to the fields with Jagga Singh to pluck *ber*s. About one kilometre away from the village stood an old *ber* tree which was called *Bathan Di Beri* in the field of Jagga Singh's family. This majestic tree on the top of a mound of sand would yield a lot of *ber*s. There was no other tree within a radius of about 200 metres, and birds and animals like jackals and squirrels would feast on the *bers* at night. The name *Bathan Di Beri* must have come as the field where the tree had been standing had belonged to someone called Bath. Some enterprising person from that family must have planted this tree and taken a lot of trouble to water it as there was no water source near it. Believed to have been planted in the 1910s, this tree withstood the fierce wind storms of Punjab because of its balanced trunks and uniform growth on all sides.

It was a safer option for me to visit *Bathan Di Beri* since the field belonged to Jagga Singh's family and there was no fear of anyone chasing me away. Moreover, the field was near the village settlement and the main path leading to Balian, frequently travelled by people on foot or bicycles. I would take a small bag and gather about one kilogramme of *bers* from *Bathan Di Beri*.

My grandmother would then dry and store them in airtight jars so that I could eat these berries even a week later.

Standing proudly like a milestone in the area, 'Bathan Di Beri' held a notable reputation. However, the villagers have now levelled the land for paddy and wheat cultivation. An electric water pump has also been installed. Despite these transformations, the Beri still stands tall, its base and trunk protected by a bricked plinth on all sides. Even after 110 years, it continues to bear fruits!

Every year, the Ram Lila was performed in the cities of Dhuri and Sangrur. The final act of the Ram Lila was the burning of Ravana on the Dussehra day. After Dussehra, the Ram Lila troupe would disperse into villages to present their dramatic rendition. My grandmother would donate about one *panjseri* (equivalent to five seers) of wheat to support the Ram Lila artists.

In Kanjla, the Ram Lila took centre stage in the locality known as *Bania Vehda*, inhabited by businessmen and other communities. After dinner, we would gather on the ground to watch the Ram Lila. The performance, accompanied by hymns, songs, harmoniums and drum beats, made the entire atmosphere very lively. The Ram Lila would start at about 8 p.m. and end at midnight. Since it took place in November or December, and we had to sit in the open on the ground, we carried *khesi*s (cotton blankets made in the villages of Punjab) to shield ourselves from the cold. Our feet would become cold and numb, but we would watch the Ram Lila till the end.

The Ram Lila always cast a positive spell over the village for about one week and we often discussed its various incidents and characters even in school. We were fascinated by the performers' ability to showcase their talents on the stage in the light of kerosene lamps, as electricity had not reached Kanjla till then. Returning home late after the spectacle, I would wake up my grandmother. The street dogs echoed the conclusion of the Ram Lila, signalling the return of spectators to their homes.

Jalsa refers to traditional plays performed by rural folk artists in Punjab villages, either during the day or at night. These plays usually revolved around romantic themes, occasionally incorporating language that may be considered inappropriate. That is why the primary audience for such plays tends to be young males. Although the majority of *Jalsa* artists hailed from the Marasi community, people from other castes also participated, based on their interest and skills. *Jalsa* plays mostly depict romantic tragedies of Punjab, recounting tales of iconic lovers such as Heer-Ranjha, Sassi-Punnu, Mirza-Sahiban and Laila-Majnu. During my time in Kanjla, I also saw a few *Jalsa* plays and was captivated by the artists' ability to recollect dialogues and sequences from memory.

The first time I saw a *Jalsa* play was in Kanjli village, when I was in Class VI. The news reached us in school that a Jalsa performance was scheduled for the afternoon in Kanjli. My friends and I walked about 3 km through narrow paths in the fields, crossed water drain and channel to reach the venue. The drama unfolded, and I was surprised to see that the *Jalsa* actors seemed more interested in entertaining the crowd with practical jokes. After the performance, I reached home late, unintentionally incurring the displeasure of my grandmother, who had been searching for me throughout the village. I had gone to another village to see the *Jalsa* without informing her.

Mohinder Singh, my cousin, was also fond of organising *Jalsa* plays. On one occasion, while preparing the venue for a *Jalsa* play with his friend Bant Singh, he invited me to join them at night. Mohinder was tasked with carrying a burning torch to illuminate the arena. He moved gracefully amidst the performers, who were attired as men and women, skillfully directing the torchlight to ensure the faces of the performers remained visible to the audience. We returned home together well past midnight.

Memorable Toys

Tall wild grass, known as *kane* in Punjabi, thrived along the boundaries of the agricultural fields, pathways leading to the fields and open spaces. This particular type of wild grass was used in constructing roofs throughout Punjab. Since the stem of the wild grass is strong, farmers used it to make *chhajj* (husk and grain separators), small bowls for storing cotton and grains, as well as coverings for roofs. This raw material is freely available to the villagers who have been using it since time immemorial. A few inventive villagers and toymakers would make toys from the stems of the grass. Among these, two toys that fascinated me were the rotating wheel and the ringing hand toy. Seeing villagers create these toys inspired me to try making them myself. Even though the process of toy-making was simple, I had to go to the fields and collect fresh grass stems. However, I was scared to go alone.

One day, after mustering courage, I went to the fields to collect about a dozen stems, which were enough for creating two toys. As I plucked the stems, I noticed colourful patterns on the ground among the grass weeds near my feet. When I looked down carefully, I saw it was a snake which had coiled up because of the cold. Luckily, I had not stepped on the snake, but when it felt my movement, it raised its head and began to uncoil. Filled with fear, I quickly grabbed the collected stems and ran back home.

In the 1950s, palm and date trees adorned our villages. In Kanjla, some of these trees flourished in a desolate area near the village pond, stretching towards *Lakha Vehda*. The branches of these trees would cascade down, and inventive boys would repurpose them as toy sticks for running. These branches, with their curved shape, allowed for easy rolling on the ground while walking or running. I wanted to get one such branch so that I could also play like my friends. However, it was easier said than done because to reach the palm trees I had to cross two streets, each guarded by half a dozen stray dogs. I had to choose a time when these dogs were napping, usually during the summer afternoons. The second challenge involved climbing up the approximately 5-metre-high palm tree to harvest a branch, all the while being vigilant about the potential risk of the branch falling onto my head. The third obstacle was clearing the leaves around the palm tree and then dragging the branch home.

I was sure that even though I may sneak to the palm tree quietly, coming back through the street dragging the palm tree branch would definitely make noise and alert the owners of the trees as well as the stray dogs. I did not want to be caught by the tree owner or, worse, bitten by the dogs. But whenever I saw other boys wandering the streets, joyfully playing with the curved palm tree branches, my longing to get one for myself would intensify.

June brought sweltering heat, and the streets were nearly deserted as hardly anyone ventured outdoors. Meanwhile, farmers were busy harvesting wheat on the village outskirts. One afternoon, I sensed a good opportunity to grab a palm tree branch. So, after lunch, I headed for the palm trees. I found climbing up the tree difficult, as I had never tried it before. Nevertheless, summoning courage, I ascended the tree and quickly grabbed the hanging dried branch with a sudden jerk. The branch snapped and fell to the ground. I quickly came down, picked up the branch and without wasting time, ran along the streets towards my house. Behind me, I could hear the barking dogs of the palm tree owner chasing after me. Fortunately, I managed to cross their street and reach our *Vadda Vehda* street. After that I was out of danger and reached home with my prized possession. When my grandmother saw the palm tree branch, she became angry because its thorny leaves could cause cuts on the hands and feet.

I allowed her to scold me, then sat down on the roof of our house and removed the leaves with a knife. By evening, I was the proud owner of the palm tree branch and happily played around in the street with my friends.

Neighbours Who Will Always Be Remembered

Our closest neighbours were Ajaib Singh and his family. Right from Class I, I aspired to emulate the success of his son Kirpal Singh, who stood out as the first successful student and top ranker, eventually becoming a lecturer at Government Ranbir College in Sangrur. Ajaib Singh had retired as a Havaldar from the army. Because of family connections, I called him *Bhai* (brother). He possessed a remarkable awareness of world events, so I would meet him every day to listen to his stories. He shared anecdotes about Indian politicians and other notable figures. I wondered about his wealth of knowledge, as in the early 1950s, he did not have a radio or other means to stay informed. He relied on *Sainik Samachar*, a magazine he received once a fortnight and read it carefully. Despite not actively participating in agriculture due to his advanced age, he had successfully provided for his family and was educating his children very well. He had given land to other farmers for cultivation, thereby earning income to meet family expenses—a feat that some of his relatives admired and envied.

Ajaib Singh was well-versed in religious scriptures, frequently reciting hymns from the holy Sikh texts. In the early morning, after waking up, he would recite the hymns loudly in a melodious voice that was very soothing to the ears. Since our house was just opposite Ajaib Singh's, we could hear him clearly. Even today, after a span of 60 years, I still remember the beauty of his singing. My grandmother often advised me to listen carefully to Ajaib Singh every day. Sometimes, we would wake up only after hearing him singing hymns. I had never seen him quarrelling or arguing with anyone. Throughout my years in Kanjla, from 1954 to 1961, I spent a lot of time in Kirpal Singh's house, either learning from him or listening to the stories narrated by Ajaib Singh.

An Unpolished Performance

Our new PET was quite fond of teaching various physical exercises to students and procured the necessary equipment for physical education activities. He told us that our school would participate in the School Games at Sangrur, the district headquarters, and we had to get white vests and white half-pants for the event. Over the course of two months, we diligently practised and prepared ourselves for the annual competition. On the day of the competition, we assembled at our school before dawn. That day, my grandmother had packed two rotis with pickle for me to take to Sangrur for my lunch.

From Kanjla, we walked through Changal and Haredi villages and reached Sangrur around 9 a.m. Our PET informed us that our competition was scheduled to start around lunchtime. We were supposed to showcase our physical exercises within a 20-minute timeframe.

There were four schools participating and we were the last team to perform. While the preceding teams had captivated the audience with splendid musical accompaniments, we solely followed the verbal commands of our PET when it was our turn. We did well, but the overall impact of our physical exercises didn't match the polished performances of the other schools. The result was announced, and we came last! Despite this outcome, our headmaster and PET were pleased that we had done the physical exercises flawlessly.

After the ceremony concluded, our PET rewarded us with two bananas each as refreshments. We commenced our journey back to Kanjla on foot after eating lunch. By the time we reached near Haredi, the sun had already set. It was well past midnight when we finally arrived in Kanjla, where my impatient grandmother awaited my return.

CHAPTER 5

A Great Loss

In April 1961, my mother visited us. When it was time for her departure, my grandmother and I accompanied her till the village *phirni*. On our way back, my grandmother told me about her severe stomach pain. Back then, I did not imagine that it was serious. My grandmother used to have headaches quite often due to migraine, and I thought her pain was similar to that. We reached home and she made tea for both of us. I then brought her medicine from Parmananda, a local medical practitioner, and thought my grandmother would soon get well. But she continued to experience pain. Unable to manage household tasks or cook, my aunt Labh Kaur came from Kakarwal to help us.

As the pain persisted, we took my grandmother to General Hospital, Sangrur where the doctors found that she was suffering from stomach cancer. This was a big shock to us! The civil surgeon advised radiation treatment, which was only available at Christian Medical College (CMC), Ludhiana. My grandmother had no money to go for the necessary treatment at CMC. So, she returned to Kanjla, determined to endure the illness stoically.

However, witnessing her suffering, my parents couldn't bear to stand idly by. They provided the essential financial support and took my grandmother to Ludhiana for treatment. During the course of her treatment, my aunt, Dhan Kaur, remained by her side. While patients were admitted, it was mandatory for their attendants to remain outside. We did not know anyone in

Ludhiana, so my aunt slept on the roadside with other attendants. My grandmother spent about 45 days at CMC. I was not sure whether she would come back to Kanjla alive or not.

While my grandmother was in Ludhiana, I went to Balian for a few days because I needed money to buy books from Dhuri. My grandfather Alwail Singh had planned to visit my ailing grandmother in Ludhiana, so it was decided that I could accompany him to Dhuri and from there walk down to Kanjla on my own. My grandfather occasionally took the train to Dhuri from Alal village, which was about 7 km from Balian.

One early morning, around 3 a.m., my grandfather and I left our house in Balian for Alal village. As there was no direct path to Alal from Balian, I followed my grandfather blindly, unaware of where we were going. We first reached the drain towards Kumbharwal, and then continued eastward for about an hour, expecting to reach a footpath that would take us to Dhandiwal village. But in the darkness, my grandfather lost his sense of direction, and we found ourselves sitting by the drain. He told me that he was not able to see things clearly, which alarmed me in that isolated place. After about 15 minutes, he regained composure, and we resumed our journey in the same direction. He knew that Alal was located to the north-east of our village, and heading in that direction would lead us to Dhandiwal and Alal villages. By this time, it was dawn and we could see our surroundings clearly. We followed the track to Alal and kept walking. After about an hour, we reached the small Alal railway station, where my grandfather purchased train tickets. A passenger train came from Barnala and made a brief stop, but no one got down. We boarded the train and reached Dhuri within half an hour.

In Dhuri, my grandfather purchased books, clothes and a pair of shoes for me. Luckily, a neighbour from Balian, who was also in Dhuri for household shopping, had brought a camel to transport goods to Balian. Around lunchtime, my grandfather boarded the train to Ludhiana, and I started my journey back to Kanjla on foot with the neighbour. We reached Bugray village in about two hours.

From there, I continued solo along the water channel towards Kanjla, while my companion proceeded to Balian. Carrying a packet on my head containing books and clothes, I walked for another two hours and reached Kanjla by evening. On that day, I must have covered about 45 km, mostly under the hot sun. Being young allowed me to endure the exertion.

Our family members went separately to visit my grandmother in Ludhiana. I accompanied my aunt Labh Kaur and my uncle Mal Singh. At that time, Bhola Singh, Labh Kaur's son, was about one year old. We boarded the train at Dhuri, and on the way, the train stopped at Malerkotla station for a few minutes. My aunt went down to the platform to fill a drinking water bottle, but the train started moving, and she had to quickly enter another compartment. I was holding Bhola, and he started crying. Seeing his distress, a young lady came forward, took him in her lap, and miraculously, he stopped crying. Unfortunately, he ended up urinating on her. My uncle apologised to the kind lady who, in good spirits, remarked that such incidents were expected when dealing with children.

We reached Ludhiana and were able to locate the CMC Hospital with the help of an acquaintance. In the evening, I saw my grandmother from a distance since we were not allowed to go near her. That day, she had been exposed to radiation and needed rest.

In the evening, I explored the Ludhiana Bazaar, which was much bigger and more beautiful than Dhuri. During my visit, I purchased a hockey stick for Rs 4, a cherished possession that I kept with me for many years. The next day, before leaving, I met my grandmother. She tightly clasped my hand and urged me not to trouble Labh Kaur. She also advised me to study hard and aspire to become a DC. I could see tears in her eyes. After spending two nights, we returned to Kanjla.

After spending about 45 days in the hospital in Ludhiana and getting full treatment, my grandmother came back to Kanjla. While the upper portion of her stomach had been burnt by radiation, her pain had significantly reduced. She could sit and eat well, occasionally walking around the house and going out for short distances. The doctors had told her that there was little possibility of her survival as the cancer had already reached an advanced stage, but she took her disease sportingly, determined not to burden anyone, especially her daughters and their in-laws.

As time passed, her weakness increased, and she struggled to eat and digest food. Even though the doctors of the CMC Ludhiana had advised her to come back for further radiation, she was too frail to undergo treatment. Sensing her impending death, she conveyed her wish to my mother that I be the one to offer her the last sip of water before her final breath.

Having shared seven years of my life with her, she became more precious to me than my own mother. By the end of October 1961, my grandmother did not have the energy even to get up and sit on the bed. My mother and aunt remained in Kanjla to take care of her as her final moments drew near. Every day, before heading to school, I would affectionately touch her. She would gaze at me with tear-filled eyes while lying down. After coming from school, I would sit by her bedside and drink tea. Although she could open her eyes, she could no longer speak. All her strength had waned, and she survived solely on water, devoid of calories.

One morning, my mother told me that my grandmother had become unconscious. Sensing that she could pass away anytime, she suggested that I skip school. Around 2 p.m., as I sat near the village *darwaja*, my aunt hurriedly approached me and instructed me to come home immediately. Fearing the worst, I ran home, where my mother handed me a spoon to gently drop water into my grandmother's mouth.

Tears streamed down my face as I cautiously poured a few drops of water into her wide-open mouth with trembling hands. Her eyes were closed, and her legs lay straight. Her body was draped in a white cloth. I touched her head and sat beside her, consumed by grief. She had just passed away, a devastating loss that left me stunned.

Later that evening, she was taken to the village cremation ground and cremated. Mohinder Singh and Joginder Singh, her nephews, were her pallbearers and helped in the cremation. Mohinder Singh later shared with me the difficulty of burning one portion of her body, suspecting it to be the cancer-affected part. After the cremation, there was a big storm with thunder, lightning and rain in the evening. I did not sleep the whole night.

My grandmother meant everything to me. Every day, she ensured that I had morning tea and all my meals. When I attended school, she would prepare my lunch and have it ready. Upon returning from school in the evening, she would serve me tea in my favourite brown bowl. Despite her age (she was over 70 years old in 1961) and a tough life, she never made me feel like a burden.

After she died, it felt as if darkness had descended all around me. I experienced a sense of helplessness and solitude. Without her, Kanjla held no significance for me. In the days following my grandmother's death, families and relatives visited our house to offer condolences. As they shared their memories of my grandmother, I couldn't help but cry. I found it unbearable to accept her death. We had spent seven years together in this house, and her loss left an irreparable void in my life.

CHAPTER 6

More Memories Unfolded

Every year, the summer vacation from mid-May to the end of June meant a break from school due to the intense heat. Some years, floods caused by monsoon rains prolonged the holidays. From 1954 to 1961, when I stayed with my grandmother in Kanjla, my holidays routine remained consistent. During this break, teachers burdened us with a heavy load of homework, which I diligently completed within the first 15 days. Since I didn't have any support or companionship in Balian, it was important to finish the homework in Kanjla. I would sit on the street next to our neighbour's house or on the sheltered staircase of Gurdial Singh, another neighbour, to complete the homework. The staircase, functioning like a wind tunnel, provided a welcome relief, as the swift air movement made the heat more bearable.

After completing my homework, I would go to Balian to stay with my parents for about a month. Before going, I would sow maize and other seeds in our courtyard patches, leaving them for my grandmother to water in my absence. Whenever my father came to fetch me, we would reach Balian on his bicycle in about an hour. However, when my grandfather came, we walked the distance in about three hours through our Patianwala and Tahlianwala fields. Occasionally, I stumbled upon feathers shed by peacocks during our journeys on foot. At times, peacocks gracefully took flights from tall trees in our Tahlianwala field, and landed on the trees along the Kotla Branch canal.

During one such journey with my grandfather, I decided to bring along a ball. Since the paths were deserted, I enjoyed throwing the ball ahead and sprinting to retrieve it. However, near Kanjli village, my playful toss along the *kacha* road took an unexpected turn when the ball ended up in a roadside ditch filled with weeds, rendering its retrieval impossible. I cried when I lost the ball, but my grandfather consoled me, promising that he would get two more balls for me.

Floods in the Monsoon

During the summer vacations of June–July 1958, heavy monsoon rains led to flooding in Balian and its surroundings. The *kacha* road from Balian to Kila Hakima, which was on the way from Balian to Kanjla, was submerged. Despite the floods, I was determined to attend school in Kanjla once my holidays were over. My father decided to drop me off in Kanjla a day before the school started. After considering various routes, he chose a safer but longer path, travelling along the Kotla Branch canal to reach our Tahlianwala field. From there, we followed the water distributary channel towards Kila Hakima, eventually reaching the road to Kanjla.

I packed my schoolbag and carefully wrapped it in a plastic sheet. We set out early in the morning, wading through water right from our village. In deeper areas, my father hoisted me onto his shoulders. After crossing the Tahlianwala field, we reached the distributary channel that supplied water to our fields from Hasanpur side. After covering a distance of about one kilometre, we encountered a wide gap in the water distributary channel. This gap, created to drain water from Kanjli towards Batuhe village, was approximately 100 feet wide, with a substantial volume of water flowing through it. Crossing this gap proved challenging due to the need to maintain our balance in the fast water current.

My father took my bag and a stick, and started wading through chest-deep water. As he was a good swimmer, he could skilfully navigate such water currents. After a few minutes, he reached the other side where he deposited my schoolbag, then came back to

take me across. Seated on his shoulders, with my legs dangling in front, I tightly clasped his hair knot for balance. He entered the water and started wading through the currents. Midway across, he gestured to our left, showing me a snake searching for a safe spot amidst the rushing waters. My father told me not to be scared and urged me to hold on to his head. Luckily, the swift current carried the snake away from our path. After a few minutes, we reached the other side. My father squeezed water from his clothes and we resumed our journey on foot. This memory of my father's courageous crossing, wading through chest-deep floodwaters with me perched on his shoulders, always remains fresh in my mind. I was happy that I reached Kanjla and would soon be able to attend school once the classes started.

Everyday Happenings in Kanjla

In the 1930s, the supervisor of the Kotla Branch canal conducted inspections on a bicycle. Villagers would gather along the canal bank to see this uncommon sight, as bicycles were a rarity during that time. While some villagers relied on horses, camels or carts for transportation, the majority simply walked. By 1950, a handful of villagers had purchased bicycles, using them to travel from one place to another.

We had an old Hind bicycle that was used only by my father. There is a unique story behind acquiring this vintage bicycle. It all began when we sold sorghum to a village shopkeeper for Rs 20. The shopkeeper, unable to make the payment, offered his old bicycle as compensation. I have vivid memories of my father taking me on our bicycle from Balian to Kanjla. Seated on the front horizontal rod just behind the handlebars, I often marvelled at how the bicycle went in the right direction and made quick turns. My father, wearing a playful smile, would jest that our bicycle inherently knew the way from Balian to Kanjla and back!

Inder Singh, a carpenter from Kanjla, frequently took up carpentry jobs in Balian. His helpful and amiable nature earned the affection of my grandmother Shyam Kaur. Quite often, he would stay at our Balian outhouse and have meals in our house. As Inder Singh hailed from my mother's village, he became Inder *Mama* (maternal uncle) to me. Every year, at the start of the new school session, he would take me to Dhuri or Barnala on his bicycle to purchase new books, notebooks and other stationery for my new class. As we pedalled along water channels or roads, he would sing loudly, with me seated behind him. Year after year, he willingly shouldered the responsibility of taking me to the city, ensuring that I had everything essential for my studies.

I needed a table to keep my books and place a kerosene lamp during nighttime study sessions. Earlier, the kerosene lamp had to be propped on a bag of wheat. This setup was rather inconvenient because I couldn't easily relocate the bag. Instead, I had to shift my seat closer to the light and the bag whenever I wanted to study. Keeping this in mind, my grandmother asked Inder Singh to make a small table for me. After about a week, he brought the table he had made, measuring 2 feet by 1.5 feet. Although it had a slight stability issue, causing it to shake when I rested my feet on its footrest, it effectively served its purpose during my nighttime study sessions. I used this table till Class XII. It is still kept at Balian.

Some friends in Kanjla had turning wheels, each with a diameter of around 15 inches, and made of iron rods of about half an inch thick. These wheels could be propelled forward by a hook equipped with a handle measuring around two and a half feet in length. It was great fun to run long distances pushing these turning wheels. Although it was difficult to make a turning wheel, I requested Inder *Mama* to create one for me and promptly forgot about it. A few days later, when I returned home from school, I was surprised to find a turning wheel and a pushing hook hanging on a peg in the verandah. My grandmother shared that Inder had brought them, leaving me momentarily speechless with joy. None of my friends had such a finely crafted turning wheel and pushing hook. I was in Class IV then and happily played with the turning wheel for about four years. It was one of the best toys ever given to me by anyone in my childhood.

Tales About Balian

In Balian village, we had rented a piece of land about one kilometre away from the village. This field served as a source of animal fodder for my family due to its convenient proximity to our home. However, being near the village meant that in the early mornings, a number of stray animals would roam around, spoiling the fodder crop. During summer vacations, my father would often send me to to guard this field. Armed with my drawing board and geometry equipment, I would spend my mornings creating drawings while keeping a vigilant eye on our field from the minor canal bank.

One day, as I sat on the bank of the minor canal, gazing over our field, I saw a male goat making its way towards our plot from a distance. Before reaching our field, it had to cross another field guarded by a young boy and girl. Despite the girl's attempt to shoo it away, the goat unexpectedly assumed a threatening stance. Terrified, the girl ran back to her brother, who was about

10 years old. A male goat, proud and unyielding, can rear up on its hind legs and forcefully strike its opponent with its horned head. Undeterred, the boy armed himself with about a five-foot-long stick and bravely confronted the goat. As the animal positioned itself to butt him, the boy swiftly struck its face with the stick and strategically stepped back, staying just out of its reach. The goat repeatedly attempted to butt the boy. However, the boy confidently stepped forward, delivering precise blows to the goat's head before retreating safely. This back-and-forth battle went on for a while until the boy landed a powerful strike that finally forced the goat to retreat, defeated.

I admired the boy's courage and skill in fearlessly confronting the aggressive goat. It was evident that had the goat succeeded in landing a blow, the boy could have been seriously injured. Luckily, he had the presence of mind, courage, and a skilled approach in dealing with such stubborn animals.

During my summer stays in Balian, I occasionally accompanied my grandfather, my uncle Chattar Singh or my father to our fields. Out of all our four fields, I liked our Tahlianwala field, even though it was more than 3 km away from our house. In this field, a row of about a dozen *Shisham* trees, planted by my father and my uncle some 40 years ago, stood tall. A number of peacocks, vultures and other birds had made their nests on these trees. The lush green field bordered by *Shisham* trees was my favourite spot.

My uncle Chattar Singh took charge of various tasks in our fields, while my father focused on ploughing with oxen. When accompanying my uncle, I assisted with small chores, such as removing weeds from the cotton, groundnut and sugarcane crops. Standing amid the five-foot-tall cotton plants in the scorching heat and humidity of July was uncomfortable, almost like a form of punishment. However, my uncle was a tough person who could withstand the summer conditions. Occasionally, he allowed me to rest beneath the *Shisham* trees, although the frequent presence of snakes made me uneasy.

In the afternoons, my uncle Chattar Singh would proudly display his tea-making skills, earning praises from my father as the finest tea maker in the area. To maintain the milk's freshness, he had a unique method—burying the milk bottle in the ground to prevent it from souring. During these tea sessions, he would regale us with tales of our family's trials and triumphs in the fields. One such incident involved a neighbour constructing an irrigation channel through our Patianwala field. He recounted how my grandfather, trusting the *kanungo* and the land settlement officer, was deceived, leading to the channel encroaching upon our land. This dispute escalated into a legal battle, embroiling my family in both criminal and civil cases that persisted for about three years.

We had about 10 domestic animals, including buffalos, cows and calves. To manage them, we employed a 15-year-old shepherd boy tasked with leading them to the fields during the day and bringing them back by evening. He usually led them towards our Lehiwala field, where many uncultivated land parcels and water sources were available for grazing. Back then, the minor canal was not brick-lined, making it easily accessible for both animals and humans to enter, along with the Kotla Branch canal.

One day when the shepherd fell sick, my grandfather took charge of leading our domestic animals to our Lehiwala field. Since I was on vacation, I accompanied him. Walking alongside my grandfather, I wondered how the animals instinctively followed the correct path on their own. We reached our destination in about two hours, and once in the field, the animals began grazing. The temperature was rising. Surprisingly, in those days, there was just one *jand* tree in our neighbour's land where we found respite. We sat in the shade of its trunk, shifting with its changing positions in alignment with the sun's movement. To cool off in the heat, we took baths in the minor canal, and my grandfather brewed tea for us under the open sky.

While we sat beneath the *jand* tree, my grandfather told me a story about an incident that took place in the summer months of 1945, about two years before the Partition of India. The central character was my father's elder sister Inder Kaur. Her husband belonged to a poor family in Hamidi village, situated about 18 km from Balian. Inder Kaur, left with only one son, had lost her husband at an early age and managed the household with the income from a small piece of land. In the year 1945, when roads were scarce, travellers navigated through paths that wound across fields and standing crops to move from one village to another. With limited irrigation facilities, large tracts of arid, sandy land often remained uncultivated, and very few people could be seen in the fields. During the hot summer months, some pedestrians walking alone would fall victim to robbers who exploited such situations. Such incidents were quite common in the Malwa region of PEPSU during that era.

On a hot summer day in 1945, my grandfather was taking a milk buffalo and her calf from Balian to Hamidi for his daughter Inder Kaur. As he reached a desolate and arid stretch of land, midway through his journey, four well-built persons surrounded him and demanded to hand over the buffalo and calf without any resistance. Luckily, my grandfather was armed with a spear for protection. As soon as he was surrounded by the robbers, he aimed the spear at them, challenging them to engage in a duel. He asserted that he could pierce a body in a matter of seconds. Confronted by my grandfather's unwavering posture, the robbers chickened out. They had not anticipated the need to shed blood to snatch a buffalo! After my grandfather's daring challenge, the robbers claimed they were only joking and hastily retreated. My grandfather recounted this incident to me several times, emphasising that courage was often more crucial than sheer strength in moments of crisis.

When I would go back to Kanjla after summer holidays, my grandmother and I would be happy just to see greenery in the courtyard, the result of her efforts in regularly watering my plants. Once by chance, I planted a few castor seeds near the staircase, and to our surprise, the castor plants started growing rapidly. Over the course of two years, two plants soared to a height of about 25 feet, attracting birds that perched on them.

Likewise, my grandmother once planted gourd seeds in the courtyard, and they grew profusely, scaling our roof along the staircase. Within a few weeks, a number of yellow flowers appeared, accompanied by large black ants collecting nectar, inadvertently aiding in the pollination process. Gradually, these plants yielded vegetables for about a month. Every day, we harvested four to five gourds, and my grandmother included them in our meals. It was a wonderful experience for us, as we had never imagined reaping vegetables from plants grown in our own courtyard. I found joy in counting the new yellow flowers and the vegetables likely to be available for us in the next few days.

Cultural Activities

In the late 1950s, around 15 students from Government High School in Kanjla came together to establish a poetry club. They would gather every evening on the school premises to recite their newly written poems. I was in Class VI and regularly attended these sessions. I found them to be a delightful blend of entertainment and creativity. The poems were often satirical and humorous, focusing on various characters in the village. A common target of the satirical verses was an elderly doctor at the Kanjla animal dispensary, who was known for his aggressive style of playing hockey. The poems vividly portrayed his unsportsmanlike conduct during hockey matches. Slowly, this club became an important meeting point in the evening.

At Balian, as mentioned earlier, my family members were followers of Swami Ishwarananda. Every day, we offered food or milk to his disciples. Although I seldom visited the Gurdwara situated on the other side of the village, we had kept the holy book, the Guru Granth Sahib, in our house. One of our family members would open the almirah daily and pray for a few minutes before it. In our Kanjla house, we did not possess any sacred texts. But I observed the villagers had become very religious, initiating annual

Akhand Paths (continuous reading of the Guru Granth Sahib from the beginning to the end) during the winter months. Families in the localities, known as *Vehdas* in Punjabi, collectively contributed to support these *Akhand Paths*. These occasions were highly exciting for us, as we attended night sessions to listen to the recitations of religious hymns by Sant Amar Singh and other important religious singers. Sant Amar Singh, with his melodious voice, would recite holy hymns for two to three hours each night during the *Akhand Path*. While my grandmother, due to her age, couldn't sit for long hours, I would go after dinner and return around midnight.

At the end of the *Akhand Path*, the Gurdwara organised ceremonies to baptize numerous young boys and girls, who then became Amritdhari Sikhs. These individuals embraced the rigorous Sikh religious traditions, including the observance of the five 'Ks': carrying a *kirpan* (small dagger), maintaining *kesh* (long hair), donning long *kachhera* (half-pant worn by Sikhs), using a *kangha* (small hair comb) and wearing a *kadha* (steel bangle). In fact, the period from 1955 to 1960 saw the real resurgence of religious fervour among the villagers. This revival was partially propelled by the upcoming SGPC (Shiromani Gurdwara Parbandhak Committee) elections. Villagers wanted to associate strongly with their religion, prompting Sant Amar Singh to contest the election as an independent candidate. The residents of Kanjla actively campaigned for votes in neighbouring villages. Despite the united efforts of the entire community, he lost the election.

Even though the majority of the villagers were Sikhs, they observed several Hindu customs and rituals, including the worship of Hindu deities. In response to a widespread foot disease affecting cows and buffaloes, a grand *hawan* (religious ritual) was organised, and holy water was sprinkled to seek the blessings of Bajrang Bali Hanuman. The entire community actively participated in worshipping Lord Hanuman and paying homage to his statue near our village *darwaja*. The villagers believed that Lord Hanuman was *Sankat Mochan* (a deity who grants relief from troubles) and safeguarded the villagers from diseases. There was also a Lord Hanuman temple in the village which we visited every Tuesday.

During the Kanjla fair, Kavishri and Dhadi groups enthralled the crowds with Punjabi folk songs for three to four consecutive days. These singers would stay in the Gurdwara complex, and take turns to entertain the public. Their performances often extolled the virtues of Sikh Gurus, the Sikh religion, the sacrifices of the Sikhs in service to their beliefs, the protection of Hindus and the relentless pursuit of the country's independence. They would narrate historical events and the heroics of our forefathers and Sikh warriors. The singing sessions usually commenced around 10 a.m. and continued into the late hours of the night.

The Gurdwara was about one kilometre from our house. At night, we, as a group, would go to the Gurdwara to listen to the mesmerising tales spun by these folk singers. As a precaution against dog attacks on the way back, I would carry a small stick. Since these folk stories were popular in the area, the shops at the village fair also offered brochures containing the lyrics of songs and narratives recounted by these performers.

CHAPTER 7

Back with My Parents

The result of the Middle Standard Examination had shaken me. Despite facing a disruption in my studies due to my grandmother's illness and subsequent death, I refused to use it as an excuse. Instead, the setback fuelled my determination to excel in Classes IX and X at the high school level.

Following my grandmother's demise, my parents locked her Kanjla house, and I permanently relocated to Balian. Every day, I commuted from Balian to Kanjla for school. In Class IX at Kanjla School, new students, mostly from the Government Middle School in Ladda, joined. During the initial few days of class, I observed that the students from Ladda, especially Piyara Lal, were sharp and hard-working. Piyara Lal, who had outperformed me in the Middle Standard Examination, was an extrovert and friendly, possessing all the qualities of a topper, and most of the teachers liked him.

In Class IX, I opted drawing as a subject over Hindi, akin to the engineering drawing taught in the first year of the Bachelor's degree programmes in engineering colleges. Alongside drawing, I had five more subjects: mathematics, science, social studies, English and Punjabi, each carrying a maximum of 150 marks, totalling 900. Accompanied by my uncle Inder Singh, I went to Dhuri to buy my books and stationery. I also needed a new bicycle and a watch for punctuality, so my uncle Sukhdev Singh took me to Barnala and bought me a new Army Brand bicycle and a Titus watch.

In the new class, I was made the class monitor by the class teacher. A new science teacher, who spoke with a Haryanvi accent, had joined the school. Known for his diligence, he commuted to school on a scooter, a novelty in those days, from his rented house in the village. A new English teacher from Malerkotla also joined the school.

Bicycling to and from School in Kanjla

During the summer months, my father would wake up at 4 a.m. After a while, my mother would prepare tea for the family. After drinking his tea, my father would carry tea for my uncle Chattar Singh and grandfather, who slept in our outhouse. My father and uncle would then attend to the oxen, providing them with fodder and leading them to the fields for ploughing. Around 4.30 a.m., my mother would rouse me from sleep. Before heading to school, I would drink a tumbler of buttermilk—a nutritious concoction of milk and curd. By about 6 a.m., I would leave my house on my bicycle and reach the Kanjla school before 7.30 am. For my lunch, my mother would pack *churi* (wheat rotis crushed with sugar and ghee and made into a ball) for me. *Churi* is similar to the energy food that athletes consume after practice. I eagerly waited for the lunch break so that I could eat *churi* while sitting on the school's boundary fence, overlooking the road.

During my daily bicycle commute to school, I made it a habit to carry a stick for protection against stray dogs or wild animals. There were two routes to reach Kanjla. The first option involved following the Kotla Branch canal and passing through Kila to reach Kanjla. The second route led along a newly aligned, albeit *kacha* road. From there, I would navigate through long grass, weeds and bushes to reach the minor canal and eventually the Kila Bridge of the Kotla Branch canal.

On the 3-km stretch through the overgrown vegetation, I frequently encountered foxes, jackals, rabbits and snakes that swiftly disappeared into the undergrowth as I approached. Occasionally, I also spotted wolves and hyenas. My father had advised me never to cycle in desolate paths surrounded by bushes when wolves or hyenas were present. He warned me that these aggressive animals could attack, pull me down from the cycle and kill me. His guidance was clear: stop cycling on spotting a wolf or hyena, take out the stick and be prepared to defend yourself if attacked. I followed his advice diligently.

Even on occasions when I encountered wolves and hyenas, they never attacked me. I made it a practice to stop cycling upon sighting them and brandish my stick. Whenever I went through the longer route, I often came across these animals due to the dense forest growth along the 4.5-km canal stretch. Sometimes, I would also see otters playing on the canal bank.

I had come to accept the notion that there was no family for me in Kanjla. Yet, whenever nostalgia crept in, the taste of my mother's delicious *churi* would uplift my spirits. After school, I would set out on my solitary ride back to my village on my bicycle, as I was virtually the only student from Balian. Even though there was another senior student from Balian, his inconsistent attendance forced me to plan my own school-going routines. I rushed back to Balian to finish the homework given by the teachers.

The return journeys during the sweltering summer months at 1.30 p.m. in the April/May heat were difficult because I had to ride the bicycle against hot westerly headwinds. Every 15 minutes, I would pause my cycling to drink water from wayside handpumps, pouring water on my forehead and turban for relief. I would reach home dead tired in about 90 minutes or so. I did not have time to rest under the shade of trees, as I had to reach home and do my homework. Reflecting on those challenging days, I take pride in my unwavering determination. I never felt disheartened, always willing to complete my solitary journeys in the blistering 45-degrees Celsius heat, cycling against strong westerly headwinds and enduring dust storms.

In the chilly and foggy months of December, January and February, the sun would be visible only after 8 a.m., and temperatures occasionally dropped below zero degree Celsius. As

My daily cycle journey to the Kanjla school from Balian village during 1962-64.

I left for school before 7 a.m., the sun would begin to rise only when I reached the midway point. The biting cold would numb my hands, making it difficult to grip the bicycle handle. I would quite often meet two vegetable vendors, Barkat Khan and Mohammad Ali, who brought their produce from Malerkotla to sell in my village. They probably left Malerkotla around 5.30 a.m. in the freezing morning, cycling along the Kotla Branch canal. Whenever I took that route to school, I would come across them, huddled around bonfires made from grass weeds along the canal. I would often join them and warm myself.

Apart from these encounters with Barkat Khan and Mohammad Ali, the 4.5-km canal journey was usually solitary. Perhaps, the experiences of navigating through both intense cold and hot weather during my school journeys strengthened my resolve to work hard and achieve my goal of scoring high and securing the top position in my class.

I was deeply attached to my grandmother Nihal Kaur and when she died, it felt as though I had lost everything. Each day, on my way back to Balian after school, as I approached the cremation grounds of Kanjla, an indescribable sensation overcame me. I don't know whether it was only my imagination, but I often heard her voice, urging me not to go to Balian as I cycled home. Despite looking towards the cremation grounds, I never found anyone. I sensed that these sounds came from a specific area within the three-acre cremation grounds.

Driven by curiosity, I asked Mohinder Singh, my cousin who had been present during my grandmother's cremation, to show me the exact spot where she was cremated. That evening, he took me to a location covered with weeds and bushes. To my surprise, it was the same spot from where I had often heard my grandmother's voice calling out to me. Knowing her love for me and trusting that she would do me no harm, I felt no fear. I believed that my grandmother's presence or her soul would always protect me from any negative influences in my life.

During my journeys to school, two peculiar incidents involving snakes left me astonished. The first occurred on a hot summer day as I was returning home. Near the Kanjli village water channel, I stopped to drink water from a handpump. A few shepherds stood nearby, gazing up a tree. Mynas were screeching, and upon looking up, I saw a snake that had climbed the tree to devour the myna chicks. The shepherds brought the snake down by hitting it with a stick. With a full belly, it move sluggishly. The shepherds killed it and began extracting the chicks by pressing the snake's belly. After a few minutes, four chicks came out. Three were already lifeless, and one, though slightly moving, was as good as dead. This was the first time that I saw food being expelled from a snake's belly.

The second snake-related incident occurred along the Kotla Branch canal, which had run dry. While returning to my village, I noticed a group of shepherds standing in the dried canal, sometimes running towards and then away from a particular object with sticks in hand. Intrigued, I stopped to investigate. To my surprise, the shepherds were trying to hit a small snake with their sticks. However, the snake was able to jump quite high, evading their attempts. Amidst the commotion, an elderly man passing by informed the shepherds that it was a flying snake, capable of jumping high and delivering bites. To avoid being bitten, he advised the shepherds to use a bush or a large tree branch. This would entangle the snake when it tried to jump. Quickly, one of the shepherds fetched a tree branch and successfully hit the snake. It got caught up in the branch and was killed by the shepherds. Witnessing this unique snake, which was able to leap and bite, was a novel experience for me.

Since I would set out early for school, the narrow and desolate paths were rarely travelled by others. Cycling alone on these secluded trails meant I had to handle any potential emergencies on my own. Villagers often shared eerie tales of ghosts being sighted in such desolate places, and, like others, I was scared of the supernatural. Aware of my fear, my father assured me that all ghosts and departed souls feared Lord Hanuman. To instill a sense of protection, he gave me a Hanuman *chalisa* (verse), which I would recite on Tuesday afternoons or whenever the fear of ghosts surfaced. While crossing these solitary paths, surrounded by tall grass weeds, I would invoke Lord Hanuman and pedal through. The mere remembrance of Lord Hanuman dispelled my fear, giving me the strength and energy needed during my journeys through desolate stretches.

Studies as a Priority

In Class IX, I faced competition from a few peers, namely Piyara Lal, Mohan Lal Sharma, and Sukhdev Singh. However, with consistent effort, I gradually improved my performance in examinations. Since I was excellent in drawing and mathematics, I aimed to establish a lead in these subjects. While Piyara Lal was brilliant, his tendency to hastily answer questions resulted in occasional errors due to carelessness. This impulsive approach often led to mark deductions, which were compounded by a less-than-impressive handwriting. In contrast, I adopted a meticulous approach, making frequent revisions before appearing in the examinations. This method ensured that I did not make unintentional mistakes that others generally made.

The mid-term examinations in November 1962 marked a turning point. With the appointment of a new science teacher and the initiation of systematic science teachings and practical sessions, the academic landscape evolved. After a few days, the results of the mid-term exams were compiled and I emerged first, with Piyara Lal securing the second position. Sukhdev Singh was not in contention. This outcome seemed to be shaping the situation in my favour, providing further encouragement and motivation.

The stretch of road from Kila to Kanjla was reasonably smooth. Despite being a *kacha* road, I could comfortably ride my bicycle on this stretch as there was almost no traffic in the early morning. Every day, while riding from Kila to Kanjla, I devoted my time to learning English essays by rote and reading my exercise books and notes, ingeniously placed on the bicycle handle. This peculiar routine became a daily ritual, except during the rainy seasons when keeping exercise books on the handle proved challenging. I had no fear of falling down or colliding with anyone, as the road was straight and I rarely found anyone travelling on it. I had a clear view of anyone approaching from over one kilometre away. Studying on my bicycle compensated for the time spent on travel.

My Fiery Paternal Grandmother

One day, upon returning to my house in Balian after school, I sensed a heightened tension among my family members. Unaware of the cause, I found my grandmother Shyam Kaur arguing with my father and grandfather. Just as I arrived, my grandmother told me that she would take me to our outhouse. A few minutes later, my mother revealed that two persons had been killed in the village by their rivals. A group of policemen led by the Deputy

Superintendent of Police (DySP) had reached the village to investigate the matter. The police had detained the suspects and planned to interrogate them.

Initially, the police had planned to set up their camp in the empty premises of the former Cooperative Bank. However, at the request of the *sarpanch* (head of the village panchayat), the DySP opted to conduct interrogations in our outhouse. As a result, we had to move our domestic animals to accommodate the police. Alarmingly, the police resorted to third degree methods, including beating the suspects, with their cries audible even at the village *darwaja*, which was about 75 metres away from our outhouse.

Adding to the discomfort, the village panchayat supplied liquor and chickens to the police personnel stationed in our outhouse. As a vegetarian family abstaining from alcohol, this action was viewed as a breach of our family values by both the police party and the village panchayat. Despite the discomfort, my father and my uncle hesitated to ask the DySP to vacate our outhouse. Eventually, it was decided that my grandmother would take the lead, with me accompanying her.

Upon entering our outhouse, we saw two persons sprawled on the ground, enduring blows from constables wielding sticks. Reacting to this, my spirited grandmother voiced her protest in Punjabi, 'Who gave you permission to enter my house? This is my house. We follow a vegetarian lifestyle, abstaining from both alcohol and meat. Yet, here you are consuming alcohol and preparing meat. Moreover, you are assaulting villagers. If you wish to stay as guests in my house, I'll arrange vegetarian meals for all of you—no meat, no alcohol.'

In response to my grandmother's impassioned remarks, the Dy SP spoke respectfully and conveyed in Punjabi, '*Mata ji*, the village *sarpanch* requested us to use this house. If it belongs to your family, please accept our apologies. We will vacate immediately.' After this, the Dy SP instructed his team to stop the interrogation of the suspects and shift to the bank building.

I was very scared during the exchange between my grandmother and the Dy SP, apprehensive about how the officer would react. However, as I listened to the conversation, coupled with the authoritative tone of my grandmother, I was taken aback. We stood there, and within a few minutes, the police party left along with the suspects. Shortly after their departure, the *sarpanch* came to our house to apologise to my grandmother. This was the first time I had witnessed the immense courage of my grandmother. I could imagine how strong she must have been in her youth. It became clear to me that the stories of her bravery, as narrated by my father, were indeed true. Once the police party left, we came back to our house. My father and uncle heaved a sigh of relief, as they had not expected the outhouse to be vacated by the police so quickly.

Hockey Match and Examinations

The hockey team of Kanjla School was rated as one of the best in the area, enhancing its prospects of clinching the top position in the district tournament scheduled for December 1962. Our school team had won all preceding matches, and was set to compete against the formidable team from Government High School, Gharachon, in the final. Recognising the significance of this occasion, our school authorities sent us to Sangrur to support our team. Most of us walked from Kanjla to Sangrur to witness the final match.

On the day of the match, commencing around lunchtime, the atmosphere was charged with excitement. Even though I anticipated an easy victory for our team, the formidable performance of the Gharachon players made the outcome uncertain. Some of their forwards were very fast in dribbling and running. After a while, Kirpal Singh (popularly known as Pala), the centre forward of the Kanjla school team, scored the first goal with a powerful shot that resonated loudly as it hit the wooden plank behind the goalkeeper. We all jumped with joy. Our principal, Durga Parshad, rushed onto the ground to congratulate the players and urged them to score more goals for a decisive victory.

The match resumed, and our team netted two more goals. As the match concluded, we emerged victorious with an impressive 3–0 score. It was the most thrilling match I had ever witnessed, making me feel as though I were also playing.

The Class IX examinations were held in the last week of March 1963, and to ensure that I did not miss them, I consistently arrived at school approximately two hours before the scheduled time. After the examinations, the results were announced in the school assembly. Once again, I stood first, with Piyara Lal coming in second. My science teacher told me that he had been diligently searching for mistakes in my science answer paper but couldn't find any. My competitors were left behind. When I came home, I shared the news of my success with my father.

A few days later, my father shared with me about his visit to our Patiawala field. There, the tube-well operator (mentioned earlier) congratulated him. The operator told him that surpassing my academic achievements seemed like an impossible feat for anyone, including his own brother Sukhdev Singh. He also disclosed that he had been providing intensive coaching to Sukhdev for the last four years. Yet, his brother couldn't outperform me in any exams from Class VI onwards. In a light-hearted exchange, the operator playfully enquired about the secret to my intelligence. My father jokingly responded that I consumed a full tumbler of buttermilk every morning, and it had sharpened my brain!

My Father's Influence

For about 19 years, my father dedicatedly visited the *dera* (dwelling) of Swami Ishwarananda and actively contributed to its maintenance. As previously mentioned, Swami Ishwarananda was proficient in Sanskrit and had a deep understanding of the *Ramayana* and *Mahabharata*. My father, in turn, would narrate stories from these epics that he had heard from the Swami.

My father's storytelling method was both simple and captivating. He always included vivid descriptions of the central characters, emphasising the overarching message that morality and truth always win. The primary objective behind these narratives was to instil in me a sense of determination and courage, while imparting the virtues of honesty and sincerity. He had not studied in any school or college; therefore, whatever he had learnt was during his time spent in the *dera*.

One story my father often recounted, highlighting dedication and unwavering focus, was that of Dronacharaya, the revered guru of the Kauravas and Pandavas. This narrative from the *Mahabharata* depicted an important moment when Dronacharaya challenged his disciples to shoot the eye of a bird with an arrow. Initially, he asked them about what they saw, and while most described the tree, its branches, leaves and the bird, Arjuna of the Pandava stood out by stating that he could only see the bird's eye and nothing else. Arjuna's clarity of his objective and his focus enabled him to be the sole archer to hit the bird's eye. The lesson conveyed was clear: to achieve one's goal, undivided concentration on the objective is key, preventing the mind from wavering.

Inspired by this tale, my father set the objective for me to stand first in my class with high marks. His guidance included not only studying hard but also adopting strategies to stay ahead of my peers. Using everyday logic and anecdotes from the epics, he underscored the importance of perseverance and having clear objectives. He would draw parallels between running on different surfaces and tackling questions of varying difficulty levels. Just as a runner faces challenges on a muddy or uneven ground, a student encounters difficulties in answering complex questions.

While many students opt for easier questions, my father stressed that to stand out as well as to obtain first rank required tackling the tougher ones. Similar to an intelligent and skilled competitor in a race, a successful student distinguishes himself by attempting challenging questions, thereby getting a significant lead in marks compared to his competitors.

Following his advice, I paid special attention to difficult questions and ensured that I covered the entire syllabus for each subject without omitting anything. This approach ehnanced my chances of scoring high marks in examinations.

I learnt that it was crucial to practise writing answers as often as possible. The ability to complete a task within the allotted time depends on consistent practice. A person who has thoroughly revised beforehand can effortlessly accomplish a task within the set time without any hiccups. The more the revision, the less time a student needs to write answers in an examination.

Students are generally under a lot of stress when they write their examinations. Therefore, they are more likely to make unintentional mistakes and get lower marks due to rushing through while writing the examination answer paper. A simple remedy for this is for students to review their answers at the end of the examination, rectifying errors and preventing losing marks. My father's counsel included completing the examination answer paper at least 10 to 15 minutes before the designated time, allowing ample opportunity to recheck my answers. He also underscored the importance of ensuring a restful night's sleep before the examination, highlighting the contrast with the prevalent habit of late-night studying, which often results in increased stress and fatigue on the day of the examination.

I followed the sound advice of my father, and found that it not only helped me score higher marks but also proved beneficial during the Combined Competitive Examination (CCE) for the IAS in 1973 and throughout my tenure in the IAS.

I had just completed my pre-university examinations and come home to Balian. It was the hot month of May in 1965, and the farmers had been busy harvesting wheat. Our family had gathered the wheat in bundles, subjecting them to the trampling of cows and buffaloes for three to four days to crush them. The resulting mixture of wheat grains and chaff was then tossed into the air so that the wheat grains were separated from the chaff by the wind. When I reached the wheat thrashing site, I saw my father sitting in a corner, sweeping wheat grains to one side. After this task, he sat on the ground with a small stick, attempting to extract a few wheat grains lodged in soil crevices. As I joined him, he told me that a good farmer would not waste a single grain and would take out every grain. This incident served as a vivid reminder of the immense hard work he invested in producing food for the family. The lesson imparted to me was that, witnessing my father's meticulous work and dedication, I should follow his example in my studies. Even today, though he is no more, I still visualise him sitting in the hot noon of May, trying to take out a few grains from the soil wedges.

My father was not only proficient in reciting *Gurbani*, the compositions of the Sikh Gurus, but he could also read the Holy Guru Granth Sahib. Even though I knew Punjabi well and had studied till Class X, I found it difficult to read the Holy Guru Granth Sahib. This is because all alphabets are intricately connected within sentences, making it challenging to discern the beginning or end of a particular word. Only experienced people, who read the Holy Guru Granth Sahib regularly, could read it fluently. My father, having dedicated 20 years to reading the sacred text, was one such individual. He was often sought after by people to recite it in his melodious voice.

I was pleasantly surprised to discover that my father was a good folk singer too. I witnessed this aspect of his talent during a visit to Chhannan village for the wedding of my cousin, Harnek Singh. Following a customary tradition in Punjab, the ladies from the bride's side began singing folk songs when it was time for the marriage party to eat. According to the custom, no one could start eating until someone from the groom's side responded with songs. To my surprise, it was my father who stood up and responded with folk songs to the ladies' songs. Although I had never heard him sing before, it seemed my father knew those songs well. After a lively exchange, the village elders thanked the marriage party, advised the ladies to stop singing and signalled the groom's side to begin the dinner.

Higher Classes

In Class X (then referred to as matriculation), I continued with the same six subjects as in Class IX. However, the syllabus became more difficult and comprehensive. By this time, I had gained confidence in excelling in drawing and geometry, including solid geometry, which was part of Class X curriculum. My attendance remained impeccable at 100 per cent, never having missed a single day. Acknowledging my dedication, the school authorities honoured me with a certificate for my punctuality.

In preparation for the Class X examinations, I set six specific goals for myself: thoroughly cover the full syllabus of all subjects, revise each subject's syllabus every fortnight, solve the last 10 years' question papers, maintain perfect attendance, use bicycle journeys to school for revising answers, and memorise as many English essays as possible. To enhance my preparation, I visited 'Chaichey Di Hati' in Dhuri, where the bookseller recommended supplementary books on all subjects. He advised that going through these additional resources would help in securing more marks, as questions in the final examination might be asked from these books as well.

The science teacher who began teaching us in Class IX was both dedicated and earnest in fulfilling his role. He informed us that out of the 150 marks, 15 were allocated to questions about various salts (also known as compounds) in chemistry. In previous years, these salts had been omitted by science teachers, resulting in students struggling to respond to related questions. Our new science teacher took the proactive step of compiling detailed notes on around four dozen salts, covering a spectrum of information, including their preparation methods, properties, reactions with key metals and acids, and their practical applications. He wrote comprehensive notes on the blackboard, which I copied diligently.

During my daily bicycle commute from Balian to Kanjla, I would place my science copybook on the handlebar and repeatedly went through these salts, committing them to memory.

Being the sole student coming from Balian, I had the freedom to study whatever I wished during the journeys to school. I had identified about 25 essays in English and memorised them. I believed these essays could be adapted for use in any essay or letter with suitable modifications. This form of rote learning was essential to avoid mistakes in sentence construction and organising arguments correctly when attempting to write an essay in my own words during the examination.

I also heeded my father's advice, and I found it helpful in scoring higher marks. Here are the key points I adhered to:

(i) Cover all questions included in the syllabus without any omissions.

(ii) Practise writing answers repeatedly before the examination to ensure writing them correctly in the shortest time possible.

(iii) Always review the answers at least once before leaving the examination hall.

(iv) Approach the examination with a fresh mind, ensuring to get adequate sleep early on the previous day of the examination. This required being fully prepared well before the actual exam date.

I used to play hockey and served as a standby player, ready to enter the hockey ground only if any player was injured. To strengthen the school team, a practice tour was planned for December 1963, covering half a dozen villages where we would play hockey and kabaddi against other school teams. The proposed tour included schools in Dhanaula, Barnala, Bhadaur, Raikot and Mahil Kalan. This tour required me to be away from my village for about five days. Despite my parents' concerns about the potential distraction from studies, I decided to accompany the Kanjla school team. However, I did not participate in any matches as all players were available. Our school team performed well in hockey and kabaddi matches at Dhanaula, Barnala, and Mahil

Kalan, returning exhausted after the five-day tour. After that, I stopped participating in hockey, choosing to focus on my studies, especially since matriculation was a tough examination. I agreed to abide by my parents' advice.

I aspired to surpass the score of 713 marks in Class X, out of a total of 900 marks. This target aimed to match the achievements of Kirpal Singh, who had scored 673 marks out of 850 in 1959, setting a seemingly unbreakable record. Teachers wondered whether any future student could break this remarkable record. The Class X examinations, conducted by Panjab University, were widely perceived as a challenging milestone for students. After matriculation, students were expected to join colleges and select science or non-science streams based on their Class X marks. Given the crucial role these marks played in determining career options, my parents did not let me do any household chores.

In the mid-term examination held in November 1963, I performed well and secured the first position. In January 1964, my mother relocated to our Kanjla house so that I did not have to travel every day to and from Balian. My parents believed that a two-month stay in Kanjla before the final examinations would be beneficial for my studies. This period was deemed crucial for my academic preparation. For our stay in Kanjla, we brought along a buffalo that provided milk. I maintained a perfect attendance throughout my Class X studies, a commendable achievement.

Final Examinations

During my time in Kanjla, I adhered to a rigorous study schedule that often stretched into late hours. My friend Jagga Singh and two neighbours, Kirpal Kaur and Pritam Kaur, would join me in our collective study sessions. As they were slightly weak in certain subjects, I helped them in understanding difficult concepts. While most houses in our neighbourhood had electricity, our home lacked this amenity due to the financial constraints faced by my grandmother, which prevented her from obtaining an electric connection in 1959-60. So I relied on a kerosene lamp for my

Class X preparation. With just one kerosene lamp at our disposal, the four of us shared the cost of the kerosene oil. After our study sessions, the girls would return to their houses, while Jagga Singh opted to stay overnight at our house. To keep us alert during the night, my mother would prepare tea. Mohinder Singh, my cousin, also started sleeping in our house to provide additional security. On some occasions, he entertained us by skillfully mimicking the sounds of drum beats using only his mouth.

The matriculation examinations were held at Mastuana for all four neighbouring schools, including Kanjla Government High School. Panjab University had sent special supervisors and invigilators to check cheating. The examination schedule spanned approximately 20 days. For our stay at Mastuana, four of us rented a room with four beds at the Gurdwara. The Kanjla school authorities instructed us to relocate to Mastuana at least two days before the exams, and took our attendance every day. Similar to our Class VIII examinations, Jagga Singh's uncle Kartar Singh diligently brought our meals daily from Kanjla.

Amidst my diligent preparation and commendable performance in previous exams, misfortune struck suddenly. In the midst of the examinations, I fell ill. I promptly informed my father, who rushed from Balian. I had high fever when I appeared for the science paper. After the exam, my father took me to a well-known medical practitioner in Bahadharpur village. The doctor administered an injection and prescribed medications. Because of my fear of injections, I panicked, prompting my father to comfort me by holding me in his lap. The doctor presumed my condition was exam-related stress and reassured that I would recover once the exams concluded. After dropping me back at Mastuana, my father cycled back to Dhuri to purchase some agriculture seeds.

While en route to Dhuri via Ladda, my father met three elderly men who were also travelling on bicycles from Mastuana to Ladda. He joined them for the journey. These men happened to be the parents of my classmates from Ladda village and had come to meet their children. One of the gentlemen was particularly confident that his son would secure the first position in Kanjla school. In response, my father mentioned that he had travelled to Mastuana to show his son (me) to a doctor as I was unwell and had fever. To this, one of the three men casually remarked that children of farmers, who supposedly don't study throughout the year, tend to develop examination fever out of fear of faring badly during exams.

Then one of them asked my father the name of his son who was appearing in the examination. My father told them that his son's name was Jarnail Singh. Suddenly, with great surprise, the same gentleman said that his son had told him that Jarnail Singh would stand first. My father narrated this discussion to me several times later on, just to let me know how proud he felt when people said that Jarnail Singh was the best student in the school and unbeatable in studies.

Despite facing health setbacks, I performed exceptionally well in the examinations. I felt optimistic about achieving 100 per cent marks in mathematics. I also excelled in the science and drawing papers. With the completion of the Class X examination, there was no reason to continue staying in Kanjla. As I anticipated joining a college after Class X, and with both my mother and I prepared to return to Balian, it seemed inevitable that the Kanjla house would remain locked indefinitely. So, my mother and aunt Labh Kaur decided to sell the house to one of our relatives. The next step involved transporting our belongings to either Balian or Kakarwal, where my aunt lived. My mother and aunt divided the moveable properties among themselves. My father brought a cart from Balian to transport our belongings.

It was a sad and emotional experience for me to leave Kanjla permanently. I cherished the Kanjla house where I had spent my childhood. The house held sweet memories of my time there and my stay with my grandmother. Every aspect of the house—its walls, rooms, staircase, courtyard and the street—reminded me of the joyful and sorrowful moments of those days. I touched the mud floor at the spot where, on that sorrowful day in October 1961, I had put drops of water in my dying grandmother's mouth. In the evening, I visited the *halti* for the last time and sat on its boundary wall in a pensive mood, crying inconsolably. Emotionally, one chapter of my life's journey was coming to an end. I had friends and classmates in Kanjla, whereas in Balian, I had almost no friends. I was leaving behind all my friends in Kanjla. The next day, I left with my parents from Kanjla to Balian, never to sleep again in our Kanjla house. I recall my father's advice not to feel sad, as life goes on. However, I couldn't help but feel deeply emotional and sad at leaving behind the house that held memories of my grandmother, who had tolerated all my mischief and supported me during my formative years of study.

The results of the matriculation examination were announced by Panjab University in June 1964. I had scored 682 marks, securing the top position not only in Kanjla but also at the Mastuana centre. In Sangrur district, I stood second, with one student getting a slightly higher score. Piyara Lal was the second-highest scorer in Kanjla School. I ranked high on the merit list of Panjab University, bringing immense joy to Durga Parshad, the headmaster of Kanjla Government High School. He received numerous congratulatory messages from headmasters of other schools in Sangrur town. Despite the special tuitions organised by these schools, no student from Sangrur town outperformed me. In those days, each of the four high schools in Sangrur town aimed for their students to stand first. However, in 1964, a student from a rural area had outsmarted them. That was why Durga Parshad, a resident of Sangrur town, felt proud of my achievement. A significant portion of the credit for my achievement goes to my school and teachers, especially the headmaster and the science teacher. I came to school and met my teachers and friends. Durga Parshad inquired about my plans for further studies. I informed him that my future course of action depended on my family's decisions. His son Mohinder Kumar had also excelled in studies, and Durga Parshad intended to send him to Panjab University in Chandigarh for an MSc degree in physics.

On that hot day, I celebrated my success by eating *kharbujas* (cantaloupes) and taking a refreshing bath in the irrigation water channel on the eastern side of Kanjla village. Accompanying me was Dharam Pal, a junior and a brilliant student. As the sun began to set, I went back home. I reached home in the late evening, and by then, my family members had already heard about my remarkable academic success. My father, in the midst of relishing a bowl of *dalia* (porridge), beamed with pride and happiness. Eager to know about my peers' scores, he asked me how many marks Sukhdev Singh and Piyara Lal had scored. I informed him that Piyara Lal had obtained more than 600 marks and was second in the school, while Sukhdev Singh had scored less than 600 marks. After hearing me, my father recounted about the efforts of Sukhdev Singh's brother to ensure Sukhdev stood first. He also briefly recounted the conversations he had with the parents of students from Ladda during his bicycle ride from Mastuana to Ladda.

During dinner, I shared my desire to attend college in Sangrur or Ludhiana. There were heated discussions, and my grandfather, sceptical due to my uncles' lack of success in studies and unemployment, suggested focusing on agriculture instead. He stated that farmers' children generally struggle to get good jobs after completing their studies. Despite his advice, I was determined to pursue higher education, and I contemplated attending Government Ranbir College in Sangrur.

I went to the rooftop to sleep, but sleep eluded me. I tossed and turned throughout the night, thinking about my next move to join Government Ranbir College. Around midnight, a severe dust storm forced me to move indoors, where concerns about my future kept me awake. That was how I spent my first night after securing the top rank in my school.

PART II

PREPARING FOR THE FUTURE

CHAPTER 8

Joining College for Higher Studies

Despite achieving excellent marks in Class X and finding my name in the merit list of the top 200 students in the Panjab University examination, my grandparents were hesitant to send me to college as they were unsure if higher education would truly benefit a farmer's son. Moreover, the substantial expense of college fees added to their reservations. The day after the results were announced, my headmaster Durga Parshad addressed the student assembly, and mentioned the congratulations he had received from numerous people in Sangrur regarding my impressive rank. When he learnt that my family was not keen about my college education, he took the initiative to meet my parents and grandparents.

I was taken aback when, in the sweltering summer of June 1964, Durga Parshad arrived at my village, approximately 25 km from Sangrur, riding his bicycle along the dusty *kacha* track. As word of his visit spread, our neighbours also came to meet him. He wanted to talk to my parents and grandparents together, so I called my father from our outhouse. An old wooden chair, long neglected and piled with worn clothes in one corner of the room, was hastily dusted off and cleaned for Durga Parshad. With everyone assembled, he congratulated my parents and urged them to send me to college for further education. He told them not to worry about financing my studies, as he was confident that

I would secure scholarships to cover my expenses. I vividly recall his words to my father, '*Main Jarnail jinna mehnati, hosyar atey imandar ladka nahin dekiaya. Isnu agey padao. Thonu paise di koyi mushkil nahin ayegi. Main suniya hai ke tusi isnu padana nahin chahundey. Eisee galti kade na karna. Eh munda thoda atey pind da na roshan karega. Tusi mere eh bol yaad rakhoge* (I have not come across any student who is as hard-working, intelligent and sincere as Jarnail. Support him for higher studies. You will not face any difficulty in financing his studies. I have heard that you do not want him to pursue higher education, but do not make such a mistake. This boy will bring laurels to your family and your village. You will remember my words in the future.)'

After having lunch at our house, my grandmother packed some *desi ghee*, a favorite of his, in a small tin for him. He then went back to Sangrur on his bicycle, a journey that must have taken about two hours. After Durga Parshad had gone, my family discussed the matter and finally decided that I should join college. I felt a sense of relief, knowing that Durga Parshad's advice and reassurance effectively dispelled my grandparents' hesitancy. His spontaneous visit had a profound impact, as he had come on his own to talk to my family.

I received a letter from DAV College, Jalandhar, (DAV stands for Dayanand Anglo-Vedic), inviting me to join Class XI, commonly referred to as 'pre-university' at that time. The letter also included an offer of a scholarship covering all tuition and hostel lodging expenses. DAV College was renowned for its ability to attract top students and athletes from across Punjab. In fact, more than half the students featured on the merit list of any examination were from this institution. The college also used to organise special teaching classes for high achievers to ensure their consistent presence on Panjab University's merit lists year after year.

Despite receiving the offer, I hesitated to apply to DAV College due to concerns about adapting to the bustling life of a top-class college in a city like Jalandhar, located in Punjab's well-developed 'Doaba' region. After careful consideration, I decided to fill out the admission forms for Class XI at Government Ranbir College in Sangrur. This college had impressive buildings and a vast campus, generously donated by Ranbir Singh, the Raja of Jind State. It is worth noting that Sangrur was the capital of the erstwhile princely state of Jind. Spanning approximately 100 acres, the college grounds were adorned with numerous guava trees. Several benches were strategically placed around the campus, providing students with comfortable spots to study in the shade of these trees.

Pre-university Days in Government Ranbir College, Sangrur

On 6 July 1964, I left my village before dawn on my bicycle and reached Government Ranbir College in Sangrur a few hours before the scheduled counselling session. Most students were accompanied by their parents, but I was the only one who had arrived alone, wearing a white kurta-pyjama while most were dressed in pants and shirts. After some time, a list of students was posted on the noticeboard of the hall. To my delight, I discovered my name at the top of the list, along with my impressive score of 682 marks in Class X. The second person in the list had 606 marks. As my name topped the list, I was the first to be called for counselling and admission. After presenting my original testimonials and certificates, I was admitted to the physics, chemistry and mathematics (PCM) stream, commonly referred to as 'non-medical'. I paid both the admission fees and hostel fees.

Classes were slated to begin on 13 July 1964, a Monday. As I was advised to reach the hostel at least two days in advance, I planned to be there on 11 July. Furthermore, I was instructed to wear either a white kurta-pyjama or a pant and a shirt, as brightly coloured kurta-pyjamas were discouraged in the college. My mother had three sets of white kurta-pyjamas tailored for me, and she also purchased a steel trunk for my belongings. I took my father's old shoes, which fit me comfortably.

On 11 July 1964, I left early in the morning on my bicycle for Sangrur. Following my parents' advice, I chose the Kotla

Branch canal route, heading first to Harigarh Bridge and then continuing along the road to Sangrur via Badbar, Mastuana and Badrukhan. This route, from Harigarh Bridge to Sangrur, served as the primary path for all vehicular traffic from Barnala to Sangrur. I proceeded cautiously on my cycle. After about two hours, I reached the outskirts of Badrukhan, where I saw a large crowd gathered on the road, with several vehicles parked on both sides. Along the roadside, a man was bleeding profusely from a deep wound resembling a sword cut. As I stopped my bicycle, I noticed a young man lying crushed on the road. From the agitated discussions of the villagers, I learnt that he had attempted to cross the road when a speeding PEPSU Roadways bus ran over him. The enraged villagers, holding the driver responsible, surrounded the bus, and one of them attacked the driver with a sword, causing injuries. Some elders and bus passengers were trying to intervene and sort out the matter. With the police yet to arrive, there was considerable confusion, and the risk of further injuries during the heated discussions was imminent. After staying there for about five minutes, I quickly resumed my journey to Sangrur.

I reached the hostel, which was in the college complex itself. I later learnt that the hostel building had once served as a stable for the Raja of Jind State. The plinth of the hostel building was about four feet high. I had been allotted Room No. 12, which I would share with Ravinder Pal, a student from Dhuri enrolled in the pre-medical course (Class XII for students studying physics, chemistry and biology), a stream that paves the way for admission to the Bachelor of Medicine and Bachelor of Surgery (MBBS) degree programme.

Upon entering the room, I found Ravinder Pal and his father already there, and he warmly welcomed me. The hostel caretaker gave me a bed, table and chair, but I was asked to arrange for my own fan. I kept my bicycle in the verandah so that it would be safe. There were only 10 rooms allotted for students, the other rooms serving as storage for the NCC (National Cadet Corps), a dining room and a kitchen. A total of about 25 students could occupy the hostel at a time.

On 12 July 1964, about six students were present in the hostel as it was a Sunday, a college holiday. In the evening, a group of senior boys confronted me near my room and started questioning me about my attire and the presence of my bicycle on the hostel verandah. Whenever I tried to respond, they would cut me short and shout at me. I had not expected such behaviour from senior hostel mates. One demanded I deflate my bicycle's tyres and move it to the lawns. Fearful, I complied quietly. They continued questioning me about my manner of speaking, dress and turban-tying style for about half an hour before going away. At that time, I was unaware that senior students in colleges engaged in the practice of 'ragging' newly admitted students.

The experience of my first day in the hostel frightened me. I thought of leaving the hostel and commuting daily from Kanjla to Sangrur on my bicycle. Before making a decision, I decided to seek advice from Kirpal Singh, another student from Kanjla. He was visiting Hazura Singh, a senior teacher at Raj Higher Secondary School in Sangrur, who had previously taught at Kanjla Government High School. After about 30 minutes, I reached Hazura Singh's house in the Patiala Gate area of the town. When I reached, Hazura Singh and Kirpal Singh were enjoying tea. I shared my concerns with them, recounting how I was ragged by a few senior boys. When I told them that I would prefer to commute from Kanjla daily, both of them advised me to continue staying in the hostel. After a brief discussion, Hazura Singh offered to accompany me to the hostel and see what he could do.

We reached the hostel within 10 minutes on Hazura Singh's scooter. Upon our arrival, I spotted the senior boys having tea at the canteen. I pointed out the four students, indicating that they were the ones who had threatened me. Hazura Singh approached them and, in a commanding voice, questioned why they were tormenting me. He then singled out one of them, who had a slightly dark complexion, and said in Punjabi, 'You look like a drum of coal tar. Why are you threatening our boy? Do you know Ballee? Should I send Ballee to set you right?' As soon as Hazura Singh mentioned this name, the senior boys looked scared. They immediately apologised and promised never to bother me again. As a parting shot, Hazura Singh warned them that he would come again to check on their behaviour.

The mere mention of Ballee's name proved to be a powerful deterrent, and no one ever troubled me in the hostel. Intrigued by the impact this unknown figure had wielded over a group of senior boys, I set out to learn more about him. It turned out that Ballee's full name was Baljit Singh, a celebrated boxer in the region. He was a student at the Raj Higher Secondary School in Sangrur and had won gold medals in boxing competitions across Punjab. Shortly after, I met Ballee's elder brother Jagjit Singh, affectionately known as Jagga, who was also a well-known boxer in Punjab. With Hazura Singh's intervention, I was able to settle down in the hostel. The senior boys, who had ragged me, now behaved politely, fearing the repercussions from Ballee!

I purchased all the required books and notebooks for physics, chemistry, mathematics, and English. However, my initial days at college were disheartening, largely due to the difference in the medium of instruction. Having been schooled in Punjabi, the transition to English-medium instruction was tough.

During the first physics lecture delivered by Professor Manmohan Kalia, I felt completely lost. While some classmates effortlessly grasped what was being taught and asked questions, I struggled to understand what the professor was teaching. This situation filled me with anxiety, especially considering my aspiration to excel academically. Moreover, the professor's English pronunciation differed from what I was accustomed to.

Similar challenges arose in the mathematics class with Professor Yadav, who spoke too quickly, making it difficult for me to grasp the concepts effectively. Fortunately, Professors Gurbachan Kaur and Ranbir Singh, who taught chemistry and English, respectively, were patient and understanding, making it easier for me to comprehend their teaching.

After a few days in the college, I discovered that many of the active participants in the physics and mathematics classes were repeating students from the pre-university programme. They had already covered these subjects in the previous year, but had not appeared in the final examinations as they wanted to score better marks for admission elsewhere. Once I understood the reasons behind their familiarity with the professors teaching physics and mathematics, I felt more at ease and started working hard. I completed all my homework daily and regularly reviewed the syllabi, focusing particularly on the differential and integral calculus of mathematics, which was quite new and required repeated revisions.

The syllabus for Class XI subjects differed significantly from that of Class X. Physics became a separate subject, whereas in Class X, it was part of the broader science curriculum along with chemistry. In physics, separate sections, such as mechanics, heat, light, electricity and magnetism, were introduced, each accompanied by numerical questions. One had to study all sections in detail as they were not interlinked. Mathematics introduced advanced topics like trigonometry, differential calculus, integral calculus and Euclidian geometry, significantly elevating the complexity of mathematics and requiring dedicated efforts. Chemistry was divided into physical, inorganic and organic branches, with organic chemistry particularly demanding rote learning and frequent review.

In essense, the Class XI syllabus diverged significantly across physics, chemistry and mathematics from that of Class X, necessitating a fresh start for students. This shift posed challenges for students, with some who had excelled in Class X struggling in Class XI. To manage this, I adopted a structured approach, dedicating time every day to revise the lessons taught. Despite English marks not being considered for BSc or engineering college admissions, with only passing marks required, I still paid special attention to the subject. My goal was to surpass the previous pre-university record at Government Ranbir College, set by a student named Rawat with 600 out of 800 marks a few years earlier.

My roommate Ravinder Pal was very studious and introverted, providing me with the inspiration to follow suit. He dedicated himself to late-night study sessions and would never go out to gossip or chat. Like him, I too refrained from engaging in social activities or watching films with other students. Ravinder's determination to secure high marks for admission to a medical college influenced my own commitment to solitary study.

Together, Ravinder and I adhered to a disciplined routine, starting our days with tea and homemade biscuits. He would get up in the early morning and wake me up too with a cup of steaming tea made on his kerosene stove. My mother had given me a tin full of homemade biscuits which we both ate.

Our hostel life was well-structured, with nightly attendance checks, stringent rules and a clean, secure environment. Those wishing to stay out late had to seek approval, and any unauthorised absences were promptly reported to the hostel warden. Alcohol consumption was strictly prohibited. My classrooms were close by; it took me less than five minutes to reach there from my room.

The mess, overseen by a contractor, offered affordable meals, priced at just 50 paisa (half a rupee) for lunch and dinner. In addition, the canteen provided morning tea and snacks. My monthly mess expenses were less than Rs 40. However, the lack of hot water for bathing made it challenging during the freezing winter months. Life in the hostel was tough, as were the studies, but I enjoyed it.

A Topper Again!

The initial difficulties I faced in physics and mathematics only fuelled my resolve to work hard and maintain a disciplined study routine. Following the mid-term examinations in November 1964, where I secured the top position in the class, a significant gap separated my marks from the second-ranking student. This success motivated me to aim higher and break the previous record of 600 marks set by Rawat. During holidays, instead of going to my village, I chose to stay in the hostel for focused study.

By this time, several of my teachers had become confident in my ability to score very high marks, and anticipated my inclusion in the merit list of Panjab University, which, at that time, covered the present states of Punjab, Haryana, Himachal Pradesh and union territory of Chandigarh. Due to my intensive and painstaking preparation for the examinations, I excelled in the final pre-university examinations held in April–May 1965.

After the pre-university examinations, I came home to Balian and eagerly waited for the results. Every day, I made a trip to Kanjla to check *The Tribune* newspaper for any announcements. In those days, this English newspaper used to be available only at the Government High School in Kanjla. One day, during a bus journey, I noticed a passenger with a copy of *The Tribune*. I inquired if I could take a look, and to my delight, the results had indeed been declared, with my name appearing in the merit list of the pre-university examination. I had scored 615 marks, securing the 15th rank in Panjab University. The first position was held by Anand Dev, a student of Government College, Hissar.

Filled with excitement, I went to Government Ranbir College, where I was informed about being awarded the Panjab University merit scholarship of Rs 50 per month for Class XII. In the evening, I returned to my village and shared the news with my parents, who were already aware of my achievement. My excellent score had also brought laurels to Government Ranbir College and its teaching faculty. Everyone who saw my namc among the top 25 students in *The Tribune* congratulated me, my parents and the college principal.

Crucial Pre-engineering Studies

After completing the pre-university examinations in June 1965, I joined Class XII (which was known as pre-engineering) at

Government Ranbir College, despite receiving an offer from DAV College in Jalandhar. During the academic year 1964–65, I discovered that with dedicated efforts, I could achieve excellent marks even while continuing my education at Government Ranbir College. At that time, there was no entrance test in most of the engineering or medical colleges; admissions were solely based on Class XII marks. Only the Indian Institutes of Technology (IITs) conducted entrance tests for admissions. Keeping in view the crucial nature of marks in pre-engineering, I concentrated on mastering my studies once again. I had four elective subjects—English, mathematics, physics and chemistry—each carrying 150 marks. In addition, I chose Punjabi as my optional subject, which carried 50 marks.

I was allotted Room No. 3 in the hostel and was glad to have Jagga Singh, a former schoolmate from Kanjla, as my roommate. It was the best room, located adjacent to the warden's office. To facilitate late-night study sessions, I bought a kerosene stove and arranged to have milk delivered for making tea. I diversified my book collection by adding works from various authors to ensure that I could cover all types of questions and be thoroughly prepared for the examination. I also restricted my trips to my village so that I could get more time for studies in the hostel. In this way, my pre-engineering studies started at a brisk pace.

One day, when I was having tea in the canteen, the head clerk approached the canteen manager seeking my whereabouts on behalf of the principal, N.K. Aggarwala, who urgently wanted to see me. Leaving my half-full cup of tea behind, I followed the head clerk to the principal's office. He did not tell me the reason for the meeting, so I felt somewhat uneasy, especially since I was wearing only one shoe due to discomfort from the other.

Upon entering the principal's room with the head clerk, he introduced me by stating, 'This is Jarnail Singh, who secured 615 marks in the pre-university examination, and his name had featured in the newspaper you were reading.' The principal immediately stood up, congratulated me, and took notice of my one bare foot. I explained the reason behind wearing only one shoe, and the principal gracefully shifted the conversation. He said that the college was proud of my academic achievement and he had called me there only to extend his congratulations. With a pat on my back, he concluded the meeting. After a few minutes, I went back to the canteen for another cup of tea.

Based on my academic performance in the pre-university examination, I was awarded a merit-cum-means scholarship by Panjab University. However, it was given to me subject to the condition that I would continue my studies in Class XII. I also had to obtain a certificate from the income tax department confirming that my father was not an income tax payer. After filling out the necessary forms, I accompanied my father to Dhuri, our *sub-tehsil* (revenue sub-division). However, the tehsildar informed us that the forms had to be signed by the income tax officer located in Sangrur. Without delay, we set off on our bicycles towards Sangrur, which is about 11 km away. My father's bicycle was old and did not have an efficient speed-breaking system.

As ill luck would have it, while we were still in Dhuri, a boy attempting to cross the road without checking for traffic, collided with my father's bicycle. Fortunately, the boy suffered only minor injuries. Immediately, a crowd of locals surrounded us and threatened us, but a witness from the other side of the road clarified that the boy was at fault for not observing the traffic rules. My father gave Rs 10 to the boy, and we quickly left, cycling as fast as we could towards the income tax office in Sangrur.

Since my father was not an income taxpayer, he informed the official at the income tax office about his engagement in agriculture. Following a few questions, the official signed the application form, confirming that agricultural income in India is exempt from taxation. This endorsement secured a scholarship for me for the next 12 months.

Patrolling as Member of the NCC

In the early 1960s, India grappled with a shortage of foodgrains and relied on imports of wheat and other foodgrains from the USA under Public Law 480 (known as PL 480). To reduce this dependence, Prime Minister Lal Bahadur Shastri popularised the slogan '*Jai Jawan Jai Kisan* (Hail the Soldier, Hail the Farmer)'. This slogan was aimed to prioritise both the farming community, for working hard to ensure enough food production, and the soldiers, who safeguarded the nation's borders. To reduce food consumption in the country, Shastri also exhorted Indians to skip one meal every week. Even the hostel mess did not serve one meal in a week. The Prime Minister did not want Indians to depend on the US-supplied foodgrains under PL-480. He also wanted to have a non-aligned foreign policy for India, a stance that the USA did not favour.

In 1965, the India–Pakistan war erupted following Pakistan's Operation Gibraltar, aimed at infiltrating forces into Jammu and Kashmir to incite insurgency against the Indian government. India retaliated by launching a full-scale military attack on the then West Pakistan. During those days, I was staying in the hostel. To guard against air raids by Pakistan Air Force, strict blackout measures were enforced at night. Being a member of the NCC at college, I was tasked with patrolling the areas surrounding the college. The college authorities had made teams of four students each for patrolling at night. Armed with sticks, we would patrol the eastern perimeter of the college to ensure that people obeyed blackout rules.

Day or night, we would see air force planes flying over Sangrur but could not make out whether they were Indian or Pakistani. Rumours circulated of damage inflicted by bombs dropped by the Pakistan Air Force on the fields where farmers worked under torchlights during nighttime irrigation. There were also whispers of Pakistani spies parachuting into the region, who would then signal from the ground so that the planes could bomb strategic targets. In such an atmosphere, even a flicker of a torchlight or the glow of a cigarette sparked suspicion of being a spy of Pakistan. Throughout our night patrols, we remained vigilant, and kept a watch on anyone who violated the blackout protocols.

During the India-Pakistan war of 1965, Lieutenant General Harbaksh Singh, the general officer commanding the Western Command, was in the news quite often. Hailing from Badrukhan village, which was about 4 km from Sangrur towards my village, Singh's leadership was notable amidst the conflict. Spurred on by interventions from the USSR and the USA, Shastri went to Tashkent to negotiate a ceasefire with Pakistan President Ayub Khan. Anticipations were high before his departure for Tashkent, with hopes that Shastri would not concede to any ceasefire terms that involved returning the stretches of Pakistan's territory measuring about 1840 square kilometres. Pakistan had occupied about 520 square kilometres of Indian territory. However, despite these expectations, Shastri signed the Tashkent Declaration on 10 January 1966, agreeing to comply with UNSC Resolution 211. This resolution aimed at restoring the status quo ante, necessitating India's return of occupied territory to Pakistan. There have been many theories about the cause of Shastri's mysterious death in Tashkent, which occurred a day after the signing of the agreement. Some had suggested that the stress of these negotiations might have led to his untimely demise, possibly due to a heart attack.

Every week, I had to dedicate two hours to NCC training. Additionally, a 15-day NCC camp was organised for us in December 1965 in the army cantonment. We would get up early in the morning at 5 a.m. and get ready for the NCC parade. During the camp, we undertook a demanding 35-km trek to Mahlan village, aiming to familiarise ourselves with the rigourous cadet life resembling that of the army. We were also trained to shoot with rifles used by the army. These NCC activities consumed a lot of my precious time, which I had intended to dedicate to studying for the pre-engineering examinations. Participation in NCC camp and weekly parades was mandatory for pre-engineering students, leaving me no option but to take part in these activities. Without adequate attendance in the NCC, I could be barred from sitting for the final pre-engineering examinations.

Experiments in Physics and Chemistry

During the pre-engineering course, physics and chemistry experiments proved difficult. In chemistry, our task was to identify the components of two mixed salts through experiments. Despite clear procedural instructions for identifying the radicals, there was always a risk of error as certain elements exhibited similar properties. Handling diluted acids and alkaline solutions often led to spills on our clothes, causing burns, especially on the front of my shirt, despite wearing an apron. These burn marks were difficult to mend, frustrating my mother. Physics experiments were quite comprehensive and demanding, requiring significant efforts. While evaluating our experiments, the professors would question our understanding of various concepts. Since the marks for these experiments were quite substantial, I was always apprehensive of making unintentional mistakes and losing marks. This fear lingered as I approached the pre-engineering examination. A small misjudgement in identifying salts in chemistry experiments could have serious consequences.

My Delayed Result

In March 1966, I took the pre-engineering final examinations and felt confident about my performance in the theory papers of physics, chemistry and mathematics. Despite a minor stumble in the chemistry experiment, I managed to rectify the error in the final minutes. However, I was not satisfied with the English paper, especially the essay section.

The results of the pre-engineering final examinations were announced by Panjab University on 20 May 1966. To my surprise, my result was not declared! Instead, next to my roll number, it was mentioned 'Marks Late (ML)'. Even though I had passed, my marks were withheld by Panjab University, and I was not issued my marks certificate. Without it, I could not apply to any college or university, putting me in a difficult situation. I visited the college office to inquire about the reason behind this delay. However, they were unable to provide any explanation for the delay.

My aspiration in life was to become a professor of physics. Inspired by my neighbour Kirpal Singh from my maternal village Kanjla, who had achieved this feat, I aimed to enrol in the BSc (Hons) School programme of the physics department of Panjab University in Chandigarh. My plan was to complete the MSc (Hons) course thereafter and pursue a career as a college lecturer. However, my dream of joining the BSc (Hons) physics programme was shattered by the delay in receiving my Class XII result. Every day, I cycled from my village to the college, hoping for news of my result, only to be met with the same disheartening response: 'no information'. As the days passed, my anxiety grew. Newspaper announcements detailing the closing dates for college admissions added to my apprehension. With each deadline that passed, my opportunities for applying to various professional colleges and programmes diminished.

By 23 June 1966, over a month had passed since the declaration of the pre-engineering result. Yet, there was still no news about my result. Determined to seek answers, I approached the principal of Government Ranbir College. Upon meeting him, he promptly summoned the head of the office administration, who advised me to go to Panjab University, Chandigarh, with a letter from the principal without delay.

A letter addressed to the registrar of Panjab University was swiftly composed and signed by the principal, then handed to me. However, the thought of going to Chandigarh alone filled me with trepidation, as I had never ventured beyond the familiar surroundings of Sangrur. I came back to Kanjla and sought counsel from Ajaib Singh. As we deliberated, tears welled in my eyes at the fear of missing crucial opportunities due to my delayed result. Amidst my distress, Amar Singh, a respected elder in our community who affectionately called me 'Zaildar', consoled me and urged me to go Chandigarh the next day. In the evening, Amar Singh provided the necessary funds for the journey to Chandigarh. I found a newfound resolve when Kirpal Singh agreed to accompany me. I still fondly remember that day when Amar Singh and Ajaib Singh offered their counsel and unwavering support during my time of need.

In 1966, only one private passenger bus operated between Sangrur and Chandigarh. This bus would leave Sangrur town at 7 a.m. for Chandigarh and return to Sangrur by 7 p.m. On 25 June 1966, Kirpal Singh and I cycled from Kanjla to Sangrur and boarded the bus bound for Chandigarh. This was my first visit to Chandigarh, a city renowned for its serene beauty and elegant architecture. Throughout the journey, my anxiety heightened whenever the bus slowed down or stopped for unusually longer periods since I wanted to reach Chandigarh as quickly as possible. About 20 km from the city, distant hills came into view on the horizon. The changing scenic vistas from Kharar towards Chandigarh were captivating. Around noon, we arrived at the city's bus stand. Without delay, we boarded an autorickshaw and headed towards Panjab University. Four aspects of Chandigarh impressed me: its wide roads with tree-lined footpaths, the uniformity of buildings and shops across different sectors, its cleanliness and the beautiful hills in the backdrop. Notably, unlike other Indian cities, there were no encroachments by vendors on the roads.

We reached the grey administrative building of Panjab University. After obtaining passes, we entered the section responsible for handling pre-engineering results. Once there, I handed over the letter from the principal of Government Ranbir College Sangrur to the relevant assistant registrar of Panjab University and inquired about my result. After a brief check, the clerk confirmed that I had passed. Surprisingly, despite my result being ready for the past 10 days, it had not been dispatched. I learnt that this was due to the negligence of the clerical staff, who neither provided it to a newspaper nor sent it to my college. It was only upon my physical presence at Panjab University that I received my provisional mark sheet from the assistant registrar.

When I examined it, I saw that I had scored high marks in all the subjects, except English, where I just managed to pass. In physics, chemistry and mathematics, I got 385 marks out of 450, which was 85.56 per cent. We guessed that Panjab University might have granted me grace marks in English. Fortunately, admissions to the BSc (Hons) and Bachelor of Engineering degree programmes were primarily based on marks in physics, chemistry and mathematics (PCM). Since my marks were high in PCM, I could get admission in any colleges in Chandigarh or Punjab, provided there was still time to submit my admission forms.

Shift in My Career Option

We went to the physics department of Panjab University to submit admission forms for the BSc (Hons) School programme in physics, my first choice. However, we were informed that I was late by about a week. Disheartened, tears welled up as I contemplated my options, especially since admission deadlines for most colleges had passed. For someone coming from a rural background with parents lacking formal education, finding a suitable career option was difficult. I had been following the career trail of my neighbour, but now it felt like my plans were crumbling. Back at the university's administrative building, I was still wondering what to do when a person standing near us suggested that we try Punjab Engineering College (PEC), Chandigarh, conveniently located nearby, as they had extended their admission deadline by about a week. We rushed to PEC and got the admission application forms. I quickly completed them and was instructed to attend counselling at PEC in Chandigarh on 11 July 1966, as part of the admission process.

CHAPTER 9

Destined for an Engineering College

For the counselling session scheduled on 11 July, I needed to be at PEC by 9 a.m., with all my original certificates. On 10 July, my father accompanied me until Dhuri, where we slept in a shop until midnight. Around 12.30 a.m., my father dropped me off at the Dhuri railway station. I boarded the Chandigarh Express Train, departing from Dhuri around 1.30 a.m. and arriving in Chandigarh before 7 a.m. After freshening up and having breakfast at the railway station, I reached PEC on time, only to be surprised to find that most of the other students had brought their guardians along. We convened in the auditorium for the counselling session.

Counselling followed the merit list, taking into account the aggregate PCM marks. There were students from various colleges, such as DAV College, Jalandhar, and institutions in Amritsar, Chandigarh and Ludhiana. I was the only one from Government Ranbir College, Sangrur. A few students from other colleges in Punjab, Haryana, Himachal Pradesh, Uttar Pradesh and Delhi were also present. Anand Dev, the top scorer in pre-engineering at Panjab University, was the first person to be called to the dais. After a couple of hours, it was my turn for conselling. To my relief, after verifying my certificates, I was immediately granted admission. Although I had initially chosen mechanical engineering as my branch, we were informed during the counselling that specific branches would be allotted based on first-year marks.

In the auditorium, I met Inder Partap Singh, a student from Sangrur and an alumnus of Punjabi University, Patiala. Accompanying him was his father, an important revenue officer in the Punjab government. Interestingly, his marks were almost the same as mine. Post-counselling, I headed to the counter to pay the tuition fee. As there was a chaotic rush to pay both tuition and hostel fees, the clerk did not listen to my request for Inder Partap Singh as my roommate, and he was allotted another room.

After paying the fees, I rushed with my documents to General Hospital for the mandatory medical examination. The process involved measuring various body statistics—height, weight, chest, chest expansion, eyesight testing, chest X-ray, a urine test and hernia check. It was a time-consuming affair, navigating through different rooms for various tests and ensuring the corresponding entries in my medical form. Almost all the hospital staff was present, as they had been requested by PEC officials to work late hours to expedite the medical tests on the same day. The sun had already set, but I was still in the hospital waiting for the doctor-in-charge to submit my test report. By about 8 p.m., I completed all the formalities and was free to leave. Inder Partap was also there with his father, but I did not know whether they had planned to go back to Sangrur that day.

My understanding led me to choose a train journey over a bus ride, believing it to be safer at night. Arriving at Chandigarh railway station in an auto-rickshaw, I boarded a train to Ambala Cantonment railway Cantonment, where I had to wait for about six hours for my train to Dhuri the next morning. I spent the night in a nearby park. Despite the monsoon season, luck was on my side as it did not rain that day. Exhausted after a day of bustling around, I spread my towel in the park, tucked my briefcase containing my important documents under my head as a makeshift pillow, and slept. I woke up at around 5 a.m. and had a cup of tea before boarding the train to Dhuri. Arriving there,

I waited until evening for the bus to my village, finally reaching home past 6 p.m. Despite the taxing 36-hour journey, overcoming challenges such as a delayed pre-engineering examination result and handling admission formalities single-handedly, I felt a sense of accomplishment upon securing admission to the top engineering college in the northern region.

A New Start in Chandigarh

I got some new clothes stitched, packed them carefully, and on 16 July, left for Chandigarh. By 3 p.m., I reached the Jawalamukhi Hostel. To my surprise, there were only a few students in the hostel. My room was on the first floor in the front block, tucked away in a corner. The ground floor was occupied by final year students from the electronics department. Later that evening, two senior students dropped by my room, extending an invitation to join them. I silently followed them to their room, where they inquired about my studies, village and background. As the conversation progressed, they asked me to untie and retie my turban. Thankfully, their questions remained respectful, steering clear of any vulgarity or indecent requests. After the mild ragging session, which centred on my rural roots and Punjabi accent, they eventually allowed me to return to my room.

During dinner at the mess that evening, I observed only about a dozen students, sparking my curiosity about the whereabouts of the others. It occurred to me that they were perhaps avoiding ragging and opted to stay elsewhere in the city. After the meal, I came back to my room. Leaving the door slightly ajar, I switched off the lights. Throughout the night, I could hear footsteps and hushed voices in the corridor. However, upon seeing the partially open door and the absence of lights, they likely assumed that the room was unoccupied and went back. Surprisingly, I managed to sleep undisturbed on my first night in the hostel.

The next morning, a large number of first-year students came to the hostel. My intuition proved correct—most of them had spent the night outside the hostel to avoid the dreaded ragging.

After breakfast, I went to the college to jot down the timetable, taking the opportunity to explore the sprawling campus. Returning to the hostel for lunch, I found myself swiftly whisked away by another set of senior boys to their room, where they asked about my academic background. It was there I met Inder Partap again. Since he had an imposing personality, no one behaved indecently with him during ragging.

I distinctly recall that day where I was asked to scale an almirah. I removed my shoes, clambered up the almirah and sat on top for a good 10 minutes until they said I could come down. By this time, the seniors had deduced that I was a simple country boy and let me go. Their focus shifted to ragging students from cities, especially those not adept in physical activities and projected themselves as oversmart. As evening fell, a different group of senior students approached me, demanding a folk song performance. I told them that I did not know any song, but knew a fellow student who did. When I asked Inder Partap to oblige, he sportingly sang for them and received appreciation.

On the third day, rumours spread about the seniors planning rigorous ragging of first-year students at the Jawalamukhi Hostel. Hearing this, most first-year students hastily left the hostel after dinner. Deciding to follow suit, I packed my towel, locked my room and left. I went to a park in Sector 11 near the main market, but swarms of mosquitoes made it impossible to sleep. I got into an auto-rickshaw and went to a *dharamshala,* only to be rudely turned away by the manager. I had only two options—either the Chandigarh railway station or the bus stand. As the railway station was far away, I decided to try the bus stand. I found a cemented bench and spent the night relatively undisturbed—except when a police constable woke me to ask me why I was sleeping there. After hearing the circumstances, he left with a word of caution about safeguarding my belongings. This ordeal persuaded me never to leave the hostel and sleep outside. Henceforth, I adopted the same strategy: I repositioned my bed to one corner of the room, left the door half open and turned off the lights. This tactic proved effective, as I could hear the footsteps and hushed conversations of senior students in the corridor looking for someone to rag. Thinking there was no one in my room, they would go away.

The college authorities had admitted a total of 360 students, organising them into 12 sections, each comprising 30 students. Two sections, totaling 60 students, attended lectures together, while for practicals, only one section of 30 students performed experiments at a time. The names of all 360 admitted students were arranged alphabetically, and roll numbers were allotted. My roll number was 93/66, which remained the same throughout my studies at PEC and served as my primary identification.

For practical experiments, my group consisted of Indresh Kumar Garg, Jugal Kishore Khanna and Jasbir Singh Arora. Indresh, hailing from Kaithal in Haryana, was interested in the activities of the Rashtriya Swayamsevak Sangh (RSS). He once took me along to attend an RSS meeting in Chandigarh. Later, Indresh joined the RSS and rose to a prominent position. Jugal, belonging to a family of engineers in Amritsar, had three elder brothers who were colleagues of some professors at PEC. On a visit to Delhi, he brought me a shirt, stating that my Sangrur-stitched shirts lacked stiff collars! He was a confident person and well-acquainted with the challenges of engineering studies. On the other hand, Jasbir, a native of Saharanpur in Uttar Pradesh, was simple and mild-mannered, often conforming to others' opinions without frequent arguments.

Living in the Hostel

I lived with two roommates in my hostel. The administration was overseen by a warden, who was also a professor in the college. In addition, there was a caretaker who played a crucial role in maintaining the hostel's cleanliness, overseeing furniture, ensuring water availability, and managing electricity supply. The hostel had an efficient laundry service and offered clothes ironing facilities. Near the mess, a private contractor ran a fruit stall where residents could buy juices or fruits. A dedicated club room provided recreational amenities such as newspapers, magazines, a radio, table tennis, and carom. The uniformed hostel mess cooks and serving staff were well trained. The mess operated on a cooperative basis, with monthly expenses divided equally among the students. The mess management committee consisted of students who supervised the mess. One of the students served as the general secretary, while others were assigned various tasks such as maintenance and menu finalisation. Every week, the mess menu was displayed on the hostel noticeboard, emphasising the significance of cleanliness and dining arrangements. The food served was both nutritious and delicious, with special praise for the *rajma* (kidney bean) curry and rice. Even now, when we gather after five decades, the outstanding quality of the mess food remains a cherished memory.

Tightly Packed Schedule

The engineering college's schedule was quite demanding, requiring us to stay engaged from 8 a.m. to 4.30 p.m. with a one-hour lunch break. To adhere to this timetable, I had to wake up before 5 a.m., get ready by 7 a.m, and hastily head to the mess for breakfast. After breakfast, we promptly made our way to the classroom by 8 a.m. There was no respite even after seven-and-a-half hours of classes, as the evenings were dedicated to studying and completing homework assignments.

In each semester, 50 per cent of the total marks were allotted for homework, internal assessment, class participation and practical experiments. The emphasis placed on this internal assessment compelled students to consistently work hard throughout each semester. If any student missed classes or practical experiments, he would not get adequate marks in the internal assessment, which meant failure or low marks in the final examinations. In my first semester, I had five subjects—applied mathematics, applied chemistry, applied physics, surveying paper-I, and practical geometry and graphic statistics. Engaging in interesting experiments and fieldwork, especially in the survey paper and applied physics, made these subjects particularly enjoyable for me.

Practical Geometry and Graphic Statistics

I had studied drawing from Classes VI to X. To my surprise, the syllabus for practical geometry and graphic statistics in the first year of the Bachelor's Engineering programme was similar to the drawing topics covered in Classes IX and X. The only notable difference at the engineering college was the transition to full-sized drawing sheets, a departure from the half-sized ones in my school days. The drawing instruments used in the engineering college were more advanced than those I had used in high school. I had honed my drawing skills over five years in school. Professor H.M. Singh was our teacher for the subject in college. Our engineering drawing sessions took place in the halls on the top floor of the college building.

One day, as Professor Singh was inspecting the students' drawings, he paused at my table and examined my work carefully. After a few moments, he applauded and invited fellow students to see my drawing. He appreciatively remarked, 'How clean and beautifully done his drawing is!' He then expressed his intention to frame and display it on the classroom hall's wall after completion so that everyone could see it and learn to do clean drawing work.

In addition to producing neat work, I had a clear understanding of drawing various perspectives of objects. I acquired the skills for drawing elevation (front), side views and top views of objects during my school days. However, the concepts became more intricate in engineering college. Objects—generally machine parts—were cut by planes at different angles, and we were tasked with illustrating the elevation and side views observed post-cutting, along with the top view. Depicting the various views of the cut portions required imagination, and certain lines had to be drawn as dotted lines to represent those portions not visible otherwise. These inner portions of objects would have been apparent, as illustrated in different views on the drawing sheets, had the machine object been cut at that specific plane. Successfully tackling this required students to conceptualise and portray the views of the cut sections without physically dissecting the objects. I enjoyed the subject and excelled in it.

Survey Fieldwork

Practical work for the survey paper involved going to fields and colonies to map various objects and their distances along our designated routes. Employing measuring chains, instruments for distance/angle measurements, and flag-posts, we would meticulously record daily survey details in our individual notebooks. Different symbols represented trees, roads, poles, buildings and bushes. I always looked forward to field survey work for the opportunity to be outdoors and witness captivating views. I took pride in maintaining a tidy survey notebook and executing fieldwork with precision. After each fieldwork, the overseeing professor would evaluate the previous day's work by checking the survey notebook and posing questions about survey terminology and concepts. I got an 'Alpha Plus' grade every day for my performance. Achieving high marks in the internal assessment rested solely on my punctuality, sincerity, and adeptness in practical work and accurate answers during assessments.

Applied Physics Laboratory

Of all the laboratories in the college, the applied physics experiments lab left a lasting impression on me. Each week, we had to perform a new experiment utilising the machinery and equipment at our disposal. A concise write-up, outlining the experiment's objective and necessary precautions, was kept handy near each machine or equipment. Post-experiment, we analysed the results to determine if the set objectives were achieved or not. It was in this laboratory that I grasped a multitude of physics concepts, including the measurement of static and dynamic frictions. I consistently achieved excellent grades in these experiments, which strengthened my understanding of various topics in physics.

Workshop Practicals

We were tasked with hands-on work, crafting objects chosen by the instructors in seven workshops that were set up in the college. These workshops included the Smithy Shop, Machine Shop, Carpentry and Pattern Making Shop, Electrical Shop, Welding Shop, Fitting Shop and Foundry Shop. The use of hammers and other tools was initially unfamiliar to us. The workshop environments mirrored those found in Punjab cities. Each workshop was headed by a senior instructor, supported by helpers to guide us through assignments. Some students, physically less robust, developed blisters while working in the Smithy Shop, Fitting Shop and the Machine Shop. Despite repeated warnings from the Smithy Shop instructor to avoid touching recently heated iron pieces, some students couldn't resist and ended up with burn injuries. The Carpentry and Pattern Making Shop, along with the Foundry Shop, helped me understand the processes behind making intricate objects and machine parts. As the second semester concluded, eight intense weeks of full-time workshops awaited us.

My German-made slide-rule, purchased for Rs 150, proved handy for calculations throughout my engineering college days. Remarkably durable, this slide-rule, made from fine materials, has stood the test of time without a single break or defect, even as we step into 2024. In this slide-rule, one scale slides between two fixed scales, with about half a dozen scales on both sides of the two fixed scales. There is a cursor with lines drawn that is used to align the slides and read the results by bringing the cursor to the desired position. It took me a few days to learn the use of slide-rule for calculations, such as multiplication, division, trigonometrical functions, finding roots and powers of numbers, and so on. Its usefulness can be imagined from the fact that every student would carry a slide-rule to every class. Since taking a reading from the slide-rule is subjective, slight variations in calculations done by different people, especially when dealing with readings beyond three digits, were possible and acceptable.

Quick Home Visits

I enjoyed my time studying and living in the hostel. However, during the initial months, I would often feel homesick, especially on weekends when I longed to visit my home in Balian. Although it meant sacrificing two valuable weekend days that could have been dedicated to studying and relaxing in the hostel, the yearning for home pulled me back every alternate weekend. My journeys to my village were partly by bus and partly by train, with the Chandigarh Express being my preferred train for the return leg to college. Departing from Dhuri railway station around 1.30 a.m., it would reach Chandigarh around 7 a.m. The overnight train journey was quite tedious, leaving me feeling weary upon reaching Chandigarh.

Generally, I would leave Balian at about 5 p.m. and reach Dhuri past 7 p.m. Since the Chandigarh-bound train's departure time was at 1.30 a.m., I had about seven hours at my disposal at Dhuri. During some journeys, I passed the time watching Hindi feature films in the local cinema hall. On a few occasions, I stayed in Kakarwal with my aunt, who would then drop me off at the Dhuri railway station around midnight.

The Chandigarh Express typically arrived at the Chandigarh railway station around 7 a.m. From there, I would rush directly to my college to attend classes. Monday's first class often involved chemistry practicals, making it occasionally challenging to persuade the laboratory-in-charge to permit late entry. The situation would worsen during heavy morning rains, which disrupted vehicular movement from Chandigarh railway station to the city due to the lack of bridges over rivulets along the route.

The midterm examinations took place at the end of September 1966. Even though I had worked hard and did well in the exams, I harboured uncertainty about my ranking. At the time of admission, my position was at about No. 80 and I aspired to better it. About a week after the midterm exams, the results were posted on the noticeboard. I had scored 421 marks out of 500, which was 84.25 per cent. Surprisingly, only one student, Ravinder Kaur Dang, outscored me. Professor Tara Singh Kamal, an assistant professor in the electronics department and hailing from my district, congratulated me near the Jawalamukhi Hostel. The results surprised my fellow students, causing my standing to soar. My classmates acknowledged the potential in me to be a dark horse, boosting my confidence. Feeling that I could surpass anyone, I resolved never to look back but only to look ahead.

The college authorities had announced the availability of 90 merit-cum-means scholarships, to be awarded to deserving students based on the midterm examination results. This sought-after scholarship not only covered tuition fees for four years but also provided a monthly stipend of Rs 75. As this was an attractive opportunity, all students aimed to secure the scholarship. Luckily, my high marks paved the way for me to be selected for this prestigious scholarship.

The process, however, proved to be more intricate than expected. I was required to submit a form signed by the SDO at Malerkotla, my area. After filling out the form, I sent it to my father to obtain the SDO's signature. After about 15 days, I received the form back with the signature. However, my excitement was short-lived, as the administrative officer refused to accept it due to the absence of the seal of the SDO.

Undeterred, I sent the form back to my father, requesting him to secure the SDO office's seal. Another 15 days later, I received the form, but this time it had about a dozen seals affixed to it. When the administrative officer saw it, he chuckled. Sorting through the seals, he identified the correct one from the SDO, Malerkotla, circled it, and invalidated the others.

Curious about the multitude of seals on the scholarship form, I decided to inquire with my father. He shared a fascinating tale of his journey to Malerkotla, a 25-km cycle ride from our village, to get the seal affixed. When he reached the office, he learnt that the SDO was having a meeting in his office. The peon at the gate told my father to wait until lunchtime, as the tray containing the seals was inside the SDO's office. However, at lunchtime, the SDO left for his home for lunch. To expedite the process, the peon accepted a bribe of Rs 20 from my father and entered the office where a tray with about a dozen seals was kept on the table. The peon told my father to choose any seal he wanted, but neither of them was aware of which seal was the correct one. Complicating matters, the SDO of Malerkotla held multiple roles, such as sub-divisional magistrate, land acquisition officer, chairman of the Malerkotla Town Committee, officer for determination of surplus land and registrar of marriages. Consequently, all these seals were in the tray. As a precaution, my father and the peon sat on a bench and affixed every seal from the tray onto the scholarship form!

After the first semester exams in December 1966, it was time for holidays, but we were asked to come back to college for the NCC camp. Inder Partap Singh and I planned to go from Sangrur to Patiala by bus, and then take the Chandigarh Express train from Patiala to Chandigarh at 2.30 a.m. Little did we anticipate the biting cold of the night on a moving train. We boarded the nearly empty train in Patiala, and as it gained speed, the cold wind penetrated through the windows. Both of us shivered, as we had not worn adequate warm clothes to protect ourselves from the chilling midnight cold of December. With each passing minute, we eagerly awaited the end of this frigid train journey. By 7 a.m., we reached the Chandigarh railway station, our limbs numb and stiff. Luckily, we did not suffer from hypothermia and survived the perilous four-hour night ordeal. After that bone-chilling experience, I pledged never to travel by train at night during winter.

Change in Fortunes

After a few days into the second semester, the results of the first-year first semester final examinations were declared. I secured 396 marks out of 500, which was 79.20 per cent, and ranked among the top five students in the university. This success turned me into a sought-after resource as my peers began seeking my assistance with assignments and studies. Some students had not studied engineering drawing during their school days, so they struggled and resorted to copying with the help of a glass and a table lamp. This peculiar method led to many students working on their assignments as late as 2 a.m. or even the whole night.

My strong academic performance not only instilled lasting self-confidence but also transformed my interactions. Earlier I was timid and nervous when engaging with students from Jalandhar, Amritsar or Ludhiana, but now I interacted from a position of strength, changing my behaviour towards both fellow students and teachers. Whenever assignments were given, I always completed them within a day or two. Some students waited for days to obtain my assignments, intending to borrow or copy them. While I selectively shared my work with close friends, many classmates continuously sought my help, prompting me to set my terms for sharing my written work.

The final examinations of the second semester were held in April and May 1967. The papers were tough, with external examiners conducting viva voces of nearly all subjects. My thorough preparation left me feeling confident throughout the exams. In the summer of May/June 1967, we attended workshops daily from 8 a.m. to 1 p.m., enjoying free afternoons. Evenings were spent at Kaku Shah's shop in Sector 11, where we enjoyed savouring cold lassi or milk. The results of the first-year second semester examinations were declared in July 1967, with me scoring 1,589 marks out of 2,000, equivalent to a commendable 79.45 per cent. Securing the fourth rank in Panjab University marked a significant milestone in my academic journey.

Allocation of Electrical Engineering

Even though I had chosen mechanical engineering as my branch when I joined PEC in July 1966, during my first year, I realised that electrical engineering held better employment opportunities in the Punjab State Electricity Board (PSEB). With the PSEB rapidly expanding its reach and aiming for 100 per cent village electrification, coupled with a surging demand for electricity across various sectors, electrical engineering became an enticing prospect.

Branch allocation for the second year was based on first-year marks. I was the first person in the order of merit who was allotted electrical engineering, as three students higher in merit than me opted for different engineering branches. As the highest-ranked student in electrical engineering, I was designated the role of class senior for the branch in the second year. Though not a class monitor akin to my school days, being the class senior brought a sense of responsibility. Teachers sought my inputs on practical and academic-cum-administrative matters, solidifying my position as one of the top performers. I started enjoying my studies, and focused on developing concepts rather than learning by rote.

In the second year, I was allotted a single occupancy room on the first floor of the third block in the Kurukshetra Hostel—a privilege extended to only about 100 out of 360 students. The rest stayed in dormitories. For me, practical experiments in both mechanical and electrical engineering laboratories were particularly interesting. The college administration even consulted me on setting the date sheets for both midterm and final exams, marking a recognition of my growing influence.

Lucky Escape for Inder Partap

I was against ragging, so I never participated in it. Some students, including Inder Partap, liked ragging the newly admitted first-year students. One night, I was sound asleep when a loud, insistent knocking interrupted my slumber. Switching on the light, I opened the door to find Inder Partap standing outside. He swiftly entered, closed the door, turned off the light and urged me to stay quiet. He sat on the chair, while I lay down on the bed. After about five minutes, I could hear some persons running on the ground floor, as if a search was underway. A flashlight beamed through my window, and shortly after, the footsteps shifted towards the Jawalamukhi Hostel. Then, there was silence.

Inder Partap then explained that he and a few batchmates had gone to the Vindhyachal Hostel to rag the first-year students. The situation turned violent when the first-year students resisted. The groups came to blows, beating each other up, resulting in physical injuries. The college principal, alerted by the commotion, tasked the chief warden with identifying the troublemakers. When the chief warden and other professors reached the Vindhyachal Hostel, the second-year students fled towards the Himalaya and Kurukshetra Hostels. Some were caught by the chief warden and detained in the Himalaya Hostel.

Inder Partap told me he sought refuge in my room as it was difficult to find a hiding spot elsewhere at midnight. He left my room early in the morning, knowing it was a narrow escape for him. I, too, felt relieved, realising the potential problems I could have faced if Inder Partap had been caught in my room that night.

Spending Time at College

I had assembled a single-circuit local radio capable of receiving signals from the local radio station. It lacked volume control and tuning arrangements. I affixed the radio circuit to hard cardboard and named it the 'Pammi' radio. Every evening, I would listen to the Hindi songs played on the 'Vividh Bharati' programme from the Chandigarh radio station. The music created a lively atmosphere, helping me study better for extended periods. However, the absence of volume control posed a disturbance for others who wished to sleep or study without disruptions. One day, while playing my radio at full volume, a senior student residing on the top floor above me requested that I lower the volume as it was too loud for him to concentrate. As I was interested in listening to Hindi songs, I had to find a solution to continue enjoying them without causing inconvenience. Luckily, the next day, a final-year electronics engineering student helped me modify the radio circuit to include volume control. From then on, I used the self-assembled 'Pammi' radio for about three years.

Professor Gurlabh Singh, a young professor of mechanical engineering, taught us 'Strength of Materials'. This subject demanded a conceptual frame of mind and, fortunately, I found it fascinating. In the classroom, I was active and often asked questions to deepen my understanding. Professor Gurlabh Singh made the teaching as interactive as possible. He was quite impressed with my enthusiasm and was very supportive. He also taught us 'Engineering Drawing and Design – Mechanical'. When he saw my first engineering drawing assignment, he congratulated me on the exceptional quality of my work. In fact, he mentioned that he had rarely seen assignments done with such keen interest and meticulousness.

In my second year, I began playing hockey, greatly influenced by Gurpreet Singh, a final-year mechanical engineering student and the captain of the college hockey team. As he stayed in the middle block of the Kurukshetra Hostel, he often crossed paths with me. He encouraged me to participate regularly in the practice sessions, and eventually included me in the team. During a match against another college at the hockey ground near Tagore Theatre of Sector 18, I suffered an injury to my nose from a hockey ball, resulting in profuse bleeding. I had to be carried out on a stretcher, but thankfully, I recovered soon.

During the winter vacation of December 1967, the final-year mechanical engineering students went for a study tour to see factories and engineering establishments in Calcutta (now Kolkata). Tragically, Gurpreet Singh met with an accident while trying to cross a railway track as an electric train approached. A misjudgment led to a fatal collision, and Gurpreet lost his life instantly. The study tour was cut short, and the students came back. In his memory, the students and college authorities developed a rose garden in front of the middle block of the Kurukshetra Hostel, and named it 'Gurpreet Park'.

I approached the first semester of my second year with meticulous preparation across all subjects. As the class senior and the top-ranking student, I was determined to uphold my position. When the results of the first semester were declared, I proudly achieved 83.60 per cent with a score of 418 out of 500, securing the top position in the electrical engineering branch. My academic journey was on a steady track, and everything was going smoothly.

The second semester of second year commenced in January 1968, but shortly thereafter, an all-India strike by engineering college students started, protesting against the widespread unemployment among engineering graduates. Our college actively participated in the strike, with students boycotting classes and joining protests in Sector 17. Following the instructions of the student leaders, we wore our engineering college's blue blazers. However, police barriers halted our progress at the Sector 17 entrance due to prohibitory orders under Section 144 of the Criminal Procedure Code (CrPC), which restricted the assembly of more than five persons in the Sector 17 market area from the junction near the then Piccadilly Restaurant. Positioned at the Sector 17 main crossing, student leaders directed us to breach the police cordon and enter the Sector 17 market main road.

Under pressure, the police briefly relaxed the cordon, allowing our entry into the sector, but abruptly started lathi-charging us. Fleeing in various directions, we scattered into the market and shops. Easily identifiable by our college blazers, we couldn't blend into the crowd. During the lathi-charge, I sustained a blow to my right leg below the knee, causing considerable pain. Seeking refuge in a nearby building, I removed my blazer, wrapped it in a paper, and then made my way towards Jagat Theatre. From there, I sprinted directly to my college through the Rose Garden. It was a harrowing day, with many students arrested by the police.

In February, the strike gained momentum. Within a few days, the principal took the decision to shut down the college temporarily and instructed students to vacate the hostels. I went home after locking my room. With idle time in my village, I took up teaching at the local school. Both students and teachers appreciated my mathematics instruction. After approximately one month, the strike ended, and I returned to rejoin my college.

In the college, there were students who independently tackled their assignments, while others relied on their peers for assistance. Some formed tight-knit groups, sharing assignments within their circles to ensure everyone met their deadlines. This collaborative approach proved effective, ensuring timely completion of assignments. I, too, also participated in this assignment-sharing system, but with a unique twist. I always did my assignments on my own and started working on them right on the dates they were given. My ability to independently handle homework made me influential among my friends. When students from outside my circle sought to copy my work, I would suggest they obtain it after my friends had utilised it. Sometimes, I even negotiated for treats like milkshakes from Kaku Shah's shop in exchange for the assignments. This way, I took pride in being in demand and always holding the upper hand!

In the second semester, we had a paper called 'Engineering Drawing and Design – Mechanical', in which we were tasked with drawing cross-sections of various mechanical parts. The course material drew inspiration from A.C. Parkinson's book, *Geometrical and Mechanical Drawing: Solid Geometry and Mechanical Drawing*. Professor P.C. Sood, a mechanical engineering professor at our college, had also authored a book on the same subject. Since we were taught from Parkinson's book, our drawings of machine parts and associated techniques were based on the contents provided in his book. Among these drawings, there was one important drawing of the tail-piece of a lathe, responsible for gripping objects during lathe operations. This well-designed component moves forward through the circular motion of the wheel attached to the tail-piece.

I thoroughly studied and accurately rendered its different sections on a drawing sheet, as given in Parkinson's book. Some of my classmates sought my assistance and created their drawings similar to mine. In addition, we drew about 15 other important machine parts. Unfortunately, on the day of our viva voce, Professor Sood was in charge of taking our oral examination. Interestingly, the model of the tail-piece in Professor Sood's book differed from that in Parkinson's, particularly in the mechanics used for the forward movement of the tail-piece.

Two of my classmates, who followed Parkinson's tail-piece model, went inside first for the oral examination, one after the other. When Professor Sood asked them questions about the mechanism driving the tail-piece forward, they confidently opened their drawing sheets and explained it accurately. However, to their dismay, Professor Sood told them that their drawings were incorrect because they did not follow his book. He gave them Minus Beta marks, which was low. Meanwhile, I observed the unfolding drama from the distant corner of the mechanical engineering laboratory, and was curious about their evident perturbation. When I inquired, they recounted the whole conversation and what had happened during their viva voce.

After some time, it was my turn. I went inside and sat in front of Professor Sood who asked me a few questions. As he reviewed my drawings, he came to the contentious tail-piece drawing. I provided my explanation, but he disagreed with my conceptualisation. Unyielding, I asserted my stance, insisting that I was 100 per cent right because it aligned perfectly with Parkinson's book. Hearing this, he raised his voice in anger.

Our heated exchanges were heard by Professor Gurlabh Singh, who happened to be examining other students about 15 feet away. Intrigued, he approached our table and asked me to explain my drawing once again, this time in front of both him and Professor Sood. After a thorough explanation, both Professor Gurlabh Singh and Professor Sood acknowledged that I was correct. I felt immense gratitude towards Professor Gurlabh Singh, who, despite being in the midst of his own viva voce sessions, interrupted to inform Professor Sood that I was his best student. I was awarded a Plus Alpha grade in that viva voce, the highest level of marks.

Appreciative of Professor Gurlabh Singh's unwavering support and trust in my abilities, I apprised Professor Sood of my colleagues' similar drawings. To my satisfaction, he agreed to reassess their grades. I have never forgotten this incident because my courage paid off. My boldness not only helped me in securing the marks that I deserved but also aided my two classmates. If I had been timid, the outcome might have been vastly different.

The final examinations, delayed by about a month due to the strike, finally took place. When the results were declared, I was elated to discover that I had scored 1,604 marks out of 2,000 marks, which was 80.20 per cent. I was ranked first in the electrical engineering class at Panjab University. I had successfully reached the goal I had set for myself!

CHAPTER 10

Continuing with Engineering Studies

In the third year, hostel rooms allotted were based on the grades achieved in the first semester of the second year. Being the topper of the electrical engineering department, I had the privilege of selecting one of the finest rooms located on the first floor of the middle block in the Himalaya Hostel. This hostel layout mirrored that of the Kurukshetra Hostel. My room faced the sun, providing a cozy spot during winter days where I could sit outside and bask in its warmth. I also purchased a table fan, a bamboo rack for keeping my books, a split curtain, and a new table lamp. With everything in place, I was well set to start the third year.

However, Panjab University's regulations brought a slight disappointment. The calculation of BSc engineering degree marks involved assigning 25 per cent weightage for first and second years, while the third and fourth years held 100 per cent weightage. Although I had excelled in first and second years, this system meant that the real competition for the top positions in various branches intensified during the final years. Nevertheless, the uniform application of rules motivated us all to strive for maximum marks in the final years.

The electrical engineering students were tasked with conducting various practical experiments involving electrical motors. The department organised groups of four students for the experimentation process. Generally, I would read the experiment details a day prior, ensuring I arrived at the electrical laboratory well-prepared. This preparation was crucial for understanding the experiments' objectives.

In my group, I took the initiative and played a leadership role. My group members relied on me for tasks ranging from documenting instrument ratings to creating circuit drawings, conducting experiments, recording instrument readings, and verifying if the results aligned with expected trends.

On the day of the practical experiments, after reaching the laboratory, I would quickly compile a list of required instruments and equipment. While my group mates fetch the instruments from the laboratory counter, I diligently set up the apparatus according to electrical circuit diagrams, adjusting voltages and other parameters, and recording the essential readings for the experiments. Once sufficient data is collected, I would deactivate the electrical setup and coordinate with my group mates to return the measuring instruments to the counter and retrieve our requisition slip. Following this, I would document the experiments, detailing objectives, procedures, results and conclusions.

During one of our experiments, a hilarious incident happened, and the memory still brings a smile to my face. The task at hand involved experimenting with a DC (direct current) series motor, where we needed to record voltage, current, load and speed. As usual, I noted down the ratings of the different measuring instruments and handed the slip to two group mates to fetch the instruments. I also prepared circuit diagrams which were to be followed for connecting various instruments. Following the routine, I connected the wires and the instruments, assembling the entire circuit for conducting the experiment. The circuit had not yet been connected to the power source on the switchboard.

This particular experiment had a special precaution due to the unique characteristics of the DC series motors when starting the experiment. What we had to keep in mind was that the speed of a series motor is inversely proportional to its magnetic field. Theoretically, with minimal field current (also its armature current), the speed of the series motor would skyrocket. To counter this, an important precaution was required while starting the experiment—placing adequate mechanical load on the motor so that there is sufficient armature current and the generation of the crucial 'back electromagnetic force' (also called 'back e.m.f').

If the DC series motor is connected to the power source without any mechanical load, then its armature speed becomes very high and the electrical motor could fly off! I stressed the importance of following these precautions and made it clear that I would be the sole operator for starting and concluding the experiment.

However, busy gossiping with each other, my group mates did not pay attention to my advice. Generally, post-experiment, we would head to the nearby canteen for tea. Eager to finish the experiment quickly so that they would have more leisure time, they neglected my warnings. While I was on one side of the table, a group mate impulsively switched on the armature current, ignoring the precautions. Instantly, the motor picked up a very high speed. Loud noises erupted as the motor was spinning very fast. Startled, my group mates hastily ran towards the exit, leaving me alone at the experiment table. The instructor, who was standing at a corner, rushed towards me. Taking charge, I loaded the motor and managed to reduce the motor speed. I called my group mates back, and questioned their disregard for my advice and the specified precautions. The comical twist of this incident was their frantic escape without a backward glance, leaving me alone at the experiment table! After that incident, I told them to read the instructions carefully before switching on the circuits. This episode became the semester's hot topic, sparking discussions throughout.

After conducting experiments, we would document the procedures, including precautions and conclusions, in our write-ups. These write-ups featured handmade drawings and sketches and submit them on the next experiment day. Our teacher would carefully review and grade these assignments after assessing our understanding of the experiments.

The grading was important for us, as we were to be awarded marks out of a total of 100 based on our experiments. Since I took the lead in conducting the experiments, I would be the first to prepare the write-ups. Subsequently, my group mates would use them as a template to complete their own assignments. Since my assignments would go through multiple hands before I submitted them, they often ended up soiled. In contrast, my group mates' assignments were neater.

During the grading session, I was given Alpha, while two of my group mates were awarded Plus Alpha. In our college grading system, Plus Alpha equated to 10 marks and Alpha was considered 9 marks. I found this unjust, considering I had not only performed the experiment but also independently wrote the assignment. Both of my group mates had simply copied my assignment and submitted clean versions. This was not fair to me, and I was not willing to accept it without addressing the issue.

After the grading, my group mates were laughing and joking with me. Within a few minutes, while still in the laboratory, I firmly stated that in the future, they would not receive any of my assignments to copy unless my marks were upgraded to Plus Alpha and theirs were downgraded to Alpha. This held considerable weight, particularly considering the importance of assignment evaluations in an engineering college. Within moments, both my group mates approached the laboratory instructor to request him to downgrade their marks to Alpha and upgrade my marks to Plus Alpha. The instructor, taken aback by such an unusual request, inquired about the issue. I explained the entire situation, and after hearing me out, he burst into laughter. Eventually, he adjusted the marks in his register, upgrading mine and downgrading theirs.

Industrial Training

As part of the academic curriculum, we had to undergo a two-month practical training at either an electrical power station, electrical utility or electrical industry during the months of May and June 1969. I opted for training at the Bhakra Hydroelectric

Power Station. After the partition of Punjab, the Bhakra Beas Management Board (BBMB) was manned by engineers from Punjab, Haryana and Himachal Pradesh. Due to security issues, offices and residences of BBMB employees were set up in Nangal. Initially, my friend Darshan Singh and I stayed at Yodhamal Di Dharamshala in Nangal. After completing the necessary formalities, we were granted permission to stay at the BBMB Officers' Guest House in Nangal and commuted daily to Bhakra Dam by bus. At Bhakra, we frequently toured the Right and Left Bank power houses and made regular visits to the interiors of the dam. We were also shown the lowest point of the dam, where indicators had been installed to monitor dam sliding.

The first few days at Bhakra Dam were filled with intrigue and adventure. However, after about 10 days, homesickness set in, making me yearn for a shift to a month of training at PSEB in Sangrur, focusing on electricity distribution systems. Moreover, the rigid security measures at Bhakra restricted our flexibility in travelling between the dam and Nangal. Public access to the dam was also prohibited due to security concerns.

With permission from my engineering college and the PSEB authorities, I underwent a month-long training under the Executive Engineer (electrical), PSEB, Sangrur. Familiarity with Sangrur town eased my stay and commute to my village. During my training at the PSEB, I was also attached to the 400 KV grid substation of BBMB in Sangrur. In this way, I completed my two months' training, with one at Bhakra Dam and one at the PSEB in Sangrur.

I had studied hard during the third year, diligently covering all subjects. In the first semester, I scored an impressive 399 out of 500 marks. Remarkably, in the 'Strength of Materials' paper during that semester, I secured an outstanding 98 marks out of 100—likely the highest in the class. As I wrapped up the final examinations of the third year, my cumulative score was 1,581 marks out of 2,000, which was 79.05 per cent. This performance earned me the third position in both Panjab University and PEC, Chandigarh. I was satisfied with my achievements.

For our final year, we were allotted rooms at the Shivalik Hostel. Located on the eastern side of the college, it faces the Sukhna Lake and the Punjab and Haryana Secretariat buildings. The Shivalik Hostel stands out among the college hostels, as it had been constructed specifically for senior students. Inder Partap became the mess general secretary and brought about many improvements in the functioning of the mess. Rajinder Manhas and his friend Som Pal Singh were also staying in the second block across the road. Adjacent to the Shivalik Hostel's boundary fence, a small tea stall had been set up to serve tea and late-night snacks to the hostellers.

Warts that first appeared on my hands in the third year had spread throughout by the fourth year. These warts not only looked ugly but also caused pain if accidentally bumped against any object. Despite undergoing a wart removal procedure at Rajindra Hospital, Patiala, the outcome was far from ideal—instead of healing, the warts multiplied wherever the surgeon's blade had touched, leaving me disheartened whenever I looked at my hands.

One day, the college librarian noticed my condition and suggested consulting Dr B.L. Manocha, a mathematics professor and homeopathy practitioner. He had cured the librarian's facial warts with homeopathy medicines in just a month. Eager to get rid of these persistent warts, I met Dr Manocha, who advised me to visit his home in Sector 22 early Wednesday morning, without brushing my teeth or having breakfast.

On Wednesday, I arrived at Dr Manocha's residence just before sunrise. The verandah was already occupied by a few patients, and I took a seat on a bench, awaiting my turn. After a few minutes, Dr Manocha joined us and distributed medicines to them. When he reached me, he instructed me to open my mouth and carefully placed a few small white pills without using his hands.

He then scheduled my next appointment for the following Wednesday at the same early hour, and emphasised the importance of abstaining from liquor and meat. I was sceptical about the minuscule size of the pills and pondered whether they could genuinely make my warts disappear. To my surprise, Dr Manocha did not charge a penny for his services.

On the third visit, he assured me that the warts would begin falling off. Despite my initial doubts, that's exactly what happened—within one month, every wart had miraculously disappeared. After six sessions, Dr Manocha joyfully informed me that my hands were now free from warts. I was grateful beyond words! He refused to accept any payment and instead suggested that I contribute to feeding the less fortunate. I am immensely grateful to Dr Manocha for the positive transformation he brought about in my life.

All-India Tour

After the first semester of the final year, we were taken on a 21-day tour to diverse destinations across India. The college authorities had organised a dedicated railway coach for our journey. Our itinerary started from Chandigarh to New Delhi and then to Bhopal, where we visited the Bharat Heavy Electricals Limited (BHEL) factory. Most of our nights were spent sleeping in the railway coach.

Our next stop was Nagpur, a city renowned for its oranges, where we spent a night. We then reached Bombay (now Mumbai) and stayed there for about three days, visiting iconic landmarks like the Gateway of India and the mystical Elephanta Caves. We also visited film studios, even managing to secure access to one where a shoot was in progress. While there, we caught sight of the legendary actor Manoj Kumar patiently awaiting his turn outside a hall. Unfortunately, we were not permitted entry to witness the film shooting inside the hall.

We then proceeded to Poona (now Pune), and spent a day to tour the Kirloskar factory, where electric motors and generators were manufactured. Next, we went to Madras (now Chennai) to visit some industrial units and the historical site of Mahabalipuram on the sea coast. From Madras, our journey took us to Bangalore (now Bengaluru) via Arkonam, where we delighted in relishing

Punjabi cuisine at a restaurant called Sher-e-Punjab in Bangalore. After touring several industrial units in Bangalore, we headed to Aurangabad and Bhusawal. Our railway coach halted at the Bhusawal railway station, from where we went to see the Ajanta Caves by road. The caves, arranged in a hoof-shaped arc, showcased intricate statues that must have taken centuries to carve in this densely forested mountain area. Finally, we returned to Delhi from Bhusawal and concluded our journey, arriving back in Chandigarh after an enriching three-week experience.

Last Semester

In the second semester, I chose electrical control systems as my specialisation. This semester also involved undertaking a major project worth 200 marks. We were given data of water flow and waterfall head, and had to design a hydropower project. Immersing myself in the project, I diligently calculated the power-generating capacity, determined the number and types of turbines and generators. I also designed the power substation to elevate the voltage. This entire process took about two months, as it involved repeated discussions with my supervisor to refine the details.

Interestingly, many of us were engaged in designing similar projects, albeit with slight variations in capacities. Once the project design was firmed up after about two months, I documented the project and compiled all the necessary information. Unfortunately, some of my friends carelessly handled my major project while copying, resulting in it being soiled. Finally, we submitted our project reports for assessment by a committee.

I was unhappy when I did not score well, especially seeing others who had copied my project getting higher marks just because their presentations were neat. I ended up with 166 marks out of 200, while some got a generous 180. Despite obvious biases in the marking process, I chose not to contest it, prioritising future contentment over dwelling on past injustices. Looking back, I believe the college should have established a more transparent procedure for awarding marks and ranking major projects.

The current method of relying on a brief five-minute interview for evaluation lacked fairness. The electrical department could have formed a committee to shortlist the best projects, letting the selected ones to present to a knowledgeable audience for 20 to 30 minutes each. Choosing the top project from this final list post-presentations would have been a more fairer approach. The existing system leaned too much on subjective perceptions and biases of individual teachers.

In our final year, several of my classmates began actively applying for jobs, exploring opportunities in the army, air force, navy, BHEL and the Union Public Service Commission's (UPSC's) Engineering Services Examination (covering railways, telecommunications, Central Electricity Authority, and Central PWD). Some even aimed for positions in the Punjab PWD while some contemplated higher studies abroad.

However, I did not apply for any of these jobs as my goal was clear: secure a position as an assistant engineer in the PSEB. Since there were no job openings at the PSEB at the moment, I decided to pursue an MSc degree in engineering at PEC while patiently waiting for job announcements. My curiosity was piqued as I observed my next-door neighbour, Y.P. Gambhir, studying late into the night for a competitive examination. It turned out that he was gearing up for the UPSC's CCE for the IAS and allied services. This discovery sparked my interest in the CCE and the IAS.

After the final year examinations were over, we stayed in the hostels for a few more days, reluctant to part ways with the familiar atmosphere and the lifestyle we had grown accustomed to. I also decided to extend my stay for a couple more days. Eventually, my uncle Labh Singh arrived with his car to take my belongings back to the village. I packed my bags, bid farewell to my friends and went with him. In my village, I felt sad and missed the college life in Chandigarh.

In June 1970, the results of the BSc Engineering programme were declared. I secured 3,854 out of 5,000 marks, equivalent to 77.08 per cent. Unfortunately, my ranking had slipped from the third position to the fourth in Panjab University. While I acknowledged my own shortcomings, I couldn't help but notice that one of the students who outperformed me had a habit of excessively pleasing the faculty members. In the pinnacle of sycophancy, he would address them with a double '*Ji*'—'*Ji* Sir *Ji*', much to everyone's amusement. Nevertheless, I gracefully accepted the results, acknowledging that I had successfully completed the BSc Engineering programme with Honours, a commendable accomplishment for me.

CHAPTER 11

A Master's Degree in Engineering

I initially opted for electrical engineering with the aim of joining the Punjab State Electricity Board (PSEB). However, as assistant engineer positions were not yet advertised, I chose to pursue an MSc Engineering at PEC. At that time, PEC offered only one specialisation in electrical engineering—'Powers System'. Before 1970, only a few students, certainly not the toppers in BSc Engineering, enrolled in the MSc Engineering (Electrical) programme each year. However, in 1970, many top rankers from the BSc Engineering (Electrical) course applied for admission to MSc Engineering, and I was among them.

We were allotted rooms in the Aravali Hostel, a place I had not stayed during my BSc Engineering degree programme. Different in both design and construction compared to other hostels on campus, it had a reserved forest area behind it, where a small tea stall was set up. This spot became a frequent gathering place for us to enjoy tea. Luckily, some of my friends from Sangrur district and Government Ranbir College, Sangrur, who were in their final year of BSc Engineering in electrical engineering, were also staying in the Aravali Hostel. Despite occasional concerns about our job prospects, we found solace in each other's company. It was reassuring to know that some of my friends were facing similar uncertainties while pursuing the MSc engineering course with me.

My Favourite Subject

Our class of 15 bonded well in the welcoming, cozy atmosphere. In the first semester, we were taught four subjects—advanced mathematics A, surge phenomenon, theory and performance of machines, and power system analysis—by senior teachers like Professor Baldev Thapar, Dr Rao and Professor Nagsarkar. We were given scholarships amounting to Rs 250 per month, a support that proved quite reasonable.

Professor Baldev Thapar taught us the subject of 'surge phenomenon', which delved into the dynamics of electrical surges propagating through power lines, especially those of high voltages. We were also taught the mechanism behind both direct and indirect lightning strikes on power lines. Professor Baldev Thapar was a very simple and polished teacher who would explain topics slowly and clearly. Even now, half a century later, I vividly recall his patient explanations of how negative and positive charges accumulate on clouds, and the dynamics of lightning strikes on power lines and tall structures.

One of the significant dangers posed by the increase in voltages on the power lines could happen due to the phenomenon of 'wave reflection', which is capable of inflicting damage to insulation materials at substations or transformers if these high-voltage surges are not safely discharged to the ground before reaching these facilities. While other subjects covered in our studies were also interesting, none quite matched the thrill of understanding the 'surge phenomenon'.

Fascinated By Physical Phenomena Around Us

While pursuing my MSc Engineering degree, I often found myself contemplating the analogies present in the realm of science, which become apparent only when we carefully examine and compare various phenomena. Much like the reflection of ripples in a pond and the subsequent travel of those reflected ripples above the incident waves, similar occurrences take place in electrical surges. When a 1000 kilo volt (KV) electrical surge travels on a transmission line and encounters a substation, it initiates a journey back through reflection. The reflected wave would maintain the same magnitude as the incident wave if there were no energy loss or dissipation at the incident point. In the absence of energy loss, the reflected wave would peak at 1000 KV, travelling atop the 1000 KV peak of the incident wave. Therefore, in a scenario where the waves endure for an extended duration, the combined peak of both waves could reach 2000 KV at certain points. This phenomenon, wherein the reflected electrical surge wave builds upon the incoming surge wave, mirrors what occurs in water and likely manifests in other physical phenomena as well.

In fluid mechanics, the head, quantity and the flow of a fluid bear resemblance to the concepts of the voltage, charge and the current in electricity. Similarly, in thermodynamics, temperature corresponds to voltage in electricity or head in fluids. The total heat content of a body is similar to the charge in electricity or the quantity of a fluid, while the transfer of heat between objects is similar to current in electricity and the fluid flow in fluid mechanics. One requires capacity, patience and a comprehensive knowledge base to understand these phenomena across electricity, thermodynamics and fluid mechanics. Upon grasping these similarities among various physical quantities, we can only wonder how great our surroundings are where the basic principles of physical phenomena are similar in most of them. This contemplation becomes somewhat philosophical as we start getting into deeper details, prompting reflection on the grandeur of the universe and the role of a divine creator in its creation.

In the first semester, I scored 620 marks out of 800 (77.5 per cent). By the end of that semester, news of junior students securing job offers would momentarily unsettle me, though I refused to let it bother me for a longer period. In the second semester, I got 627 marks (78.38 per cent), which was similar to the first semester result. I felt content knowing that surpassing 75 per cent would qualify me for an MSc Engineering degree with distinction. I was much above that threshold, but I still wanted to cross 80 per cent.

We wanted to inquire about the advertisement of vacancies in PSEB. Upon discovering that R.S. Gill, the chairman of the PSEB, was present at the Punjab Secretariat in Chandigarh for a meeting with the finance department, we saw an opportunity to meet him. A group, including Darshan Singh and myself, went to the secretariat and patiently waited. Around 6 p.m., R.S. Gill came out of the office room of Mr Khanna, the deputy secretary (IAS). Darshan took the lead and introduced himself along with the rest of us. Upon Darshan's request to expedite the advertisement of the vacancies, R.S. Gill assured us that PSEB would soon advertise them. He explained that he had come to the Punjab Secretariat to discuss financial matters and secure additional funds for PSEB, which had been successful. As we stood there, Mr Khanna came out of his room. His youthful energy left a lasting impression on me, and I was struck by the authority wielded by the IAS officer. The fact that the PSEB chairman engaged in a five-hour meeting with Mr Khanna ignited a newfound aspiration within me to pursue a career as an IAS officer, though I remained uncertain about my eligibility for competitive examinations. The vivid image of Mr Khanna emerging from his office and engaging with the PSEB chairman remains etched in my memory.

After completing the first year, we became eligible for a diploma in the MSc Engineering programme. However, driven by the desire to complete the entire course, I chose to enrol in the second year. I was hopeful that upon completing the second year, I would have a clearer picture to make up my mind about my career options. In the second year, we shifted to the Kurukshetra Hostel, and I got one of the best rooms available. During the third semester, we were introduced to interesting subjects such as power system stability, advance electricity and magnetism, high voltage techniques and nuclear physics. Professor Baldev Thapar taught us high voltage techniques so clearly that I got fascinated by a phenomenon known as 'corona loss' in bundle conductors, which later became the topic of my thesis. As the most senior students at PEC, we earned respect from our juniors. In the mess hall, we enjoyed the privilege of sitting at the guest table and receiving better service during meals. Unlike during the BSc Engineering programme, we rarely went together as a single group.

In the third semester, I studied hard, and my efforts bore fruit as I performed well in my examinations. Some weeks after the exams, while enjoying a cup of tea in the canteen, a peon approached me and informed me that Professor K.K. Suri from the physics department urgently wished to meet me. Fearing I might have made errors in my nuclear physics paper, which was taught by Professor Suri, I hastened to his room. To my surprise, Professor Suri introduced me to an elderly person seated beside him. It turned out he was a professor from Kurukshetra University and the external examiner for our nuclear physics paper.

With a reassuring tone, Professor Suri allowed the visiting professor to share his observations. The professor from Kurukshetra University remarked that when he evaluated my nuclear physics answers, he was pleasantly surprised to see how systematically they were written—a quality he rarely encountered even in MSc Physics students' answer sheets. He strongly advised me to appear for the CCE conducted by the UPSC for the IAS and allied services, and suggested taking physics as one of my subjects. He assured me that with hard work, I would certainly make it to the IAS. Despite receiving only Rs 100 for evaluating 15 answer scripts, the professor felt compelled to come to Chandigarh from Kurukshetra at his own expense to personally advise me to appear in the competitive examination. Professor Suri echoed the same advice, and both of them instilled confidence in me.

This interaction filled me with a profound sense of energy and excitement, unlike any other source. At that moment, I silently committed to pursuing the IAS, though I kept it to myself. Having already observed my next-door neighbour, Y.P. Gambhir, preparing for the CCE, I knew my approach would be different. Later on, when I started preparing for the CCE, the words of the professor from Kurukshetra and Professor Suri echoed in my mind, strengthening my determination and courage.

In the third semester, I got 675 marks out of 800, which amounted to 84.38 per cent. With this, my total marks in the three semesters were 1,918 out of 2,400, which was 79.92 per cent. Although I missed reaching 80 per cent by just two marks, I was extremely pleased with my achievement. This success fuelled my strategic planning for the next steps, which included completing my thesis and earning the MSc Engineering degree.

My Thesis on Corona Loss in Bundle Conductors

I decided to work under Professor Baldev Thapar for my thesis. He suggested that I focus on corona loss in bundle conductors in high-voltage (HV) power transmission lines. In India, the use of bundle conductors was increasing, driven by the need to transmit bulk electricity across long distances. It is imperative to increase power transmission voltages, as the power transmitted is directly proportional to the square of the transmission voltage and inversely proportional to the surge impedance of lines, which depends on line inductance and capacitance. For 400 KV lines, the surge impedance is about 400 ohms, and the maximum power transmission capacity of a single 400 KV circuit is, therefore, about 400 megawatts (MW). However, if the line is longer than 350 km, the power transmission capacity of the line reduces. To transmit power over 1,000 km, the establishment of two intermediary substations becomes necessary, incurring significant costs.

The basic principle, therefore, is that the higher the power transmission voltage, the greater the line's capacity to transmit power. However, this transmission voltage cannot be increased beyond a point due to factors such as the costs of step-up and step-down stations, equipment insulation levels and tower height limitations. Furthermore, elevating the power transmission voltage can cause ionisation of the air surrounding the conductors, resulting in faint lights or rings around high-voltage power lines, particularly visible at night or in humid conditions. This ionisation, occurring at a potential gradient of 30.00 KV per cm around the conductors, leads to power losses along the transmission lines. The illuminated rings, more pronounced near rough and sharp edges, represent energy wastage in a phenomenon known as 'corona loss.' While increasing power transmission voltage is crucial for enhancing power transmission, it also increases corona loss. To address this, one approach is the use of bundle conductors in each phase of the high-voltage line. This not only increases the power transmission capacity but also enlarges the effective diameter of the bundle, thereby reducing corona loss.

Edith Clark, the renowned American pioneer in electrical engineering, had developed an approximate formula for the calculation of disruptive critical voltage for bundle conductors. I wanted to develop an exact formula as well as calculate the power loss in bundle conductors. With the help of my supervisor, the following objectives were identified for my thesis:

A. Developing an exact formula for disruptive critical voltages for bundle conductors.
B. Establishing envelopes around the bundle conductors in which corona loss takes place.
C. Conducting an experiment in the high-voltage laboratory by placing a conductor at the centre and varying its distance from the conducting pipe to measure corona loss at different voltages of the conductor.
D. Designing the high-voltage transmission lines with minimal corona loss for various bundle conductors, by either adjusting the distances between the conductors in the bundle or by altering the height of the bundle from the ground or by modifying the spacings between the bundles.

Conducting the Experiment

The theoretical aspect of the thesis was easy. However, the real challenge lay in procuring equipment for the experiment in the high-voltage laboratory. It took a lot of time to organise and assemble the apparatus for conducting the experiment safely, especially given the high voltage involved. Extra precautions were paramount to prevent accidents during the experiment. Interestingly, a robust Russian-made bridge, donated to India for research purposes, had been lying unused in the college. This bridge proved instrumental in measuring power loss during the experiment. Its sturdiness was evident; one could lift the entire bridge, weighing over five kilograms, by gripping its knob. The results of my experiment were similar to the theoretical calculations and the hypothesis set up for the thesis. I completed my thesis in December 1972 and submitted it to Panjab University through my college. I was happy that my thesis yielded useful conclusions, laying the groundwork for future exploration by myself or others.

In 1972, Professor P.V. Gupta, head of the Department of Electrical Engineering at TIET, was appointed by Panjab University as my external examiner for my thesis evaluation. Professor Gupta suggested that I visit TIET in Patiala for the examination on 15 January 1972. He planned to host my guide, Professor Thapar, a highly esteemed figure among electrical engineers and professors in northern India, for lunch before conducting my examination at his residence. After reaching TIET around lunchtime, I went to Professor Gupta's residence and waited in the lawn. About half an hour later, both professors emerged. Professor Gupta, evidently briefed by Professor Thapar, asked me a dozen questions about my thesis. I responded to the best of my ability. He commended the innovative nature of my work in a promising area for future power transmission. With a smile, he congratulated me and told me that I could go.

The evaluation of my thesis took place on 15 January 1973, and the results of the MSc Engineering examination were announced on 18 January 1973. I obtained a score of 79.92 per cent in the written papers and received a distinction for my thesis. I was conferred the MSc Engineering degree with a 'distinction' in electrical engineering on 18 January 1973.

CHAPTER 12

My Professional Debut: A New Beginning

The Punjab Engineering College in Chandigarh experienced an annual shortage of four to five faculty members in the electrical engineering department due to delays in filling vacancies. To address this issue, PEC adopted the practice of appointing lecturers on an ad hoc basis for about nine months, from July to April. This is how I secured my first job as an ad hoc lecturer at PEC in July 1972.

Despite my lack of prior teaching experience and initial hesitancy stemming from shyness, I gradually mustered the courage to take two lectures daily. I was entrusted with the responsibility of instructing second-year electrical engineering and third-year production engineering students. While the second-year electrical engineering students were young and fresh, the third-year production engineering students, part of a sandwich programme, held diplomas in mechanical or production engineering and were pursuing BSc Engineering degrees. Despite being older than me, the production engineering students were well-behaved and composed.

Even though I possessed a solid foundation in electrical engineering, particularly in calculations, formula derivations and and engineering concepts, I soon realised that teaching was an art in itself. Effectively conveying concepts in a sequential and systematic manner was crucial to ensuring understanding among students with varying learning speeds. A teacher has to teach at a measured pace so that both quick learners and those who require more time can grasp the lecture and appreciate it. If a teacher skips steps, some students could lose track and, consequently, interest in the class. Such students might then pose problems or create disturbances as they struggle to follow the subject and, in their boredom, engage in mischief. To address this challenge, I began meticulously preparing my class lectures every day, rehearsing and systematically outlining the steps I needed to cover during the class.

My experience with the production class was positive, and I could comfortably teach them. However, the second-year electrical engineering class consisted of several unruly students who deliberately disrupted the class atmosphere. To discourage such activities, I refined my teaching approach by implementing a practice where all students were required to write down formulas during the lecture. In this way, I was able to shift their focus from merely listening to actively engaging in both listening and writing.

I was also entrusted with supervising the practical work in the electrical measurement laboratory for second-year students. The role of a lecturer required a substantial time commitment, preventing me from dedicating full attention to my thesis and causing a delay of about six months.

In December 1972, I accompanied a group of college students on a tour of power projects in Himachal Pradesh. We visited Dehar, where a 900 MW power project was under construction along the Beas River. The students entered the tunnels and shafts, and witnessed the practical application of their theoretical knowledge. We also visited the Baggi channel and the under-construction Pandoh Dam. After our stay in Mandi, we visited the holy shrine of Latan Wali Devi, commonly known as Jawalamukhi. At the temple, we marvelled at the gold crown presented by Mughal Emperor Akbar as a token of reverence to Goddess Jawalamukhi. We came back to Chandigarh via Nangal after a few days.

In January 1972, I had begun considering the option of pursuing the CCE to become an IAS officer. During this time,

I frequently interacted with Professor M.S. Ghumman, a civil engineering professor and my tutorial group supervisor during BSc Engineering days. Professor Ghumman, known for his soft-spoken and polite manner, often regaled me with anecdotes about Ajit Singh Chatha, an engineer who had joined the IAS. At that time, Chatha served as the managing director at the Punjab State Industrial Development Corporation Ltd (PSIDC). Professor Ghumman and Chatha were acquainted from their college days.

On one evening in January 1972, Professor Ghumman took me on his two-wheeler to Chatha's residence in a posh locality of Chandigarh. Around 7 p.m., we were invited into the drawing room. Chatha soon joined us, extending a warm welcome. From their interaction, it was evident that they shared a strong friendship. Although it was my first meeting with Chatha, I had often come across his pictures in newspapers. His impressive voice and authoritative conversation style made a lasting impact on me.

Professor Ghumman introduced me to Chatha, highlighting my outstanding academic achievements and my potential to succeed in the IAS. In a relaxed and amiable manner, Chatha shared valuable insights into the latest industrial initiatives spearheaded by PSIDC in Punjab. He also recounted his recent travels to Europe and various other places. He spoke about his experiences of flying aboard Boeing aeroplanes, injecting a touch of humour as he playfully compared the journeys in a Fokker Friendship plane to riding on a donkey, emphasising the comfort of a Boeing jet.

Chatha reflected on his time serving as the Deputy Commissioner of Ludhiana and recalled how he successfully cleared the city of encroachments. He motivated me to give my best shot at the CCE and aim for a position in the IAS. His words inspired me to seriously consider pursuing the CCE. I also came to realise the distinction between being a working engineer and a civil servant, the latter, with its quick promotions and perceived authority, commanded respect and offered the opportunity to take on significant roles such as district commissioners at a relatively young age, around 30 years old or so.

Appearing in Combined Competitive Examination

I began preparing for the CCE and chose physics, chemistry and applied mechanics as my optional papers. In addition, there were three compulsory papers: English essay, general knowledge and general English studies. From February to June 1972, I dedicated my full attention to all these subjects. The three compulsory English papers were new and required a lot of effort. My aim was to excel in my optional subjects to compensate for the disadvantage of receiving low marks in three English subjects. The CCE was held in Patiala in two parts. The first part included three compulsory papers followed by three lower optional papers in early October 1972. After about 15 days, we had to appear for two higher papers scheduled for early November 1972. During the CCE, I stayed with an old friend, Dr Ram Lal Goel, at the Rajindra Medical College Hostel. Dr Goel, who was pursuing MD (Doctor of Medicine) degree, was also an alumnus of Government Ranbir College, Sangrur. The examination centre was situated in the Central Library building, around 4 km from the hostel.

On the day of my applied mechanics paper, an unexpected incident occurred. I had been studying until 8 a.m. in my hostel room. After getting ready, I went outside to hail a rickshaw to reach the examination centre. As bad luck would have it, there was a general strike of rickshaw pullers in Patiala. With no alternative left, I had to run about 4 km to reach the examination centre. Unfortunately, I arrived at the centre about 15 minutes late, and the examination had already commenced. I pleaded with the centre superintendent to allow me to appear for the paper and assured him that I would not seek additional time. After some initial hesitation, he asked me to write a request, explaining my reasons for arriving late and confirming my commitment not to ask for extra time. After submitting the note, I was permitted to take the examination, albeit with a delay of about 30 minutes. This was the only engineering paper in which I could have scored high marks, thereby compensating for the lower scores in the English papers.

Unfortunately, it seemed that my strategic plan had fallen through. In November, I appeared for physics and Mughal history papers.

By this time, most of my classmates had already established themselves in various professions. While some had chosen careers in the air force and the army, others found their places in Central engineering services such as the railways, telecommunications department, Bharat Heavy Electricals Limited (BHEL), steel plants and Punjab PWD. They would frequently drop by at PEC, proudly sharing their accomplishments, and a few would even flaunt their official vehicles. I would feel a twinge of melancholy and anxiety witnessing their success stories and discussions about their jobs and bosses. At times, I questioned whether I had made a mistake by not pursuing a similar path in some service. However, having Darshan Singh, the topper of our batch, by my side offered some consolation, reminding me that I wasn't the only one navigating this journey. Despite this reassurance, the visits from my batchmates tended to lower my morale, leading me to avoid meeting them whenever they came to the college campus.

Interview in New Delhi

The result of the written CCE 1972 was declared in January 1973. To my surprise and joy, I had qualified for the interview—the deciding factor! My interview was scheduled for 13 March 1973 at the UPSC office at Dholpur House on Humayun Road, New Delhi. I began preparing for the interview, which was the most critical stage in the selection process. The final results of the CCE would be determined by the combined marks of the written papers and the interview. For the interview, my friend Rajinder Manhas accompanied me to Delhi and we stayed at the IIT Delhi hostel, where one of Rajinder's colleagues was pursuing a Master of Technology (MTech) degree.On the interview day, both of us headed to the UPSC office.

While I attended the interview, Rajinder decided to explore Delhi and visit a few historical places. Although my interview was reasonable and not too bad, there was nothing particularly exciting about it. There were some policy questions regarding electricity and subsidies for sectors like agriculture, to which I couldn't provide satisfactory answers. After the interview, during which some of my responses had been somewhat patchy, I realised that my selection depended largely on the marks I received in the written papers. If my written marks were high, I stood a chance at securing a position in the IAS; otherwise, my prospects were limited. We came back to the IIT hostel, packed our bags and boarded a late evening bus to Chandigarh. Exhausted, we reached Chandigarh past midnight.

A Short Stint at Punjab Public Works Department

In November 1972, the Punjab Public Works Department (Buildings and Roads), known as the PWD (B&R), advertised about two dozen Sub-Divisional Engineer (SDE) (Electrical) positions through the Punjab Public Service Commission (PPSC). I was anticipating the results of my MSc Engineering in January 1973. Having already met the eligibility criteria for the position, I promptly submitted my application. The interviews for the SDE (Electrical) positions in the Punjab PWD (B&R) were held in February 1973 at the PPSC office in Patiala. I reached the PPSC office at 10 a.m. for the interview, but was informed that Lal Singh, the chairman of the PPSC, would only be available in the afternoon. While waiting for my turn, hunger and fatigue set in, prompting me to rest on a bench in the compound. Finally, I was interviewed after sunset, around 7 p.m.

I entered the interview room and greeted the chairman and the members of the interview board. Lal Singh, distinguished by his grey flowing beard, sat in the centre, with board members on both sides. Positioned to his left was the interview expert, a serving superintendent engineer of the Punjab PWD. After exchanging greetings, I took my seat and handed over the folder containing my certificates and testimonials to the members. Lal Singh inquired whether I was a Jat Sikh and, upon confirmation, questioned the trimmed state of my beard. I explained that it was a common practice among young Jat Sikh men in my village. He advised me to let my beard grow as per Sikhism expectations. Following this, another board member asked about my performance in the BSc and MSc exams. I shared my marks and also informed the members that I had secured the fourth position in Panjab University in BSc Engineering and stood first in MSc Engineering with a distinction. Chairman Lal Singh smiled in approval when he heard this.

The expert then asked questions on topics related to electrical engineering, expressing disagreement with some of my answers. Despite my confidence in being correct, it became apparent that the expert, with a diploma in electrical engineering, may not have possessed a comprehensive understanding of the subject matter. I contested his objections, firmly telling the chairman that my answers were 100 per cent correct. I emphasised that the expert was not up-to-date with the latest advancements in electrical engineering. To validate my claims, I suggested that the interview board members could call a professor from the Thapar Institute of Engineering and Technology (TIET) for confirmation. The last five minutes of the interview transpired in this manner, with the chairman smiling at my courage in challenging the expert.

After about 10 minutes, my interview concluded, and I had low expectation of being selected. To my astonishment, when the results were declared, I found out that I was ranked first among the general candidates! It appeared that the PPSC had taken into account candidates' performances in both the MSc and BSc Engineering examinations for the ranking. My selection belied rumours circulating among aspirants that the Akali Dal-led government had already decided on the names of the persons to be selected and that the PPSC interviews were only a formality. The Akali Dal is a Sikh-centred political party in Punjab.

I was assigned the position of SDE (Electrical) in Amritsar, a city quite far away from my village. I hailed from the Malwa region, which was relatively less developed than the Majha region of Punjab where Amritsar is located. On 15 April 1973, Rajinder Manhas and I boarded a bus for Amritsar and reached his brother's residence in the late evening. Dr Baldev Manhas, Rajinder's elder brother, was seerving as a professor and head of the Department of Chemistry at the recently established Guru Nanak Dev University in Amritsar. A tall, soft-spoken, scholarly person with a down-to-earth attitude, Dr Manhas held an outstanding academic record and pursued higher studies in the United States, earning a PhD in chemistry from the University of Texas at Austin. While he was at the University of Texas, he was the president of the Indian Students' Association. Despite numerous opportunities to remain in the US, he chose to come back and teach in an Indian university. When I met him, he had started wearing a turban.

The next day, 16 April 1973, I reported to the PWD (B&R) office located at the Verka crossing and officially assumed the charge of the post of SDE. Initially, I stayed with Dr Manhas for a few days, and later, rented a room near my office. Once I settled in, Rajinder returned to Chandigarh. This was my first field job, and I had to familiarise myself with the processes of writing and deciding on cases documented in official files.

During this period, my friend Ashok Kumar Grover from Ambala stayed with me as he was preparing for the CCE-1973. As I did not have any official vehicle during my tenure as the SDE, I relied on rickshaws for commuting within Amritsar. I particularly recall my visits to the Wagha Border, with Pakistan on the other side, and inspecting electrical engineering works in my sub-division, particularly in the Khem Karan area.

After about two weeks, Grover returned to Ambala, leaving me feeling lonely. So I frequented Lawrence Road, a fashionable area, every day, as I had no other friends or places to explore. Meanwhile, I awaited the results of my CCE-1972 anxiously, maintaining reasonable confidence that I would qualify for the IAS.

I visited the Tarn Taran and Khem Karan areas to inspect buildings where contractors had completed internal wiring. During these visits, I saw houses that bore the scars of destruction from tank battles during the 1965 India-Pakistan war. Khem Karan gained notable prominence during the war when Pakistan executed incursions through the Khem Karan sector into India, deploying Patton tanks. Despite its attempt to penetrate deep into Indian territory, the Indian Army thwarted its intentions. I observed that the road from Khem Karan to Amritsar was well-maintained and smooth, in contrast to the roads in Sangrur district, maybe because former chief minister Partap Singh Kairon was from this area.

After a few days, the Superintending Engineer (SE) of Punjab PWD (B&R)'s electrical wing came to Amritsar by road. We welcomed him at the PWD rest house and hosted a lunch. During our conversation over lunch, the SE recognised me and informed my Executive Engineer (EE) that I was the same person who had a disagreement with him during the PPSC interview. I felt embarrassed when the SE sharply mentioned that I had insulted him in front of chairman Lal Singh during the interview. It was evident that he had neither forgotten the incident nor forgiven me. I chose to remain silent, but after a few minutes, I excused myself and decided to avoid any further interaction with the SE throughout his entire tour. I also sensed that if I continued in the PWD job, my working experiences might not be pleasant.

The CCE-1972 results were expected in the last week of April 1973. Starting from the last week of April, I visited the Hall Gate daily, eagerly scanning the newspapers for the published results. On 1 May, I saw that *The Tribune* had published the CCE results, listing the roll numbers and names of the successful candidates for appointments to the IAS, IFS, IPS and the Class I services under the Government of India. To my disappointment, my name and roll number were missing. I went through the list multiple times, desperately hoping to find my name, but it was not there.

Realising that I had been unsuccessful was a big shock for me. Overwhelmed by a sense of helplessness, I stared blankly at the Hall Gate for a few moments. As I had harboured confidence in my selection for either the IAS or IPS, I had planned to stay as the SDE in Amritsar for a couple of months only before joining one of these prestigious services. However, my failure shattered all my aspirations and plans.

After regaining my composure, I returned to my office. Following the advice of my friends, who were working as section officers in the PWD, I started staying with them and sharing my sorrow and anguish.The next day, I wrote a letter to Rajinder Manhas, who was still working as a lecturer at PEC, Chandigarh, urging him to come to Amritsar immediately. I wanted to seek his counsel before making a decision regarding whether to resign from my position as the SDE and prepare for the IAS again.

As soon as Rajinder got my letter, he arrived in Amritsar, once again demonstrating what a loyal friend he was. He consoled me and encouraged me to give it another try. So, I took leave from the office and went to my village with Rajinder. From Amritsar, we went to Phagwara, where we met Darshan Singh, who had decided to leave his SDE job and go back to Chandigarh for IAS preparation. In the evening, we reached Khanna, where Rajinder's uncle was working as a general manager at a Markfed factory which produced vegetable ghee. We spent the night at his house. From Khanna, we left for my village via Malerkotla and Dhuri. Throughout the journey, a lot of unpleasant thoughts crossed my mind. I was feeling myself in a limbo. After a long wait in the scorching summer at Dhuri, we finally boarded a bus bound for my village Balian and reached there by evening.

This was the first time that Rajinder had visited my village. Over dinner, I deliberated my future plans with my family, including my parents and my uncle Chattar Singh. I conveyed my intention to resign from the position of the SDE and relocate to the PEC hostel in Chandigarh, where I would once again prepare for the CCE to be held in the year 1973.

While my family supported my decision to attempt the CCE again, they strongly disagreed with my plan to resign from my permanent job. Given the challenges associated with securing a job through the PPSC, my relatives and friends advised my parents to dissuade me from resigning. At that time, there was a general belief in rural areas of Punjab that an individual from a backward district had slim chances of succeeding in the IAS. Despite their limited knowledge about the selection process, rural people believed that only influential persons could qualify for such prestigious services.

That evening, my uncle Chattar Singh cautioned me about our financial constraints, stressing that we couldn't afford bribes for my IAS selection. Undeterred, I insisted for one year of family support to make a final attempt at the IAS. After thoughtful consideration, my parents reluctantly consented.

On 4 May, we left my village and arrived in Chandigarh in the afternoon. I promptly submitted a request to PEC, Chandigarh, to allot me a room in the Jawalamukhi Hostel for one year. The next day, I went to Amritsar to tender my resignation from the SDE position, effective 4 June 1973, in compliance with the one-month notice period stipulated by the regulations. The decision to resign from a permanent position just 20 days into my tenure surprised the EE and colleagues at the Amritsar office. Many thought that I was making a mistake and was overly ambitious. However, I remained determined and focused on my goal of cracking the CCE-1973. On June 4 1973, I officially handed over the charge of SDE (Electrical) and left for Chandigarh, determined to pursue my goal.

Preparing for Combined Competitive Examination

On 5 June 1973, I reached PEC, Chandigarh, and was allotted Room No. 322 in the Jawalamukhi Hostel (currently numbered as J-310). I started my preparations for the CCE-1973, scheduled for October and November 1973. Among my neighbours were Rajinder Manhas, Gurnam Singh and Darshan Singh. Gurnam Singh had already joined as an assistant professor in the college. Even though I devoted my full efforts to the preparation, I harboured doubts about achieving high scores in the three English subjects. Like in my first attempt, I came to understand the importance of excelling in science subjects, particularly in physics and chemistry, to compensate for potential lower scores in English. I was aware that the interview (or personality) test in the CCE could also be a weak point for me. These factors led some of my colleagues to question my chances of success, expressing concerns that I might be wasting my time.

When I reviewed my CCE-1972 scorecard, I saw that I had scored very low marks in two English papers and the interview, particularly in the essay paper where I scored in single digit. However, upon checking the cut-off marks for the IAS, I found that I had narrowly missed the IAS selection. This was why I had been offered a Class II job in the Central Secretariat, which I declined. Reviewing my scores boosted my confidence, convincing me that I could definitely succeed in my second attempt. Meanwhile, my BSc Engineering batchmates, who had secured various jobs and services in 1970 and 1971, were advancing in their lives and careers. The thought of still being unemployed only fuelled my determination to work harder. I also knew my weaknesses, so I focused on addressing them while strengthening my proficiency in subjects where I had a strong foundation.

Routine for Preparation

I selected physics, chemistry and Indian history as my lower papers, while choosing physics and Mughal history for the higher ones. From the first week of June, I meticulously prepared a rigorous daily routine. Rising at 5 a.m., I prepared tea and focused on studying until 9 a.m., followed by a one-hour breakfast break. Baitun Ram, my room bearer, served breakfast in my room. The study session resumed from 10 a.m. till 1 p.m., with a lunch break in the mess, a brief walk and a nap till 3.30 p.m. After further studies from 3.30 to 4.30 p.m., Baitun Ram provided tea and snacks. The evening from 5 to 8 p.m. was again dedicated to studying, followed by dinner and an evening walk from 8 to 9 p.m. I would pore over my books again from 9 to 10.30 p.m., after which I would sleep till 5.30 a.m. This schedule allowed me to devote about 10 to 12 hours daily to my studies, with the help of my friends and Baitun Ram.

Gurnam Singh assisted me in obtaining books from the Panjab University Library for my higher physics paper. Predicting potential exam questions for the higher papers was relatively easy. For physics, I repeatedly revised the most probable questions. I learnt Mughal history by heart, and practised history paper writing for getting a high score. Recognising the scoring potential of the general knowledge paper, I invested in O.P. Khanna's renowned general knowledge book and memorised much of its content by the end of July 1973. If someone quoted a line from that book, I could readily tell the lines above and below it. As I knew that I would not score well in general English, I compensated by prioritising general knowledge.

A friend's advice proved invaluable for writing the essay paper. He said that after selecting an essay topic, I should spend at least 30 minutes brainstorming relevant points, organise them in a sequence, and write them out systematically in beautiful handwriting in about 10 pages. I followed his advice.

In late July 1973, Rajinder secured admission to the University of Washington in Seattle. Being a dear friend, I couldn't be happier for him, yet the impending distance tugged at my heart. I went with his two younger brothers to Delhi to see him off at the airport. As the Air France flight to Seattle took off after midnight, tears welled up in our eyes. From the airport, I boarded an early morning bus back to Chandigarh.

In July 1973, when the PSEB announced openings for assistant engineers, I decided to apply as a backup in case I did not make it through the CCE-1973. About two months later, interviews took place at the PSEB office in Patiala. Confident about becoming an assistant engineer, I sensed that my plans were falling into place, solidifying my belief that leaving the position at Punjab PWD was a wise decision.

For the CCE-1973, I stayed with Dr Goel at the Rajindra Medical College, Patiala. This time, my roll number for the CCE was 000065, as I was among the first to submit my application. The first three papers—general English, general knowledge and essay—were held at the Multi-Purpose Higher Secondary School near TIET. The optional papers of physics, chemistry and history were held at the State Public Library near the railway station. This time, Dr Goel arranged a separate room for me to study in another block to ensure minimal disturbance.

After completing the examination on the first day, I came out of the hall to find my father waiting near the gate beside a rickshaw—a delightful surprise! He shared that Dr Goel had given him the address of my examination hall. Standing there, my father told me that he had visited Haridwar with a friend and brought back an apple gifted by a revered sadhu, who assured it would ensure my success in the CCE. I ate the apple in my father's presence. Even though he did not display his emotions, I sensed his silent prayers for my success. After a brief 10-minute meeting, he left for the railway station, and I came back to the hostel to prepare for my next papers. His unexpected visit filled me with joy, and I was confident that he had gone to Haridwar to pray for my success in the IAS examination.

I appeared in all the papers in the CCE with confidence, leaving nothing to chance. During the higher papers, a strike at the Rajindra Medical College disrupted my stay in the hostel with Dr Goel. I secured a room in a hotel near the Sheranwala Gate and stayed there until all the papers were over.

I expected to qualify for the interview this time, as I was confident of achieving 5 to 10 percent more marks than the CCE-1972. Instead of joining an academy for interview/personality test coaching, I decided to delve into topics of interest and current affairs by myself. My preparation focused on gaining the confidence to answer questions accurately and present my viewpoints systematically during the interview. Now, all that remained was to await the results, intensify my interview preparation, and fervently pray for success.

PART III

MY CAREER AND STUDIES AT HARVARD

CHAPTER 13

Joining the Indian Administrative Service

In October 1973, I was selected as assistant engineer in the Punjab State Electricity Board (PSEB) and was appointed as the Assistant Director (Research). Fortunately, the research unit of the PSEB, where I was assigned, operated on the PEC campus in Chandigarh, making my stay in the hostel convenient until the declaration of the results of the CCE (including the written papers and the interview if one qualified for it), which was expected by the first week of May 1974.

I was assigned two interesting research topics, both centred around evaluating the impacts of lightning on power transmission lines. I was familiar with these engineering topics and went to install instruments for measuring lightning surges at the Ganguwal power station of the Bhakra Beas Management Board (BBMB) in mid-December 1973. These instruments, placed on high-voltage power lines in Punjab, aimed to gauge lightning surges and their effects on the lines.

After about a month into my new position, I received a transfer order to the Directorate of Thermal Design at Nangal. I learnt that the director in charge of the Directorate had requested the PSEB secretary to assign newly recruited assistant engineers with an MSc Engineering degree for faster processing of thermal designs. As I had secured the top position on the list, I was chosen for this posting. Initially reluctant, I was not inclined to move anywhere before the first week of May 1974. Moreover, I preferred Chandigarh over Nangal, as my friends, including Darshan Singh and Gurnam Singh, were all based there.

Determined to stay in Chandigarh, I reached out to influential people who could potentially stop my transfer. Fortunately, S.S. Sibia, the minister for power in Punjab, hailed from my home district. With the assistance of Rajinder Manhas's cousin Kulwinder Singh, who stayed with me in the hostel, I secured an appointment with the minister in Chandigarh. During the meeting, he rang up the PSEB chairman and instructed him to stay my transfer. He also informed him that I would meet the chairman the next day.

I travelled to Patiala and had a positive interaction with the PSEB chairman, where I explained my need to stay in Chandigarh until the CCE result was declared. Understanding my situation, the chairman enquired about my chances of success in the examination. I assured him of my optimism and pledged to relocate to Nangal if unsuccessful. The chairman agreed and rang up Mr Kansal, the deputy secretary in the PSEB and an executive engineer. He advised Kansal to reconsider my transfer, and suggested that I meet him.

I reluctantly went to meet Kansal because I had been told about his disagreeable nature. When I explained my reasons for seeking a stay of my transfer, he angrily said that the IAS was not my cup of tea and insisted that I should focus on my job in the PSEB. I firmly replied that I was confident in cracking the IAS. After a heated argument, Kansal sternly informed me that my transfer orders were only halted on the minister's directive. While I was leaving his room, Kansal added, in an irritated tone, that the IAS examination was too difficult to crack for someone like me. After an hour's wait, I got the transfer stay orders and went to Chandigarh.

Interview for the IAS

The eagerly awaited day finally arrived. It was January 1974, and the results of the written CCE of 1973 were declared. Scanning the published results, I searched for my roll number, and there it was! I had successfully cleared the written examination. After a few days, I got a letter informing me of my interview at the UPSC, scheduled for 25 February in New Delhi. This time, I prepared carefully, working hard to hone my speaking skills and practicing articulate responses to potential questions.

Dr Ram Lal Goel accompanied me to Delhi for the interview. He decided to combine the visit with his personal work in the city. Since we did not know anyone in Delhi, we decided to stay at the house of my engineering college friend Jasbir Singh Babbar in the Railway Colony near Paharganj.

My interview took place in the forenoon on the first floor of the UPSC office at Dholpur House. Armed with confidence, I faced the interview board and successfully answered most of the questions. Notably, P.N. Haksar, the former principal secretary to Prime Minister Indira Gandhi, was among the interview panel members. After about half an hour, I came out, reasonably satisfied. Following the interview, I proceeded to Safdarjung Hospital for the required medical examination. We spent the night at Jasbir's house and left the next day for Chandigarh.

A Memorable Morning

The hostel warden had allowed me to stay in what was then Room No. J-322 (now Room No. J-310) of the Jawalamukhi Hostel since June 1973. As the Chandigarh administration had decided to take over the hostel for Commonwealth students to occupy the rooms and the hostel needed repairs, the warden ordered all the residents to leave the hostel by 30 April 1974. All the furniture items in the rooms were removed. As I did not have any other place to go to, I continued staying in the same room, even though I had to sleep on the floor as the bed had been taken away. As I was awaiting the final CCE result in the first week of May, I decided to wait there.

On the morning of 3 May, as I lay on the floor, the newspaper man surprised me by knocking on the door to deliver *The Tribune* newspaper. In the past, he would just slide the newspaper beneath the door. Before coming to me, he had gone to the Shivalik Hostel, where Gurnam Singh was staying. It was Gurnam who told the newspaper man that my name was in the list of successful candidates of the CCE-1973. When I opened the door, still half-asleep, the newspaper man's excited voice revealed that my roll number was in the list of successful candidates, jolting me awake. I took the newspaper and eagerly searched for my roll number. I was overwhelmed to discover that I ranked high on the merit list, ensuring my selection for the IAS. The newspaper man delivered the best news of my life, and that fateful morning of 3 May 1974 brought good luck and forever changed my life.

Upon learning of my IAS selection, I wanted to celebrate with those who had supported me during the challenging preparation days. They were Rajinder Manhas, Gurnam Singh, Dr Ram Lal Goel, Professor M.S. Ghumman and Baitun Ram. Since Rajinder had already gone to the USA, I sent him a telegram from the Panjab University post office. I later learnt that he never got it. Gurnam was occupied with teaching, and Darshan had left to celebrate his own selection in the Indian Revenue Service. The only person with me was Kulwinder Singh, Rajinder's cousin.

Together with a few friends, including Ramanjit Grewal (popularly known as Bobby), the son of the then inspector general of police, Punjab, we visited Pinjore Garden, a beautiful 17th-century Mughal Garden about 23 kilometres away from Chandigarh, to celebrate. However, I did not enjoy it much as my friends drank beer, which I abstained from. The celebration party felt incomplete due to the absence of those who truly supported me during my struggles in preparing for the IAS examination.

On 5 May 1974, I shifted to the Shivalik Hostel until mid-July, after which I had to undergo training at the Lal Bahadur Shastri National Academy of Administration (LBSNAA) in Mussoorie. I spent three days at home, during which my family organised an *Akhand Path* (the uninterrupted reading of the entire Guru Granth Sahib) for me.

Police Verification

The police and intelligence agencies adhere to a prescribed procedure to verify the background of every new IAS entrant. My verification form reached the Sherpur police station because Balian village came under its jurisdiction. A policeman was sent from there to my village to authenticate the details provided in my application regarding my parents and place of birth. Above all, he was tasked with verifying my non-involvement in any criminal activities. Daatta Singh, the village chowkidar, was the nodal person to supply this information. However, when presented with my photograph, he failed to recognise me, asserting that no one of that name and calibre resided in Balian village. After talking to the chowkidar, the policeman started his journey back to Sherpur.

Fortunately, on the way to Sherpur, he met my uncle Sukhdev Singh who was sitting outside the *haveli*. My uncle offered him tea and while they were chatting, the policeman casually informed my uncle that he had come to verify the credentials of someone named Jarnail Singh who had been selected for the IAS. He told my uncle that the chowkidar had informed him that there was no such person in Balian. When my uncle saw my photograph on the verification form, he identified me as his nephew. Surprised that Daatta Singh could be so ignorant about his own villagers, the policeman called the chowkidar, who admitted that he had made a mistake. My uncle reprimanded Daatta Singh and told him to be careful in future. It was only after this incident that my credentials were verified by the police.

Within a few days, I received my appointment letter to the IAS, in which I was instructed to report at the LBSNAA in Mussoorie on 14 July 1974. I also received a letter from the LBSNAA deputy director who gave me a list of warm clothes and other essential items I would require for my stay in Mussoorie.

As soon as I got the appointment letter, I submitted my resignation letter to the PSEB. I went to the PSEB head office in Patiala to personally hand over my resignation letter to Deputy

Secretary Kansal in his office. After a brief wait outside his office, I was summoned in. Kansal glanced at me and asked if I was Jarnail Singh from the PSEB Research Unit in Chandigarh. With a hint of sarcasm, he then enquired if I had come for the transfer order to the Thermal Design Directorate at Nangal. However, his surprise was palpable when I revealed my true purpose—to submit my resignation letter as I had been selected for the IAS. He looked at me in disbelief, his expression priceless with an intense embarrassment he could not hide! He even extended the courtesy of offering me tea, which I politely declined, as I was in a hurry to return to Chandigarh.

On 8 July 1974, I formally relinquished my position of the assistant director at the PSEB and went to my village for a few days to collect my belongings. I wanted to leave for Mussoorie from my college in Chandigarh, where I had spent eight years building a name for myself. I had friends there who had been with me for years. The atmosphere of the PEC had been a significant part of my life, and I knew I would always have fond memories of it.

Training at IAS Academy

On 13 July 1974, I left Chandigarh to join the LBSNAA in Mussoorie. On the way, I halted at Ambala Cantonment for a night, and decided to visit a barber to become clean-shaven.

When I reached the IAS Academy, it was raining heavily. I entered the Sardar Patel Hall fully drenched and signed my joining report as an IAS officer on 14 July 1974. The initial phase at the Academy comprised a four-month foundation course designed for all Central and All-India Services. After this course, in November, members of all other services, except those of the IAS, would leave for their specialised trainings, while the IAS officers remained for their professional courses.

In the foundation course, the focus was on providing an overview of fundamental law, basic economics, political science, and physical exercises. Among the scheduled activities for the officers, horse-riding emerged as the most intimidating, with many of them expressing their fear for it. The horses seemed adept at discerning experienced riders from novice, occasionally causing novices' horses to bolt and start circling the riding ground with riders clinging to their saddles. From a distance, our riding instructor Nawal Singh would command and guide the riders, and it seemed that the horses were more obedient to him than to the riders themselves. Evening discussions often revolved around the day's events on the horse-riding ground.

Each day commenced with supervised physical exercises, overseen by an instructor. All of us were provided with room bearers who assisted us in attending to our daily needs. Some officers, who were repeaters* of the foundation course, engaged in social service in the remote areas of Jaunsar-Bawar in the Garhwal Hills of Uttarakhand for about six weeks.

The foundation course studies were not overly rigorous, and prominent persons were often invited to give lectures to us. We received special lectures and written materials emphasising the importance of ethics, etiquettes, and morality in public service. Even though we were required to pass various courses, including a horse-riding test, the marks obtained during the foundation course did not factor into our seniority determination.

The Academy introduced yoga sessions for the officers, and knowledgeable practitioners were invited to share insights on yogic education. Weekends often involved *shramdan* (voluntary manual service) in various locations around Mussoorie town or the surrounding rural areas. Some of us, who had never done manual labour, developed blisters on hands while using spades and crowbars. On weekends and during holidays, many of us frequented Harry's canteen, located about 200 metres away on the hill slope opposite the Academy's main gate. The owner of

---

* Repeaters are officers who initially attended the foundation course as members of one service but were later selected for a better service after re-examination. Subsequently, they enrol at the LBSNAA to undergo the foundation course again, this time as members of their newly assigned services.

the canteen was a resourceful person who helped us in procuring articles of our daily needs. All in all, the atmosphere at the Academy during the foundation course was generally relaxed, and the officers were in high spirits, having secured coveted positions in the premium services of the Indian bureaucracy.

In November 1974, during a lecture at the Sardar Patel Hall, the cadre allotment of IAS officers was announced. I was taken aback to learn that Manipur-Tripura was assigned as my cadre. While I had heard about Manipur, I wasn't sure about its exact location on the map. Allotment of a North-eastern cadre to any IAS officer was not considered a compliment. At the rear of the lecture hall, there was a large political map of India where I located Manipur. Cadre allotments once made were usually fixed, with the only exception being marriage. Not knowing the language spoken in Manipur, I faced a challenge because there was no one at the LBSNAA to teach us the Manipuri language, so we ended up learning Bengali instead.

As Mussoorie becomes very cold in December and January, the LBSNAA administration organised programmes for IAS officers outside the hill station. We were first taken to New Delhi, where we had the opportunity to call on the President of India, Fakhruddin Ali Ahmed, at the Rashtrapati Bhavan. After our time in Delhi, we proceeded to Nagpur for training at the National Fire Service Training College and at the National Civil Defence College.

One of the memorable adventures we experienced was the sea journey from Bombay (now renamed Mumbai) to Goa. As the ship moved away from the shoreline and entered the open sea, it encountered choppy waters. The ship's tilting and tossing became quite alarming, and many officers suffered from severe seasickness. After about 18 hours, we finally reached Panaji, the capital of Goa.

During a tour of the Raj Bhavan at Panaji, we marvelled at the Bohemian chandeliers, antique Chinese porcelain, beautiful paintings from Macau, and high-quality solid wooden furniture with intricate workmanship made from Macau teak. However, when I revisited Goa and stayed at the Raj Bhavan in August

2009, I was dismayed to find that all those impressive artefacts were missing. The only artwork was a painting from Manipur depicting the Manipuri Ras Leela, which had been brought in 2008 by Governor S.S. Sidhu from Manipur.

When I inquired about the missing items, the Raj Bhavan staff disclosed that one of the governors from north India had taken away all the valuables while leaving the Raj Bhavan. The saddest part of this incident was that the governor had used the Raj Bhavan staff to pack these precious items for him.

First Days in Manipur

After completing our Phase I Training in April 1975, the Manipur government directed us to report to the Director of the Administrative Training Institute (ATI) in Ranchi, which was under the jurisdiction of the then Bihar government. Our training at ATI took place alongside the Bihar IAS and Bihar civil service officers. The focus of the training was on revenue administration in Bihar and methodologies adopted for maintaining law and order during agitations and large processions in Bihar towns. While beneficial for the Bihar cadre officers, this training proved less relevant for the three of us from the Manipur-Tripura cadre. By the end of May 1975, our training at the ATI was concluded, and we left for Kolkata by train.

After a day spent at Kolkata's Manipur Bhavan on Rowland Road, we travelled by air to Imphal, marking my first-ever flight experience. Interestingly, IAS officer H.S. Butalia, the newly appointed chief secretary, was also on the same flight to Imphal. In those days, Imphal airport functioned from an old five-room structure located on the eastern side of the current airport building. Luggage from the plane was manually loaded and offloaded, spread out on the grass lawn for passengers to retrieve. During that time, there was only one daily flight from Imphal to Kolkata, operated by Indian Airlines.

My initial impression of the people in Manipur was very positive, as I found them to be friendly and cheerful. However, the language barrier posed a significant challenge, as I didn't know Manipuri, making communication with the locals difficult. For my initial training, I was attached to the Sub-Deputy Collector (SDC) of Kakching in the south-eastern part of Manipur for a period of two months. During this time, I learnt to handle various revenue-related cases falling under the purview of the SDC.

While staying at the PWD Inspection Bungalow at Kakching, I had limited company for the duration of two months. In the evenings, I would visit the Kakching bazaar for tea and snacks. Passing through the *Ima* market (*Ima* means 'mother'), I often overheard phrases like, '*Punjabi asi yam wangey*'. A person at the snack shop explained that it meant 'This Punjabi is very tall.'

During my journeys from Imphal to Kakching and back, I often relied on local buses for transportation. On a particular Monday morning, as I travelled from Imphal to Kakching, the bus made a stop near the town of Wangjing after passing the then Manipur Sugar Mills. Seated by the window, I was observing the surroundings when a man standing outside suddenly approached my window and made a request. As I couldn't understand what he was asking, he repeated himself, raising his voice this time. Standing on a pile of broken stones dumped by a PWD contractor for road repairs, he became increasingly insistent. Failing to grasp his request, I was taken aback when, to my surprise and shock, he unexpectedly delivered a punch to my left cheek!

A woman seated behind me immediately raised her voice in response, and a young man who was nearby quickly intervened, successfully persuading the unruly person to sit down. When the bus resumed its journey, I turned to the elderly man beside me to understand the reason behind the man's outburst. He explained that the man seemed to be intoxicated, and was likely seeking money, presuming me to be a businessman. Although I was not seriously injured, my cheek remained tender for a few days. This incident served as a valuable lesson, prompting me to prioritise learning the Manipuri language and travel on local buses with increased caution.

Warring Villagers

I completed an intensive six-week training programme in land survey and settlement in Imphal, followed by additional training under the guidance of the Deputy Commissioner (DC) of Manipur North District. During this period, a highly intense land dispute arose between Liyai Khullen, a village in Manipur, and Zhavame village in Nagaland. Despite the disputed land being located in Manipur, the Zhavame villagers asserted ownership of it. The situation escalated dramatically when around 500 armed volunteers from both villages gathered on a hilltop, prepared to resolve the dispute through forceful means. Clad in the traditional attire of Naga warriors, they exhibited unwavering determination. Fortunately, the timely intervention of district DCs from both Manipur and Nagaland successfully diffused the volatile situation, leading the warring villagers to agree to return to a state of peace.

During the reconciliation ceremony, the Liyai Khullen villagers performed a customary ritual by presenting the DC of Manipur North District with a mithun's head (a mithun or *Bos frontalis* is a large domestic ox). However, this ritual was enacted in a rather ferocious manner, as the mithun's head was severed with a sword, resulting in a disturbing and gruesome sight.

Getting to Know Manipur

In December 1975, the chief secretary directed me to accompany the Manipur Rifles' jawans, who were heading to conduct operations against Naga militants in the Haochong area. Upon joining the jawans, I stayed at the Manipur Rifles' post in Haochong, a Naga-inhabited village in western Manipur. Unfortunately, clean drinking water was not available. With no roads in sight, the driver skillfully navigated the *Jonga* (a military jeep) through rivulets, and in the course of the journey, many leeches fell on us. Vigilance was necessary against these potential bloodsuckers. That night, amidst the cold and windy conditions, I shared a tent in the jungle with the jawans.

I had to acquire proficiency in the Manipuri language and pass the Class X Manipuri test before July 1976. To achieve this, I purchased books that provided English translations of Manipuri and commenced my language-learning journey with full zeal. Learning Manipuri from books proved to be more accessible and systematic, prompting me to dedicate half an hour daily to practice. Within a few months of my arrival in Manipur, I began conversing in Manipuri. I placed equal emphasis on both writing and speaking. Initially, communicating with people from tribal communities was more manageable, as they generally spoke slowly, which helped me in understanding them better as well.

Sardar Gurbachan Singh, the author's teacher in the primary level at Kanjla School, played a significant role in shaping the author's handwriting.

Shri Durga Parshad, the headmaster of Government High School, Kanjla, made a 25-km bicycle journey to the author's village to convince his parents to support his pursuit of higher education in college.

Sardar Dalip Singh, the author's father, played a pivotal role in strengthening his determination and boosting his morale by sharing inspiring stories from religious scriptures, fostering a strong work ethic.

The study table used by the author throughout his primary, middle, and high school education.

The author during Class X final examination in March 1964.

A group photo taken during the farewell of the author's Class X at Government High School, Kanjla, in March 1964. The author (circled) can be spotted in the second row from top.

A group photo taken in February 1966 featuring hostel residents, along with Principal N.K. Aggarwala and Hostel Superintendent Prof. J.P. Aggarwal. The author (circled) can be seen in the second row from bottom.

The author during BSc Engineering studies at Punjab Engineering College, Chandigarh, in 1969.

A group photo taken in 1969-70 featuring Prof. M.S. Ghumman's Tutorial Group. The author can be spotted seated second from the left.

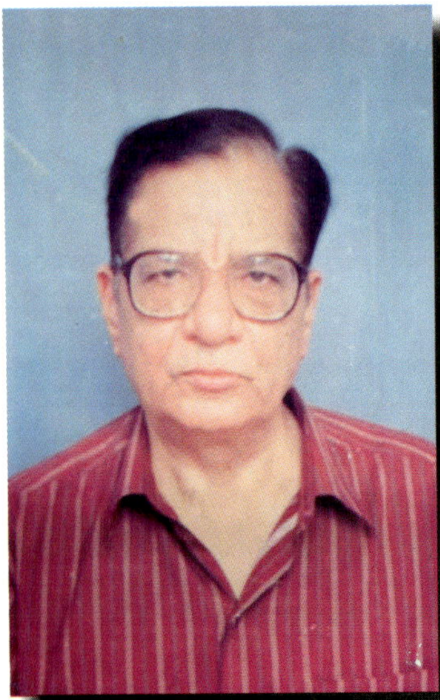

Prof. K.K. Suri from Punjab Engineering College, Chandigarh, who encouraged the author to take the Civil Services examination after assessing his Nuclear Physics paper in December 1971.

The author on the day of his joining IAS as an officer trainee at Lal Bahadur Shastri National Academy of Administration (LBSNAA), Mussoorie, on 14 July 1974. The author, a Jat Sikh, had cut his hair and shaved his beard a day before joining LBSNAA.

Mr P.H. Trivedi, Adviser to the Governor of Manipur, leading a meeting with district-level officers in Ukhrul in 1979. The author can be seen on the right side of Mr Trivedi. Manipur was under President's Rule during that time (1979-80).

The author serving as the Deputy Commissioner of Ukhrul, Manipur, in 1980.

With Mrs P.P. Trivedi, IAS, Adviser (State Plans) from the Planning Commission, during her visit to Hungdung in Ukhrul District in 1980.

The author photographed at the summit of Shirui Hill, Ukhrul, Manipur, in May 1980. Shirui Hill is renowned as the habitat of the world-famous Shirui Lily, the state flower of Manipur, characterised by its unique pinkish-white colour and exclusive presence in the Shirui Hill Range.

The author, accompanied by Chingai SDO Mr Guneshwer Sharma and Wahong Village MDC Mr Joyson, inspecting an old abandoned village site in May 1980 on Wahong Tusom Range, near the international border with Myanmar.

Celebrating the birthday of the author's son Paramjit at the DC's residence in Ukhrul in March 1981.

The author and his family, accompanied by the staff of Ukhrul DC Office, on a picnic at Sihai Phangrei in July 1981.

The author with social worker Shri R.V. Mingthing, who later became a minister, at Kongai Village en route to Wahong Village in July 1981.

The author's wife Seraphina Singh pictured with their son Paramjit at the Ukhrul DC's residence in 1981.

The author with wife Seraphina Singh and sons Paramjit Singh and Vikramjit Singh at the India Gate lawns in 1983.

Paramjit and Vikramjit, the author's sons, in front of Rajpath (now known as Kartavya Path) near Vijay Chowk in New Delhi in 1985. At the time, the author was working as Deputy Secretary in the Department of Power, Ministry of Energy, Government of India.

On the way to attend classes at the Kennedy School of Government, Harvard University in August 1988.

On a morning jog in August 1988 on the Charles River Bridge, opposite Peabody Terrace in Cambridge, Massachusetts, USA.

The author with wife Seraphina Singh and sons Paramjit and Vikramjit during their trip to the sea coast of Maine in February 1989.

The author (circled), alongside Mason Fellows, during their visit to Nicaragua in February 1989, where they had the privilege of meeting Daniel Ortega, the President of Nicaragua.

The author (third from right) with Mason Fellows during a trip to Costa Rica in February 1989.

The author seated on a ramp in Costa Rica in February 1989, with the backdrop of the Atlantic Ocean behind.

With Ms Marcia Grant, Director of the Edward S. Mason Program for Mid-Career Fellows at the John F. Kennedy School of Government, during a visit to Costa Rica in February 1989.

The author seated on one of the seats arranged along the staircases (intended for students to relax and study) at Harvard's Kennedy School in May 1989.

The author in front of John F. Kennedy's portrait at the Harvard's Kennedy School in May 1989.

The author working in the computer laboratory of Harvard's Kennedy School of Government in May 1989.

(L-R) The author receiving the Master in Public Administration degree at the commencement on 8 June 1989, on the lawns of the Kennedy School of Government at Harvard University, followed by a lunch celebration with his wife and sons.

The author's son Vikramjit (right) participating in a school play at Peabody Elementary School in Cambridge, Massachusetts, in 1992.

The author with his parents and wife at his house in Punjab in 1994.

The author receiving the 'Prime Minister's Award for Excellence in Public Administration for the year 2007-08' from Vice-President M. Hamid Ansari at Vigyan Bhavan, New Delhi, on 21 April 2009, with Union Cabinet Secretary K. M. Chandrasekhar also in attendance.

CHAPTER 14

A Posting with Many Responsibilities

After completing my training at the LBSNAA, Mussoorie, I was posted as the Sub-Divisional Officer (SDO) at Tadubi, and officially joined on 31 July 1976. Situated at a height of about 5600 feet above sea level, Tadubi was known for its strong winds. The SDO's official residence, a three-decade-old structure constructed in the traditional Assam style, had four rooms made of bamboo walls plastered with cement. The slightly tilted roof, supported by wooden pillars and rafters, faced the northern side. Electricity was sporadically available from the Nagaland side, and water had to be manually carried in buckets to the bathrooms. Adjacent to the residence was the SDO's office, a four-room complex.

After I took over as the SDO at Tadubi, M.K. Priyobrata Singh, who was the chief minister of Manipur from 1947 to 1949, had come to meet the members of the Naga National Council (NNC), staying at the Sajouba Peace Camp following the Shillong Accord. The accord, signed on 11 November 1975, aimed to stop insurgency and involved the NNC, the Government of India and the Nagaland government.

Priyobrata Singh took me to the peace camp, where he introduced me to NNC members. The purpose was to facilitate the resolution of urgent issues that may arise among the camp residents. I met Mr Athisii of Chawainu village, the self-styled Colonel and the commander of the camp. Later, I learnt he was widely regarded as a ruthless man and local people were afraid of him. However, during my time in the camp, I found him to be surprisingly polite and pleasant. The camp inmates had some issues which Priyobrata Singh took note of before departing for Imphal.

Senapati District Headquarters

The state government had decided to set up a new district headquarters for Manipur North District in Senapati, located about 4 km from Karong towards Imphal. On the evening of 3 August 1976, I got a message from the DC, directing me to be in Senapati by 8 a.m. the following morning for the eviction of encroachers from the proposed district headquarters land. In those days, the SDO of Tadubi relied on wireless messages for information since there was no telephone system in place.

On the 4th, at 5.30 a.m., I boarded a truck from Tadubi to Karong, and then proceeded to Senapati, where I met the DC and the Superintendent of Police (SP) of the district. Joined by about 25 Manipur Rifles (MR) jawans armed with sticks and rifles, along with a few civil police personnel, we conducted a survey of the encroachments and saw around three dozen huts.

Following discussions with the DC and SP, a decision was made to clear all encroachments before lunch. Our standard procedure involved entering each house, securing all weapons such as spears, and then demolishing the hut. Despite emotional moments, including a woman throwing her crying child at my feet, I followed the advice of the DC and SP to remain firm in enforcing the eviction. The operation continued for about four hours, and by lunchtime, all encroachments were successfully removed. I then signed the required letter and handed over possession of the cleared land to the assistant engineer (PWD) for the Senapati district headquarters. Thus, the Senapati district headquarters was set up on 4 August 1976.

Mystery Holes in the Walls

In my bedroom, I noticed holes in the walls, roughly seven feet above the ground, and it was evident that they had been made by bullets. The construction style of the residence, an Assam-type, unfortunately made it easy for bullets to penetrate. Yet, the origin of these holes remained a mystery, though local elders often recounted a chilling tale associated with them. According to their narrative, underground (UG) insurgents once confronted the SDO residing in that house and demanded money. When he refused, they bound him with wires taken from the military telephone installed in the SDO's residence, and locked him inside. The insurgents then posted guards at the front door. Somehow, the SDO managed to free himself and escaped through a window at the back of the house. Enraged by the SDO's escape, the insurgents unleashed a volley of gunfire at the house, resulting in the bullet-riddled walls that I now observed. As I lay in that room, the eerie sight of light filtering through those holes served as a constant reminder of the unsettling events that had unfolded in the past.

Tour on Foot

I decided to explore the western villages, consisting of about 10 villages inhabited by both Maram and Zeme Nagas. This region is sparsely populated, and the villages are dispersed over a considerable distance from each other. Since there was no direct road from Senapati to Oklong, my team and I were left halfway and had to cover the remaining distance on foot, arriving in Oklong by late evening. During my time there, I discused the government's development programmes with the village elders.

The next day, departing from Oklong, we descended the hill towards the Barak River, passing through paddy fields until we reached the Lower Rajamei village. To cross the Barak River, we made use of the footbridges built by the villagers. By evening, we reached the Lower Rajamei village, which consisted of about 20 houses. During our visit, we saw the villagers engaged in the construction of a new house, diligently crafting its thatched roof with dried grass. I was impressed by the collaborative spirit displayed by the community.

The villagers informed me that they often heard the roars of wild animals during the nights, prompting them to keep their doors securely locked as a precaution against potential attacks. The Upper Rajamei village was situated quite a distance away, and it required around 12 hours on foot to reach there. Some villagers also mentioned that, especially during the dry season, elephants from the Assam side would occasionally venture into their village through the Barak River.

Stay at Yangkhunou Village

Early the next morning, we departed from the Lower Rajamei village towards Yangkhunou. After walking a few kilometres, we decided to take a break in a hut situated in a paddy field along the Barak River. I was unaware that deadly snakes could inhabit such huts. While seated inside, a fellow villager spotted a large snake coiled in one corner of the hut, just a few feet away from where I was sitting. He quietly pulled me to another side, effectively saving me from a potential snakebite. Had I extended my hands or opted to lie down, I would have inadvertently provoked the snake to bite me. It was indeed a lucky escape!

We quickly left the hut, resuming our journey towards Yangkhunou, situated atop a hill. The ascent was steep, demanding a slow-paced climb with frequent rests. By late evening, we reached Yangkhunou, where I spent the night in the school building. The Zeme tribe inhabitants of Yangkhunou appeared notably healthier than those in the neighbouring villages. They are normally peaceful by nature, and their main occupation is agriculture.

Journey to Tamphung Village

Early the next morning, we were to leave for Tamphung village, which was a 40-km trek through dense jungles with rugged terrain.

Along the way, we were to pass Thuyeng village. In the morning, the headman of Yangkhunou village shared alarming news about frequent sightings of wild animals, possibly tigers and leopards, in the jungle between Yangkhunou and Thuyeng. Therefore, the villagers had arranged for about a dozen well-armed guards to escort us up to Thuyeng village. Many areas had no footpaths, making it difficult to trek uphill and downhill slopes. The armed villagers took the lead, providing protection both ahead and behind our group. It took us about four hours to reach Thuyeng. After a brief rest, we continued our journey to Tamphung.

Initially, we ascended a steep hill slope, and from its summit, we could see Tamphung village, situated about 12 km away. Subsequently, we trekked through tall grass weeds. Despite continuous walking, the village of Tamphung remained about 6 km away as the sun began to set. To avoid walking in the darkness, we decided to pick up the pace and began to run. While we could see lights in the villages on the Nagaland side, the Manipur side was cloaked in darkness due to the absence of electricity.

Tamphung is the last village of Manipur, nestled snugly along the border with Nagaland. From this vantage point, the glaring contrast in development between Nagaland's Peren district and the corresponding areas in Manipur couldn't escape my notice. Nagaland's villages boasted extensive electrification and well-planned road networks, laying bare a significant developmental gap with the Manipur side.

When I flipped through Tamphung's visitors' register, I was startled to find that only one senior officer had visited this village many years ago. My visit to this remote area was aimed at strategising and executing essential development projects in the region. As a result, I later on spearheaded efforts to enhance road connectivity and initiated the construction of power substations to facilitate widespread electrification across the villages, effectively addressing the longstanding disparities in development.

We embarked on our journey back to Thuyeng early the next morning. The inhabitants of Thuyeng are part of the Zeme Naga tribe, renowned for their distinctive black shawls. I visited the local school, which had been under construction for years. Despite the ongoing work, the school's roof remained incomplete, and the wooden flooring showed signs of neglect. It was evident that no one had inspected the building's progress for quite some time. Staying overnight in the school building posed a risk due to its remote location, surrounded by wildlife-filled forests. Fortunately, I was warmly offered accommodation at the village chief's house, which had a thatched roof. However, there were no beds in the house, only a long wooden plank raised about three feet above the ground, designed for the entire family. A section of the wooden plank was allocated to me, with a bamboo wall partition separating my space from the chief's family. Unfortunately, the incessant noise created by the chief's family shifting and kicking the wooden plank disturbed my sleep, leaving me restless throughout the night. Even though it was considered an honour to stay in the chief's house, it turned out to be an uncomfortable experience for me.

Before we left for Yangkhullen, the Thuyeng villagers delighted us with a short dance performance. During the dance, I was surprised to see a villager carrying his child on his back, his head adorned with an old blue toothbrush that I had discarded earlier that morning! While such acts may amuse outsiders, in these remote Naga villages, adorning one's hair with colourful objects and feathers is a customary cultural practice.

Yangkhullen Village on a Steep Hill

We left Thuyeng and reached Yangkhullen by evening. It was a tough journey because we had to ascend steep hills to reach the village. Yangkhullen, known as the hanging village of Manipur, is prominently visible from any vantage point on the hill. Situated on a cliff with an approximate 45-degree slope, there is an inherent fear of potentially rolling down if one were to accidentally slip on any village path. Certain houses even give the impression of clinging precariously to the face of the cliff with minimal support. I have never seen another village built on such a precipice.

The villagers of Yangkhullen did not follow Christianity; and were categorised as Hindus or non-Christians, they worshipped stones and local deities. In the evening, the villagers organised a brief cultural programme and wrestling matches. Among them, a tall and well-built person, known as 'Dara Singh' (named after the legendary wrestler from Punjab), stood out. The wrestling matches adhered to Naga customary rules, and I learnt that some wrestlers from Yangkhullen often went to Peren district of Nagaland to participate in matches. It was truly surprising to witness the people in this secluded village so contented, well-built and healthy. Before leaving Yangkhullen, I also visited Kanelu, a small Zeme Naga village located beyond Yangkhullen and surrounded by nearly impassable steep hills.

From Yangkhullen, our journey led us back to Willong, passing through picturesque fields and encountering massive megalithic stones. Willong is a large Maram Naga village. During my interaction with the villagers, they presented me with a goat as a token of goodwill. However, not desiring to accept it, I graciously returned the gesture by presenting the goat to the village headman.

Our route from Maram to Willong followed a mud footpath, featuring a reasonably gentle gradient and passing through grassy expanses devoid of trees. After a two-hour trek, we reached the National Highway near Maram. From there, I returned to Tadubi by jeep, concluding a memorable journey.

Fight between Makhel and Chakhomei Villagers

Makhel and Chakhomei are two Mao Naga villages that were embroiled in a dispute over a piece of land on the eastern side of the National Highway. This land dispute suddenly escalated into a volatile situation when villagers from both settlements sought to cultivate the contested land. One early morning, I got a distressing message informing me that about 700 villagers from Chakhomei and Makhel had gathered at the disputed site, ready to engage in a fight. As I had no vehicle, I quickly boarded a truck bound for Imphal. Accompanying me was Salu Mao, a diligent police constable from Tadubi police station who remained on standby 24/7. Surprisingly, upon our arrival at the disputed site, the villagers swiftly withdrew and ceased their intimidating war cries. I talked to the elders from both villages, after which they reached a mutual agreement to return to their respective villages.

The following day, around 9 a.m., I learnt that a fierce clash had erupted between the villagers of Chakhomei and Makhel at the disputed plot in the wee hours. The confrontation, marked by the use of sharp-edged weapons, resulted in two casualties and numerous injuries among the villagers. Acting promptly, I, accompanied by a police party, visited both settlements and found that most of the villagers had deserted their homes, seeking shelter in the nearby hills.

Before this unfortunate incident unfolded, I had initiated proceedings under Sections 144 and 145 of the CrPC, restraining both parties from accessing the disputed site until further orders. Since they had already violated their undertakings made under the CrPC, they were liable for a breach of commitment. It took two days to apprehend the violators of the CrPC and, as a consequence, about 150 persons were sent to Imphal jail, where they remained imprisoned for about one month. Eventually, a temporary resolution to the dispute was reached, and I issued orders for the release of those detained. This incident served as a significant lesson for the villagers, emphasising the importance of adhering to the law and refraining from taking matters into their own hands.

Visiting Chilivai and Lapona areas

In February 1977, I received a message from the DC of Senapati concerning reports of about a dozen persons missing from Chilivai and Lapona areas in the Senapati district. Despite the Shillong Accord being in effect with the NNC and the insurgents supposedly in peace camps, the government suspected that they were still secretly recruiting people and sending them to their camps in Myanmar. The DC tasked me with visiting these villages to verify the presence or absence of specific persons in each location.

Despite the rugged terrain, I perceived it as an opportunity and decided to undertake the task. I travelled to Purul by vehicle and stayed overnight in a school building. Early the next morning, I set out on foot for Kodom Khunou village via Sirong. As per the local tradition, villagers took turns to carry the SDO's luggage from one village to the next. In my case, residents of Purul carried my luggage up to Sirong village.

However, when the Sirong headman assigned a middle-aged lady to carry my luggage to Kodom Khunou, I, feeling uneasy, inquired about the choice. The headman explained the rotational nature of such duties among villagers, and this time it happened to be her turn. Though I couldn't relieve her of the task, I asked two men from my group to assist her with the load. From Sirong, we descended to a river and then climbed up a hill, which proved strenuous for someone like me who was not accustomed to hiking. Remarkably, the lady managed to carry my luggage effortlessly and rushed back to her village after delivering them at Kodom Khunou.

In Kodom Khunou, I cross-checked the list of missing persons and found that all of them were present in the village. From there, I walked down to Kodom Khullen, Khongdei Khuman, Khongdei Shimphung, and Khongdei Ngawar. Once again, to my astonishment, there were no reports of missing persons in any of these villages. I halted at Khongdei Khuman and Khongdei Ngawar. While observing the traditional shawls in Khongdei Ngawar, I observed their striking resemblances to Tangkhul Naga shawls. Even the names of the residents resembled Tangkhul names. Additionally, I could see numerous banana and citrus fruit trees, suggesting a fertile land.

I then departed for Thiwa, crossing the hill range to the east. I marvelled at the colossal wild banana trees, towering as high as four-storey buildings. After a four-hour trek, we reached Thiwa, where I found that no one was missing. Interestingly, in the Chilivai and Lapona areas, no persons from the state government's list were reported missing. This journey provided me with the opportunity to admire the scenic beauty of the entire region on foot. The next day, I left Thiwa village via Kachai and returned to Imphal. From there, I went back to Tadubi in an UNICEF vehicle.

On a separate occasion, when I returned from Oinam village after verifying names for inclusion in the electoral rolls, darkness had set in, and there was no proper road in the paddy fields near the Barak River. The overflowing river water had turned the route into a muddy, slushy terrain, causing my jeep to become stuck. We had to push it for quite a distance. After walking for about 15 minutes, a villager advised me to check my legs and hands. The river water flowing into the paddy fields was teeming with leeches. When the villager flashed his torch on my legs, I was horrified to find numerous leeches clinging to my body. Fortunately, the men accompanying me were skilled in swiftly removing them. I felt grateful that the villager had alerted me in time; otherwise, continuing for at least another half an hour could have resulted in significant harm from the leeches. It was indeed a fortunate escape!

Visiting Interior Areas Again

One cluster of villages that remained unexplored lay towards Liyai, Phuba and Koide. My primary goal was to visit this cluster to ensure that I had covered most of the villages in my subdivision. Liyai Khullen, a big village, holds significance as the Barak River originates from the hill slopes of Liyai—a captivating sight visible en route from Liyai Khunou to Liyai Khullen. The bend in the road on the eastern side marks the Barak's place of origin. The narrowness of the road near Liyai Khullen poses a challenge, with stone hills making it difficult to widen—allowing only one vehicle to pass at a time. Liyai Khullen stands as a heritage village with its ancient houses. Even the shawls made there have traditional designs that are truly unique and not found elsewhere.

After a night's stay, I left for Phuba Khuman and Phuba Thapham. Situated on both sides of a hill bend, these villages thrive agriculturally. In Phuba Thapham, I saw a unique musical instrument—it consisted of a steel wire/string of about one millimetre in diameter attached to a square plank, measuring about

2 inches by 2 inches. The player holds one side with their teeth and the other with a hand, producing vibrations in the string with the other hand. A talented young girl skilfully played this instrument, creating melodious tunes and even modulating them with her mouth while manipulating the string.

The journey from Liyai Khullen to both Phuba villages was truly enchanting. On our left, tall hills adorned with lush green forests greeted us, while on the right, paddy fields and lower hills stretched out. Perennial water sources dotted the landscape, fostering abundant vegetable cultivation by local farmers. I spent the night in Koide, one of the last villages on the hill bend opposite Liyai Khullen. In the evening, the Koide villagers organised around a dozen wrestling matches, following Naga customary laws. Their fervent enthusiasm for wrestling pleasantly surprised me, reminiscent of the spirited atmosphere in Yangkhullen.

The next morning, we descended from Koide and reached the Barak River. A brief river crossing led us to a gentle climb, bringing us to Saranamei and the Tadubi-Tungjoy road. Midway between the Barak River and Saranamei, we stumbled upon the charming small village of Khaikho, tucked away in the forest with just a few houses. A local villager shared that its name originated from the sound made by a bird in the surrounding forest, echoing the word 'Khaikho'—a delightful piece of information.

I served as the SDO in Tadubi for about one year, during which I toured almost all villages in my sub-division, mostly on foot. This immersive experience allowed me to grasp the challenging living conditions faced by the villagers and identify the infrastructural gaps hindering the economic progress of the region. My familiarity with these remote areas, combined with a deep understanding of the crucial requirements for infrastructural development, such as roads, electricity, water supply, schools, and primary health services, enabled me to actively contribute to and implement initiatives for both infrastructural and economic development.

As I rose through the administrative ranks in both state and Central governments, I was able to devise and implement major infrastructural schemes in the Chilivai and Lapona areas in the eastern side, as well as in the western side inhabited by Zeme and Maram tribes.

The important schemes that were meticulously planned and executed included the construction of the Senapati to Phaibung road, covering about 100 km, which was sanctioned and approved by the PMO during my tenure as Joint Secretary to the Prime Minister in 1996; the development of the Maram to Peron road, which passed through Willong and Bandramei (positioned midway between Yangkhullen and Yangkhunou); the establishment of a 132/33 kV power substation at Karong, along with 33/11 kV power substations at Thuyeng, Lakhamei, Maram, Mao, Liyai Khunou and Willong; and the implementation of water supply schemes for major village clusters.

My first-hand familiarity with the region played a crucial role in planning and implementing better infrastructure, a contribution that continues to garner appreciation from the local community. This was particularly evident in 2009 during a public meeting held in Senapati, where elders from Chilivai and Lapona proposed my name as a potential contender for the Lok Sabha elections, acknowledging my substantial role in their economic progress. However, their suggestion was merely for theoretical consideration, as I am not a tribal and therefore ineligible to contest elections in a reserved constituency meant for tribals. Nonetheless, their endorsement during a public meeting of village elders across the district indicated their gratitude for my efforts in planning and executing development initiatives in their respective areas.

CHAPTER 15

From Manipur State HQ to Hill Districts

In August 1977, I was posted as the under-secretary in the tribal development department of the state government. After about one month, I was asked to work as the under-secretary (education). At that time, W. Nipamacha Singh was the Minister of State (MoS) for education. In the education department, my responsibilities included overseeing peripheral tasks such as teachers' training programmes and improving the teaching of Hindi and the Manipuri languages. The main responsibilities for college and school education were delegated to other officers in the education department. G.C.K. Sharma, an IAS officer and my senior colleague in the education department, often shared anecdotes about the workings of the Manipur government in the 1960s.

W. Nipamacha Singh was a straightforward and kind-hearted person with whom I enjoyed working. His annotations on the files I forwarded to him always had something such as 'I have very sincerely read the notes of commissioner and under-secretary...' or 'I have honestly read the above notes and sincerely feel that...' He was very particular about including such expressions in official files. In meetings, he spoke softly, creating a welcoming atmosphere for all of us. At times, he found himself at a loss for words and struggled to express his thoughts openly. It would be accurate to describe him as fearless. More often than not, he would smile after he had spoken his mind.

G.C.K. Sharma once recounted a ghost story relating to the Secretariat building, sandwiched between the bank building and the North Block of the Manipur Secretariat. This building, a single-storeyed structure that had housed a printing press known as *chhapakhana* for government printing work, gained notoriety due to an employee's suicide by hanging himself from the rafter in the ceiling. Since then, rumours had circulated about the ghost haunting the *chhapakhana* building, particularly the room near the newly constructed Ministerial Block. Some claimed to have heard whispers and footsteps or to have seen a figure in a white dress, even in the absence of anyone else.

In 1976-77, there was a widespread demand for the adoption of the Meitei Mayek script for the Manipuri language. However, scholars expressed conflicting viewpoints concerning the script's alphabet count. The state government wanted the issue to be resolved so that the Meitei Mayek script could be introduced. I attended a meeting on this matter at the office of the Director of Education and was shocked by the intense debate among participants, which escalated into physical altercations. Observing the heightened emotions, I hurriedly left the meeting after a few participants suffered injuries.

I urgently needed a scooter for commuting to the office and market. However, the waiting time to purchase a Bajaj Scooter in the open market was around 10 years. Approximately 20 Bajaj Scooters were allotted monthly under the government quota, distributed directly by the manufacturer. In the Manipur government, the minister of transport allocated scooters, mainly to influential individuals. Despite my numerous requests, the minister did not allot a scooter to me. Perhaps, I wasn't important enough to get one under the quota, even though some of my colleagues had acquired scooters through it. I had to continue using a rickshaw for my daily commute between my residence in Lamphel, a suburb of Imphal, and my office.

My Marriage in Manipur

I met my spouse-to-be, Seraphina D. Lolia, during a teachers' conference at Tadubi while I was serving as the SDO there. At that time, she worked as a teacher in a village school. After seven months, we decided to marry in a simple court-registered ceremony. In November 1977, we gave the notice of our intended marriage at the sub-registrar's office in Lamphel. On 12 January 1978, we travelled in an old, rickety jeep to the office of L. Mukando Singh, the Sub-Deputy Collector and sub-registrar for marriages at Lamphel. After paying Rs 10.50 as marriage registration fee, we received our marriage certificate. I had taken half a day's casual leave for the event, and my senior colleague, G.S. Pandher, hosted a get-together at his house to celebrate our marriage. It was one of the simplest marriage receptions ever held in Manipur, with a total expenditure of only Rs 650!

More Postings in Manipur

In August 1978, I was posted as Additional District Magistrate (ADM) of Manipur Central District, stationed at Imphal. This district covered the entire Imphal valley, including Jiribam, which has now become a separate district. At that time, A. Halim Choudhary was the Deputy Commissioner (DC) of the Manipur Central District. He operated his office from his residence in Babupara, and seldom visited the DC's office in Lamphel. Halim Choudhary was a genial and approachable individual, and could not take tough decisions against land encroachers or serious law offenders. His ability to maintain amicable relations with politicians across various political parties likely contributed to his prolonged tenure as the DC in Manipur Central District.

Raj Narain—the politician who won the landmark case against the then Prime Minister Indira Gandhi on charges of electoral malpractices, ultimately resulting in the imposition of Emergency in 1975—belonged to the erstwhile Socialist Party. He was a follower of Ram Manohar Lohia, a prominent socialist political leader of that era. In the 1977 general elections to the Lok Sabha, when the Janata Party came to power, and Morarji Desai became the Prime Minister, Raj Narain was appointed as the Minister of Health and Family Welfare in the Union Cabinet.

In 1978, the Manipur state government invited Raj Narain to lay the foundation stone of the district hospital at Prompat in Imphal, and I was appointed as the liaison officer for the minister. We received him at the Imphal airport. He had a green cloth wrapped around his head and carried a small cloth bag, which he entrusted to me to give him at the Raj Bhavan, where he would stay. Interestingly, during our journey, Raj Narain chose to sit beside the driver in the front seat and insisted that I sit in the rear seat with the security guard, a departure from the usual protocol. He maintained a casual and friendly demeanour during our conversation, even enquiring about my meal preferences. Upon learning that I was vegetarian, he seemed pleased. Later in the afternoon, he laid the foundation stone for the district hospital at Prompat. At that time, the area was surrounded by paddy fields, but today, the landscape is dominated by concrete structures.

In the evening, the state government hosted a state dinner in honour of Raj Narain. The event followed traditional customs, with guests seated on the floor and food served on banana leaves. A wide array of dishes were offered, and the guests relished the diverse flavours. During the dinner, Raj Narain invited me to sit beside him. As the food was being served, he mentioned that he could smell fish. I assured him that his meal did not contain any fish, but some other guests were enjoying fish curry and a local specialty called *eromba*, made from fermented fish. The strong smell of fish in the air made it difficult for him to enjoy his vegetarian food, prompting him to be seated at a separate area free from the odour.

After the state dinner and the cultural programme, we returned to Raj Bhavan around 10 p.m. There, Raj Narain informed me that he couldn't sleep without a head massage. I did not know where to find a person who could do the massage, but we were lucky when a police officer arranged for a barber from Teli Patti, an area known for such services, to massage his head for about half an hour. Following the massage, he went to sleep.

The next day, when I met Raj Narain at the main lounge of the Raj Bhavan, he took out a small packet from his cloth bag. Inside the packet were roasted grams, which he consumed and offered me some as well. After finishing his snack, he kept the packet back in his bag and casually elevated his legs onto the table in front of the sofa. Then pointing at his partially exposed legs, he said in Hindi, 'You see the marks on my legs? These are from the tear gas shells of the Indira Gandhi government. My legs have been broken by repeated hits of tear gas shells.'

What added a touch of humour was when a Manipuri person later asked if Raj Narain was my relative. Perplexed, I enquired about the reason behind his assumption, and the reply was that he also sported a green cloth on his head, resembling my turban!

In 1978, students in Imphal had launched a number of agitations against 'foreigners' although their focus extended to all 'outsiders' in Manipur. Usually, these student groups would march through Paona and Thangal bazaars, proceeding to the Ima market, and stay put there. The routine of most protests followed this pattern. Despite the tension, the DC was very patient and refrained from imposing any restriction on agitations. My role involved accompanying the students alongside an additional SP in a vehicle.

One day, the protestors marched towards the chief minister's residence and reached the Imphal police station. About 3,000 students crowded the road stretching from the accountant general's office to the South Block of the Secretariat. The situation took a perilous turn when a fully loaded petrol tanker entered the main road from the Raj Bhavan side, posing a potential disaster. Positioned just inside the Imphal police station gate, I witnessed protestors hurling stones at the police. Some of these stones landed at Secretariat building, while others were directed towards the police and me, but I protected myself with a shield.

As tension escalated, some students attempted to set the petrol tanker on fire. The police informed me that unless they dispersed the students using tear gas or by resorting to firing, a serious tragedy could unfold—if the petrol tanker exploded, the Secretariat could be engulfed in flames. Surprisingly, the police did not have tear gas equipment. Urgent announcements were made over a mike, declaring the crowd unlawful and instructing immediate dispersal. Armed only with sticks, the police were outnumbered by the crowd, rendering their efforts ineffective. Recognising the gravity of the situation, I signed an order to disperse the unlawful assembly by firing. Immediately, the police aimed their rifles on the students, who started running into the then Bengali High School building. Within minutes, the students ran into Bengali High School and towards the Imphal River.

Soon, the roads were cleared of the students. The next day, there was a news item that 'Jittery ADM Jarnail Singh signed the firing order' and that a timely decisive action prevented the Secretariat building from being set ablaze. Reflecting on the events, I believe that allowing crowds on the road from Raj Bhavan to the First Manipur Rifles battalion headquarters' gate, which is housing sensitive buildings, was a mistake.

Another student agitation took place a few days later when the students of Thoubal College, who had been on strike for quite some time, presented a comprehensive list of demands to be fulfilled immediately. With their grievances unaddressed, the students forcibly closed all offices in Thoubal sub-divisional headquarters (Thoubal is now a district headquarter). In response, the chief secretary ordered me to go to Thoubal and manage the situation. He had also got a message from the chief minister's office to send me there as the national highway was being blocked by students and all offices had been closed. When I reached Thoubal, I found a large crowd of students advancing towards the SDO's office. Positioned at a small bridge on the national highway, I navigated through large heaps of broken stones on the roadsides (as it was being widened).

A small contingent of lady police personnel was also with me. Even though armed with sticks, they hesitated to confront the girl students in the crowd. On that day, the Rajasthan Armed Constabulary (RAC) jawans, along with some Manipur police constables equipped with tear gas shells, were stationed at Thoubal. The situation took a serious turn when the students suddenly rushed towards us and started throwing stones. Fortunately, my turban shielded my head, but I was struck by a stone. The policewomen, overwhelmed by fear, sought refuge inside the office, taking cover in the SDC's courtroom.

Unfortunately, a malfunction occurred with the Manipur police tear gas equipment, rendering them unable to fire tear gas shells at the students. We feared that the students would overrun us. Luckily, an officer from the RAC offered to use tear gas, and I consented. Seizing the tear gas equipment from the Manipur policemen, he started firing tear gas shells towards students. In panic, the students retreated. I entered the SDC's office, directed the policewomen to come out, and ordered them to arrest the girl students. Unfortunately, when I pulled out a lady sub-inspector of the Manipur police, her arm bone cracked.

That day, the police chased the students for about 2 km and arrested about 100 students. They were detained in the Imphal jail. Surprisingly, the students' strike ended the next day. I was injured on the right hand and had to keep it bandaged for several days. I later learnt that Chief Minister Yangmaso Shaiza expressed satisfaction with my firm handling of the agitation.

In February 1979, I was posted in the Public Works Department (PWD), which was one of the important departments of the state. Despite facing water scarcity in Manipur during that period, the state PWD inexplicably purchased numerous bathtubs for government quarters, far exceeding any genuine need. While a few might have been needed, the majority were procured through repeat orders. The chief engineer of the PWD and some of his officers had misused funds that could have been used for purchasing essential construction materials for buildings, bridges and roads. The fundamental principles governing government department purchases are twofold: firstly, a proper assessment of the required quantity of a specific item, and secondly, determining its price through open tender. Unfortunately, both these principles were violated. In the same way, earth rammers and water geysers were purchased without the call of tenders and assessing the requirements. I was surprised to see how the commissioner and the chief engineer of the PWD had disregarded the General Financial Rules (GFR) of the government in these reckless purchases, actions that predated my tenure in the department. My predecessor had opposed these irregularities but was overruled.

Under President's Rule, in November 1979, the state government initiated Central Bureau of Investigation (CBI) investigations into these purchases. The cases were straightforward, and the GFR violations were evident. The Commissioner (Works) was convicted for violation of financial rules and sentenced to simple imprisonment till the rising of the court, along with a fine of Rs 10,000. When his case was heard in the Supreme Court in October 1995, his sentence was increased to six months. Unfortunately, both the chief minister and the chief engineer had passed away before the court's final decision.

Deputy Commissioner of the Hill Districts

On 6 August 1979, I took over as the Deputy Commissioner (DC) of Chandel district. The DC's residence was on a hill slope and surrounded by dense pine trees. At night, we could hear the howls of jackals and foxes. During the months from June to September, Chandel is humid and hot. As it was my first posting as a DC, I tried to settle down quickly in the job. I devised plans to explore remote areas of the district and aimed to prepare a comprehensive infrastructure development plan.

One evening, I got a terse message from the chief secretary of Manipur stating that the headman of the Molcham village, situated on the India–Myanmar border, had raised concerns with the Government of India about encroachments on his village's land by Myanmar's villagers. The headman had formally requested the intervention of both the Government of India and the Manipur authorities to demarcate the south-eastern boundary of his village land. Additionally, there were previous reports of missing boundary pillars (BPs) in this region along the India–Myanmar's international border. In the message, the chief secretary had directed me to personally visit the area and submit a comprehensive report within one week.

There were two travel options to reach Molcham. The easier one involved a jeep journey along the muddy track parallel to the India–Myanmar international border from Moreh town. This kacha track ran along the western edge of the Kabo valley, just at the foothills. Initially within India, this track, after a few kilometers, partially lies in Myanmar and partially in India. This route usually took about two days to traverse. The second one, a more challenging option, required a trek from Chakpikarong to Molcham village, which is about 65 kilometres from Chakpikarong. Due to the absence of roads or kacha tracks beyond Chakpikarong, the entire distance had to be covered on foot. I opted for the hiking route, and the following morning, my official vehicle dropped me off at Chakpikarong.

Accompanied by my office staff and a district council member from Khengjoy, we commenced our journey by ascending the hill on narrow paths, reaching Mombi, a small settlement comprising a handful of houses. From there onwards, the path was mostly flat, winding along hill footpaths in the hot and humid weather.

To guard against leeches climbing up my trousers, I had tucked my trousers into my socks. Since there was a thick growth of grass on all sides of the footpath, I could see leeches perched on the vegetation. Concerned about bloodsucking worms falling from trees, I buttoned my shirt collar, ensuring it was securely closed.

Our first night halt was planned at Khengjoy, which was about 40 kilometres by foot. On plain footpaths, I could maintain a brisk pace due to my height. However, when faced with ascents or descents, I lagged behind my companions. After crossing Mollen/Mullam (the pronunciation of the name varies), we encountered a steep hill with a very narrow footpath that stretched on for about 10 metres. The hillside near the footpath was barren, with a steep slope of over 500 metres that required cautious navigation to prevent sliding down. Feeling nervous, I recognised the real risk of slipping. Observing my apprehensions, my companions devised a solution. They brought two bamboos, each about 6 metres long, and joined them to create a makeshift railing on the downhill side of the footpath. Advised to remove my shoes for better grip, with one person walking in front and another behind to boost my confidence, I slowly crossed the intimidating 10-metre stretch—a passage that was like a potential death trap. I was dismayed to discover there was no alternate footpath to bypass this patch, as the other side of the hill was also very steep.

So far, we had covered about 30 kilometres, and I was exhausted. I was told that Khengjoy was still around 10 kilometres away, and with just half an hour of sunlight remaining, our pace quickened to ensure we reached Khengjoy before nightfall. At times, we even resorted to running. By the time we arrived, darkness had enveloped the surroundings. I was exhausted, finding it difficult even to lift my legs. The villagers brought hot water for me, allowing me to take a soothing bath and eventually enjoy a restful sleep. This marked the longest distance I had ever walked in a single day during my entire service career—approximately 40 kilometres with many steep hikes.

The next morning, we left Khengjoy and reached Yangoulen in the Kabo valley. On the way, we passed the L. Bongjoi village. The Yangoulen village area is flat with teak trees all around. There was a Border Security Force (BSF) post near the village. I met the post commander, who possessed a copy of the map of the border area, certified by the surveyor generals of both India and Myanmar. This certification implied an absence of disputes on paper regarding the international boundary between the two countries. The only issue was to locate the missing BPs on the ground using this map. The post commander informed me that patrolling squads were dispatched weekly to inspect all BPs within their jurisdiction. Any suspicious activity or foul play concerning the BP's location triggered immediate reporting to the government, and the issue was promptly addressed. The post commander also informed us that the Molcham village headman had been complaining about a missing BP. According to him, the headman believed that the Tuiwang village in Myanmar was in Indian territory, and someone from that village might have played a role in the disappearance of one of the BPs.

In the early morning, I inspected the area alongside the post commander and local villagers. With the help of the map provided by the post commander, we successfully pinpointed the approximate position of the missing BP. It seemed to be near the northern bank of the Tuiwang River, suggesting that it might have been intentionally thrown into the river. Notably, this particular BP (No. 66) positioned Tuiwang, a Myanmar village, about 100 metres inside the Indian territory. It became evident that the Tuiwang villagers harboured a vested interest in ensuring that BP 66 was not fixed on the ground. They continued to reap benefits if the boundary in this area remained disputed. If the BP was fixed on the ground, then the Tuiwang village would have to be relocated to Myanmar's territory. I engaged in a discussion over tea with the headman of Tuiwang village and discovered that the people of Yangoulen (the Indian side) and Tuiwang are from the same tribe and related to each other. In fact, the Tuiwang headman expressed a willingness to become part of India if the BP were fixed on the eastern side of their village, as it would place their agricultural land within the Indian territory.

After five days, I returned to Chandel. During this journey I familiarised myself with the area and the living conditions of the people. I prepared a comprehensive report detailing the missing pillar and proposing potential solutions to settle the issue. I found lots of merit in the representation made by the Molcham headman to both the Government of India and Manipur government. Since there was no dispute about the location of BP 66 on the map, it would be easier for the teams from the surveyor generals of India and Myanmar to locate it on the ground. Based on my first-hand knowledge of this area and my subsequent report submitted to the state government, the proposed location for the Sub-Deputy Collector's office (now the sub-divisional office) was shifted from New Samtal to Khengjoy.

Sudden Transfer as Deputy Commissioner, Ukhrul

I had just settled as the DC, Chandel, when a district council member visited my office, removed his cap and took out a paper from it. With a smile, he handed it over to me. Glancing at the paper, I was taken aback by its contents—it was an order from the Governor of Manipur posting me as the DC of Ukhrul.

After serving a mere 39 days as the DC of Chandel, I handed over charge to the officer concerned and headed to Ukhrul on 13 September 1979. Though my shift from Chandel to Ukhrul was quite dramatic, it turned out beneficial for me. Ukhrul held significant political influence in Manipur, with Yangmaso Shaiza, the Member of Legislative Assembly (MLA) from Ukhrul, serving as the chief minister. I was told that I had been handpicked by him to be the DC of Ukhrul after he saw my firm handling of the students' agitation in Thoubal about six months earlier. I assumed charge as the DC, Ukhrul, on 14 September 1979, which incidentally was also my 30th birthday.

I found the people of Ukhrul to be well-educated, smartly dressed and articulate in expressing themselves. I also liked the DC 's residence, which was built by a British officer in the 1940s. Ukhrul district is famous for the Siroy Lily, the state flower of Manipur. The pale pinkish flower (*Lilium mackliniae*) is also locally known as *Kashong Timrawon* (*Kashong* is the name of the peak of the Shirui Hills in Ukhrul and *Timrawon* means lily in the Tangkhul language). The lily blooms for only three to four weeks each year, from mid-May to mid-June.

Village Development Plans

I focused my attention on preparing a development plan for each village of my district. This was essential as every village has a different resource base and potential for development and growth. A pro forma was prepared to make a database of the resources of each village, which included key aspects such as population, education levels, animal stock, cultivable land, irrigation sources, current production levels of paddy, vegetables, fruits and other crops, as well as road connectivity. After preparing these village-specific development plans, my next objective was to compile a district-wide development plan for Ukhrul and place it before the state government and the Planning Commission for funding. This was a systematic approach, but I was not sure how the state government would perceive and evaluate the proposal.

Interior Areas of Kamjong Sub-division

After about a month, I decided to explore Kamjong, a hilly area connected to Ukhrul by a road that largely resembled a kacha track. Setting out from Ukhrul in the afternoon with Ashui, my driver, we encountered heavy rainfall that resulted in the road becoming muddy. By around 3 p.m., we reached Gamnom and saw the damage to the road leading from Gamnom to Kamjong, caused by trucks transporting heavy wooden logs from the border to Dimapur via the Ukhrul-Jessami road.

By the time we reached halfway to Kamjong, the sun had already set and it was completely dark. Ashui was finding it difficult to steer the jeep straight as the wheels could not move easily on the deep, wet tracks left by heavy trucks. Suddenly, we encountered a very slushy wheel track, followed by a loud breaking sound. Ashui stopped the jeep, and discovered that the tie rod, an integral part of the steering system, had broken. Unfortunately, in the late hours, the prospect of any vehicle passing by was slim. As it was my first visit to the Kamjong area, I had no idea of the road or distance ahead.

'We are stuck for the night,' I thought. However, I had underestimated Ashui's resourcefulness in jungle scenarios. Always well-prepared during my tours, he carried a torch and a sharp *dao* (knife). After assessing the situation, he took out the torch and knife, climbed a tree on the hill slope and found a sturdy vine hanging from it. Using the *dao* skilfully, he modified the vine into a rope-like structure. He then secured the tie rod with it, enabling us to drive the jeep again. Slowly and steadily, we navigated the wet tracks and eventually reached a more manageable stretch of road, arriving in Kamjong after 9 p.m.

The first village beyond Kamjong was the colourful Grihang. Each house was surrounded by about a dozen orange and citrus trees laden with fruits. Aptly named the 'Orange Village,' Grihang resembled Kachai village in the western Thangkhul area, known as the 'Home of Lemons'. The locals in Grihang told me about Brigadier Pamrei, a key figure in the Naga underground movement associated with the NNC. They revealed that he hailed from Grihang and speculated that, had he not died, he might have ascended to the top of the Naga underground hierarchy.

After Grihang, I visited Ningchou, a small village. Little did I know that this visit would alter my destiny. I was unaware that the plans I made that day in Ningchou village would pave the way for my enrolment in the Master in Public Administration program at Harvard University. I distinctly remember standing beside my jeep in the village playground, overlooking the water supply tank and discussing the persistent issues of the non-functional water supply scheme with the villagers.

Despite months of complaints to the relevant government department, the village continued to suffer from water scarcity. Upon further enquiry, I found that the diesel engine, which was used for lifting water to the supply tank, could not be operated due to unavailability of spare parts. Even when operational, diesel shortages often disrupted the water supply. While standing in the playground, I learnt about a reliable, perennial water source approximately 200 feet below the village that could meet the village's needs. A sudden realisation struck me: why not use hydrams (hydraulic rammers)* in such areas? Drawing on my studies of hydram functioning during my first year of Bachelor of Engineering, I recalled their successful use in the Garhwal Hills of Uttarakhand for irrigation and water supply purposes.

After Ningchou, I went to Kongkan Thana, another small village that served as the boundary post of the Maharaja of Manipur. It had a small brick structure which was used as a guard room by the Maharaja's men. Kongkan Thana marked the end of the Kabo valley and the commencement of hills stretching northward. Phaikok, the last village of Manipur on the border, lacked stringent checks on people's movement between Myanmar and India.

The next day, I visited villages on the hill ranges of Kongkan and Molvailup. On the eastern side of Kongkan, one could clearly see the Kabo valley and Kongkan Thana. The villagers were growing citrus fruits and explained their plans to focus on settled cultivation near the Kabo valley if irrigation facilities could be created. After Kongkan, I went to Molvailup, where there are plenty of teak trees, which the inhabitants were trying to cut and sell as wood. On the third day, I went to villages called Kangpat Khullen, Nampisha and Choro Khunou which are situated on a long hill ridge. On the eastern side of the ridge is the Tuyungbi River and on the western side is the Kabo valley. At the end of the ridge on the hilltop is Choro village, the small Choro Khunou village being near the international border.

Choro Khunou had been in the news for two reasons. One was the proposal of the state government to exchange territories between Myanmar and India at Moreh, Molcham and near Choro Khunou to settle the border disputes with Myanmar. The second one was about the deadly clashes of October 1980, between security forces and the members of an outlawed militant organisation in which the militants had suffered heavy losses.

A Disturbing Incident At Ukhrul

The incident that profoundly disturbed my conscience was the brutal physical assault on Kangsui Luithui, the chairman of the Ukhrul Autonomous District Council, by an army officer. Even as I reflect on that distressing incident today, I am deeply shaken by the sheer inhumanity displayed. It baffles me to consider how a commissioned officer of the Indian Army could commit such a reprehensible act. This incident triggered an immediate and spontaneous uprising among the public against the Assam Rifles. The Assam Rifles Headquarters at Somsai was surrounded by enraged Naga villagers from all sides. This was the most brazen misuse of powers vested in the armed forces under the Armed Forces (Special Powers) Act (AFSPA), 1958. The Act empowered the armed forces in 'disturbed areas' to search, arrest, or even to kill anyone violating the law—all without the need for a warrant and with immunity from any prosecution or legal suit.

One early morning, I was abruptly awakened by a clamorous crowd outside my residence. When I came out to meet them, I found a highly agitated assembly, demanding the immediate arrest of Captain Sharma, an Assam Rifles officer stationed at Somsai Headquarters. They told me that on the previous night at about 10 p.m., Captain Sharma, accompanied by his escort, had surrounded the house of Kangsui Luithui. In a state of intoxication, the captain insisted that Luithui accompany him to Somsai. On the way, Captain Sharma and his escort misused their powers under the AFSPA, and subjected Luithui to severe physical assault.

In the morning, I received distressing information regarding the severity of Luithui's injuries. His condition was so severe that he was hardly recognisable—he was partially unconscious with his whole body swollen. Upon learning of the incident, Colonel Gatphou, the commanding officer of the battalion at Somsai, took prompt action by placing Captain Sharma into custody and transferring him to another location. As Luithui's condition deteriorated, arrangements were made to airlift him to Imphal for urgent medical treatment.

The enraged public demanded immediate arrest of Captain Sharma, seeking to mete out similar treatment to him as he had done to Luithui. In response, the Governor of Manipur promptly asked the major general of the army from Jakhama to go to Ukhrul and address the escalating situation.

Initially, the local public refused to meet any army personnel to discuss the matter. Finally, a meeting was held at the Ukhrul Autonomous District Council/Pettigrew College complex in Somsai. However, before anyone could address the gathering, the major general nonchalantly took out a cigar to smoke and even smiled. Immediately, an elderly lady from the front row stood up and said, 'Do not smoke in front of us. You are smiling while we are mourning. Are you not ashamed of this? Have you come here to enjoy yourself or to share our grief?' The major general was visibly stunned by her words, which amounted to a serious public rebuke. He apologised and placed the cigar back in his pocket. After intense discussions and persuasion, the agitation was called off. Captain Sharma was court-martialled for the wrongful use of powers vested in army officers under the AFSPA, 1958.

A Midnight Journey

All arrangements for the general elections of December 1979 had been made and we were expecting a peaceful polling. However, around 9 p.m. on the eve of voting, I received a wireless message informing me that the presiding officer in the remote village of Soraphung, in the Chingai assembly constituency, had decided to relocate the polling station from a school building to a church. This decision was made because the school building had been damaged in the previous night's storm. Under the Indian election laws, a polling station cannot be set up in any religious place. Since I was not able to communicate with polling officer of Soraphung, the only option was for me to go there at midnight to ensure that the polling took place in the originally designated school building. Since there were no other election-related issues reported elsewhere in the district, I left Ukhrul for Soraphung at 10 p.m. It was a dark night, and by around 12.30 a.m., I reached Chingai. From there, the journey continued for about 12 kilometres along a potholed and bumpy *kacha* track, winding through dense jungle. In the silent darkness, I could hear the roars and howls of wild animals.

Finally, through Kongai, we reached Soraphung at about 3 a.m. Once there, my driver Ashui contacted the village headman and the polling personnel. I requested the villagers to repair one room of the school building so that it could be used for polling. The villagers started working, and by 6 a.m., the room was ready for voting. I left Soraphung at 7 a.m. via Kharasom.

Ambush by Militants at Mahadev

In February 1980, Rishang Keishing, newly appointed as deputy chief minister, visited Chingai and stayed at the Chingai PWD guest house. During our morning conversation over tea, he recounted a disturbing nightmare where he saw a woman with unbound hair sitting on his chest with a dagger. Despite it being a dream, he seemed visibly shaken. At breakfast, I sensed that the deputy chief minister was expecting a visitor, but none arrived. Later, I learnt that an influential leader from the underground Naga group was supposed to meet him, but did not turn up for unknown reasons. It may be worth mentioning that the Somra Tract in Myanmar, where the Tangkhul Naga dialect similar to that in Ukhrul district is spoken, lies about a three-hour walk from the international border opposite Chingai. The underground Nagas had established camps in the Somra Tract and used to go there through Chingai. In turn, residents of the Somra Tract frequently ventured to Chingai for essential commodities such as sugar, salt and medicines.

After lunch, we started our journey back to Imphal. The *kacha* track between Chingai and Awang Kasom was about 10 kilometres, with many sharp bends. During the journey, a tragic accident took place when a vehicle carrying security guards plunged into a deep gorge, resulting in one fatality and severe injuries to some guards. The delay caused by the accident disrupted our schedule. I discontinued my journey at Ukhrul and Rishang Keishing continued to Imphal. After about two hours, I learnt that some vehicles en route Imphal had been ambushed by militants between Mahadev and Gwaltabi. Luckily for Rishang Keishing, he escaped the attack because of the delay in reaching Mahadev. The militants had fired upon a group of civilian vehicles, mistaking them for the deputy chief minister's convoy. They had even dug trenches near the bend of the road on the hill for the ambush. The darkness of the night saved Rishang Keishing and his convoy; had they arrived on time during daylight, the ambush could have resulted in casualties. The deputy chief minister was later escorted safely to Imphal.

Looting at Ukhrul

The United Bank of India (UBI) in Ukhrul, located a mere 50 metres away from the Assam Rifles post, fell victim to an unusual heist orchestrated by militants one night. The perpetrators discovered that both keys to the bank's currency chest were held separately by the cashier and the bank manager. Seizing one opportune moment after sunset when the bank was closed, the militants executed their plan. Dividing into two groups, one targeted the bank cashier's house, while the other headed to the residence of the bank manager. Skilfully, they escorted both individuals with their respective keys, to a house situated just behind Assam Rifles' post. This house was rented by district fisheries officer K. Vaiphei, who happened to be away in Imphal. Taking advantage of the vacant house, the militants locked the bank manager and the cashier inside, took the keys and proceeded to the UBI building.

Once at the bank, they opened the currency chest and looted all the cash. The following morning, the trapped manager and cashier raised an alarm, and were rescued from the locked house. Intelligence reports pointed towards the involvement of the NSCN cadres in the bank robbery. However, despite these leads, the police investigation focused on K. Vaiphei, diverting valuable resources and energy away from the actual perpetrators.

Firing at Ukhrul Treasury

It was 31 March, the last day of the financial year 1979-80. The Ukhrul Treasury, a non-banking institution holding a substantial cash reserve, bustled with activity. All bills sanctioned by the treasury needed to be settled in cash at the designated treasury counter. Departmental officials awaited the processing of their bills and the subsequent withdrawal of cash. As it marked the fiscal year's conclusion, the treasury's operations extended into the late evening, continuing after the sun had set.

Meanwhile, the Manipur Rifles (MR) jawans, entrusted with guarding the treasury, decided to create mischief and cause panic, or even intend to loot the cash. Suddenly, I heard a barrage of gunshots from the treasury side. At the same time, the Ukhrul SP rang me up to inform that gunshots were hitting his residence as well. To evade bullets, he had taken shelter under his bed. Although uncertain about the identity of the shooters, he confirmed that the loud sounds came from the treasury vicinity.

Swiftly responding, I contacted the commanding officer of the Assam Rifles for urgent assistance. Within 15 minutes, Major Sherawat of the Assam Rifles reached the spot with about 50 soldiers and surrounded the treasury complex. By 9 p.m., they had secured the treasury, enabling the departments to resume bill processing and cash withdrawals. Subsequently, the police arrested three inebriated MR jawans who had taken part in the gunfire.

While some suspected their intent to loot the treasury, I held a different perspective. I argued that if their aim was robbery, they could have harmed the treasury officer and staff, and stolen the cash, which they did not do. It seemed more likely to me that the MR jawans, influenced by alcohol, initiated the gunfire, possibly after an argument among themselves or with the treasury staff.

Adviser, Planning Commission, visits Ukhrul

Mrs P.P. Trivedi, IAS, serving as the Adviser, Planning Commission, visited Manipur to review the progress of development schemes. During her stay, she expressed a desire to visit a hill district, and fortunately, the state government chose Ukhrul as her destination. We meticulously organised her itinerary, including visits to inspect various schemes and engage in discussions with the district officers. We showed her the potential for pottery development in Nungbi, the efforts of women organisations in vegetable cultivation in Hungdung, and the prospects for the growth of the horticulture and handloom sectors.

In a meeting, I brought to her attention the Ningchou water supply scheme, which was non-functional due to unavailability of spare parts and diesel. I then told her the practicality of using hydrams in remote areas for irrigation and water supply needs. She attentively listened, being well-versed in the utilisation of hydrams in the hills of northern India. She asked me to prepare project reports for water supply schemes based on hydrams and submit them to her. I also presented the village-wise resource mapping and the draft of the Ukhrul District Development plan. Mrs Trivedi informed us that the Planning Commission was encouraging states to formulate district plans by consolidating village development plans. Extending her stay to two days instead of one, as initially planned, she encouraged us to focus on developing water supply schemes based on hydrams wherever feasible and to complete the Ukhrul District Development plan. She informed us that she would revisit Ukhrul.

Tea Amid Tiger Roars

I decided to visit Wahong, the farthest village in the north-western part of Ukhrul. The journey beyond Chingai was difficult as the *kacha* tracks were muddy. We had to cross the Chalou River and on the way, visit the New Tusom and Tusom Christian villages.

After navigating the rugged *kacha* tracks, by late evening, we reached the Lower Wahong village, nestled near a small stream at the foot of a hill. The original Wahong village is on top of the hill, a couple of kilometres away from the international border. Upon reaching the original Wahong village, enveloped by a dense forest, I discovered around 10 families residing there. It was already dark, and the hushed sounds of crickets and insects could be heard from the jungle. The village chief offered me a cup of tea while we sat around the fireplace at the centre of the house. As we sipped our tea, we heard loud roars. The chief told us that these were tigers' roars from the jungle.

Then the village chief proudly presented to me a trophy—the head of an animal he had hunted. The village chief then conveyed in Hindi, 'You are the first big officer to visit Wahong village. Neither Phizo nor Muivah has set foot in our village. All have forgotten us.' (Angami Zapu Phizo and Thuingaleng Muivah were Naga separatist leaders.) He expressed his joy at my visit, emphasising that while Lower Wahong had received visits from lower-level officials, the original Wahong had long been overlooked. That seemed to be his main grouse. I left his house after 9 p.m. The next day, I left for Soraphung, which is located amidst beautiful tall trees. This village has a unique feature—a big water body atop the hill.

I adopted a no-nonsense approach in the implementation of development schemes, and a specific case serves as an illustrative example. The headman of a neighbouring village of Ukhrul had secured a sanctioned scheme of about Rs 6 lakh for the construction of an irrigation channel and a boulder check dam. I got two to three recommendations from social workers to make the payment as the headman had already completed the required work by borrowing money. I decided to personally inspect the site along with engineers and field assistants.

Despite the headman's attempts to dissuade a physical inspection, citing the distant location and potential two-day journeys, I was adamant. The journey, though challenging, was not as extensive as it was made out to be. When we reached the site, we found only about a dozen boulders piled up. To my surprise, there was no check dam or irrigation channel; no actual work had been done. Assuming that the boulders were piled up by the headman from the water stream, I got those measured. Once back in office, we recorded entries in the Measurement Book (MB) to facilitate payment to the headman based on the supposedly completed work.

According to the Manipur Schedule of Rates (MSR), the total value of the work done at the site amounted to Rs 19.90 as against the estimate of Rs 6 lakh for the fully completed work! The headman had cut a sorry figure. Later that evening, I learnt that the headman had spent more than Rs 20,000 at Ukhrul and Imphal to get the project sanctioned. After that incident, the field staff in Ukhrul district refused to certify work completion reports without personally checking the actual sites.

Restart of Insurgency

During the intervening night of 12 and 13 February 1981, heavy rain poured over the region. Around 6.30 a.m. on 13 February, I was sitting in the outer drawing room of my residence, leisurely sipping tea. To my astonishment, I observed the national flag, which was always hoisted at the DC's residence, fluttering violently in the strong winds. Suddenly, before my eyes, the flag tore apart in a forceful gust of wind and fell down. Such a thing had never happened in the past. It seemed a bad omen. I immediately called the security guard and asked him to hoist a new national flag. Despite my reluctance to associate such incidents with omens, I couldn't help feeling uneasy.

Later that evening, around 5.45 p.m., I was standing in my compound. By then, the rain had stopped, revealing a clear sky. Suddenly, I heard gunshots from Khunjao, the old Ukhrul village. After a few seconds, I heard loud gunshots near Bob Pharmacy, just in front of my residence, and dogs barking. The gunfire was a mere 25 metres away from my location. In a matter of minutes, additional shots rang out from the Viewland area of Ukhrul. Such widespread firing in Ukhrul was highly unusual. I wondered how multiple locations in Ukhrul town could become the epicenter of gunfire. Shortly thereafter, I saw people running towards the Ukhrul police station. Within 10 minutes, the police informed me of multiple firing attacks in Ukhrul executed by the NSCN members. In Khunjao, an elderly NNC leader from Huime village had been shot and injured. In Viewland, two to three young men forcibly entered a residence, picked up a contractor from there, took him to the main road and shot him in the head, killing him then and there. The attack on a house behind Bob Pharmacy injured a person, though not fatally.

This was the restart of insurgency after the Shillong Accord of 1975. After a lapse of six years, 13 February 1981 was the day when insurgency started again in the state. At night and for the next day, Section 144 of the CrPC was imposed in Ukhrul town and surrounding areas. Security forces conducted thorough searches in Ukhrul and neighbouring areas, yet the elusive attackers seemed to have vanished into thin air.

In the wake of the insurgency's resurgence in February 1981, there were numerous incidents involving the killing of villagers by unidentified armed assailants. Tragedies unfolded in Lamlang Gate, Tusom, Paoyi, Ukhrul and many other villages, leaving the district's populace gripped with fear, uncertain about who might be the next target. Even behind my residence, a lifeless body riddled with bullet holes was discovered. One day, an unfamiliar gentleman came to my office and handed me an envelope before swiftly departing. Inside the envelope was a small booklet which contained information about a new organisation called the NSCN. Although uncertain of the motive behind sending me the booklet, I noted that the NSCN leadership therein repudiated the Shillong Accord. After this, the police posted an armed guard at my residence and advised me to take an armed escort while going outside Ukhrul to visit villages. I knew such security arrangement would not be able to protect me if I were on a potential hit list and if the militants planned to attack me. However, I received no direct or indirect threats from the militants or any other person.

The Tolloi villagers had planned to erect a big memorial stone to commemorate the silver jubilee of the unification of their two villages. However, due to security concerns, the Deputy Chief Minister, slated as the chief guest, could not attend. In light of this, the villagers requested me to preside over the function. Despite my own concerns, I attended Tolloi function with a modest police escort and found that it was a grand function. A big stone was erected near the playground to commemorate the 25 years of Tolloi village unification, and to my surprise and honour, my name was engraved on that stone. I think this was the biggest stone on which my name has been engraved anywhere in Manipur.

After his retirement from the IAS, S.M.H. Burney was appointed as Governor of Manipur. When he took charge, he expressed his desire to visit the hill district headquarters. For his visit to Ukhrul, I got a long list of essentials to be arranged for the Governor and his entourage. Deputy Chief Minister Rishang Keishing also graced Ukhrul with his presence for the Governor's meeting. I was advised to extend invitations to the headmen of all villages in the Ukhrul district to meet the Governor.

The meeting of headmen and village elders convened at the Tangkhul Naga Long (TNL) ground, where a special platform was erected for the Governor and Deputy Chief Minister. The Assam Rifles collaborated with the state police to ensure the security arrangements were robust. The Governor was seated in the middle, with me on his left and the Deputy Chief Minister on his right. It was an impressive gathering, and the meeting started on a positive note.

During the meeting, the Governor enquired whether armed militants were present among the gathered crowd. I told him that there could be. He expressed concern about the risk of firing from militants within the crowd. I assured him that the Governor and the DC were not their targets. Instead, political representatives with differing views from the insurgents were at greater risk. The Deputy Chief Minister, known for his staunch opposition to militants' activities, had been targeted by the militants in the past.

In a surprising turn, the Governor moved his chair towards me, distancing himself from the Deputy Chief Minister. However, the Deputy Chief Minister promptly followed suit, dragging his chair towards the Governor! Despite this momentary tension, the meeting went off peacefully, and both the Governor and Deputy Chief Minister delivered speeches. I couldn't help but reflect on Governor Burney's apparent lack of awareness regarding insurgent strategies, given his previous role as the Home Secretary of India.

Ruthless Killings

During my visit to Chingjaroi village, I halted at Paoyi, which is one of the biggest villages in this area. I had a meeting with the villagers where a member of the Ukhrul Autonomous District Council translated my speech. After the meeting, I went to Chingjaroi, stayed there overnight and returned to Ukhrul the next day. A few days after my visit to Paoyi, disturbing news reached me. It was reported that some unidentified men had shot the gentleman who translated my speech in Paoyi, killing him at once. A Nepali gentleman named Laxman, who had given me tea during the meeting, was also shot dead. Laxman, having learnt about the possible attempt on his life, had sought refuge by hiding on the roof among the rafters. However, he was discovered and shot while on the roof, leaving him hanging there. These incidents instilled intense fear among the general public, with uncertainty looming over who might be the next target of insurgents.

After sunset, a haunting silence blanketed the villages. The residents would lock their houses from inside. The incident in Tusom village was particularly harrowing, where four unidentified assailants forcibly pulled out two persons from their homes, bound them with ropes, took them about half a kilometre away from the village, and shot them dead. Shockingly, there was no resistance from any villager or the public. Such was the fear of insurgents.

In the year 1980-81, Mrs P.P. Trivedi, IAS, Adviser (State Plans) of the Planning Commission, visited Manipur again. Upon receiving a message, I met her in Imphal. After her meeting with state government officials, we held a meeting to delve into the projects outlined by the office of DC Ukhrul for water supply schemes and also the resource-based Ukhrul District Development plan. I provided detailed notes on the proposals for water supply schemes, including those based on hydrams, along with updates on other projects. I also explained our efforts to combat the spread of tuberculosis. Mrs Trivedi expressed regret that she couldn't revisit Ukhrul due to pressing matters in Delhi. Nevertheless, she was pleased with my work and encouraged me to continue the commendable work.

Ukhrul had been declared as a town by the state government. In the latter half of 1981, the SDO of Ukhrul oversaw the elections to choose the members of the Ukhrul Town Committee. Both the Indian National Congress and the Janata Party had contested the elections. The Janata Party got one seat more than the Congress. Additionally, the state government had the authority to nominate two persons from the unrepresented sections of the town. These nominations could potentially sway the balance of power and influence the election of the Ukhrul Town Committee chairman, who was subsequently chosen by the town committee members.

I was advised from Imphal to recommend the nomination of two persons from the Tangkhul tribe, but settled in Ukhrul from neighbouring villages. I thoroughly reviewed the regulations pertaining to the nominations multiple times. Following discussions with all relevant people, I recommended two persons from non-Naga communities (who were not represented by elected members) for nomination. The state government approved these two nominations. During the election for the Ukhrul Town Committee chairman, the nominated individuals abstained from voting. As a result, the Janata Party candidate was elected as the chairman of the Ukhrul Town Committee.

This decision displeased influential persons in Imphal, resulting in my transfer to Imphal. I handed over the charge of the office of the DC, Ukhrul, on 16 December 1981 and bid farewell to my staff. My wife and I left Ukhrul with heavy hearts, and I couldn't shake the feeling of being unjustly singled out for maintaining fairness and impartiality in the execution of my duties.

* A hydram, or hydraulic ram pump, is a water pump that uses the power of falling or moving water to pump water to a higher ground. Hydrams are self-powered and don't require electricity, generators, or wind to operate.

CHAPTER 16

Working in National and State Power Sectors

Experience in the Power Sector

In January 1982, I moved to New Delhi as part of a transfer to the Centre. I joined the Department of Power in the Ministry of Energy, Government of India. In this department, I managed various responsibilities related to rural electrification, power transmission systems, and the state electricity boards. My time here provided me with a diverse experience in the national power sector, and I fully utilised the opportunities presented to me.

I enjoyed working under Mr S. Venkitaramanan, an IAS officer who was the Secretary (Power). Known for his quick work disposal, he played a crucial role in introducing several groundbreaking schemes in the power sector. His initiatives included the adoption of high-voltage direct current (HVDC) in power transmission, the implementation of super-critical boilers, the utilisation of natural gas for power generation, and the introduction of combined cycle gas turbines in India. Moreover, he spearheaded renovation and modernisation schemes of thermal power-generating stations and the establishment of a national power grid.

Venkitaramanan was not a status-conscious bureaucrat. Notably down-to-earth, he once accompanied me to meet a section officer in the Ministry of Finance to discuss a case for foreign funding of a power project and to address the officer's concerns directly. He was business-like and not egoistic at all.

National Power Grid and HVDC in Power Transmission

In 1983-84, some states and regions in India experienced surplus of power for some hours, while others faced shortages. Unfortunately, there was no established mechanism to efficiently redistribute surplus power from regions with excess to those facing deficits. For example, surplus power in the eastern region at night went waste due to the lack of infrastructure to transmit it to the northern region, where it could have powered agricultural tubewells during nighttime.

To address this issue, the concept of a national power grid and regional power grids emerged. These grids were envisioned to facilitate the seamless transfer of power from one region to another. Subsequently, a proposal was set forth and approved to establish the National Power Transmission Corporation Ltd (NPTC), later renamed the Power Grid Corporation of India Limited (Powergrid). This entity would undertake the task of building and operating the national power grid.

A significant challenge hindering power transfer across regions was the variance in power frequencies among different grids. The initial solution involved the use of HVDC links. HVDC links were initially proposed between the northern region and the western region at the Vindhyachal and Singrauli super-thermal power stations of NTPC.

Subsequently, a proposal took shape to construct a 910-kilometre-long bipolar +500KV and -500KV HVDC line from Rihand to Dadri (near Delhi), to transmit 1500 MW of power. In April 1984, I was a member of the team that visited World Bank at Washington, and successfully negotiated a loan for the HVDC line and link. As the deputy secretary overseeing power transmission,

I took the lead and steered the HVDC projects through various levels within the Government of India.

A Lost Opportunity

In 1984, my name was proposed for an 18-month graduate study programme in 'Energy Policy and Management' at the Pennsylvania State University, USA. Unfortunately, the Department of Personnel and Training (DoP&T) of the Government of India did not grant approval for my participation on the ground that the programme was for engineers and not IAS officers. S. Venkitaramanan strongly believed that 'Energy Policy and Management' was useful to all involved in energy management, including IAS officers. He actively pursued the matter, advocating for my approval, reaching out to the Cabinet Secretary and even engaging with the PMO. But he was not successful. Eventually, he informed me that he would arrange an appointment for me with the then Prime Minister Indira Gandhi to discuss this issue personally whenever it materialised. Unfortunately, fate had other plans. Mrs Gandhi was tragically assassinated before I could meet her. The issue relating to my participation in the programme ended there.

Power Sector in Manipur

I returned to Manipur in June 1986 and assumed the role of secretary in charge of power, rural development and science and technology. At that time, the power sector in Manipur faced three significant challenges. Firstly, there were around 67 per cent power losses. Secondly, the power transmission and distribution grids at 132 KV and 33 KV levels were virtually non existent. Lastly, there was an issue of excess engagement of work-charged staff. The primary reasons for the high power losses included unmetered power supply, faulty metering, and power theft. The state had only one 132/33 KV substation at Yurembam near Imphal, with very few 33/11 KV substations. Both the 132 KV and 33 KV grids were almost non-existent. The government had irregularly appointed about 4,000 work-charged staff, leaving insufficient funds for essential projects. In addition, the department had invested in four small hydropower projects, all of which turned out to be failures.

During the annual plan allocation meetings, the Planning Commission consistently emphasised critical areas for the Manipur state government to address, with power loss reduction being a recurring topic. For the February 1987 Planning Commission meeting, Rishang Keishing, who had become the chief minister, took me along with other officers for finalising the annual plan allocation. The discussion focused on steps the state would take to reduce power losses. Rishang Keishing informed Deputy Chairman Dr Manmohan Singh that a new secretary had been appointed to the power department and he would bring about positive changes. He then introduced me to Dr Manmohan Singh. After addressing various matters, the meeting concluded with Rishang Keishing assuring Dr Manmohan Singh of the state government's commitment to reducing power losses. Dr Manmohan Singh came to me after the meeting, patted me on my back and advised me to improve the power sector in Manipur quickly.

The Greater Imphal area was responsible for consuming about 65 per cent of the total electricity in Manipur. I focused on checking power consumption by big consumers. To achieve this, special teams were formed, and senior officers were tasked with visiting all areas in Greater Imphal. In some cases, police personnel accompanied them to address instances of power theft.

There was strong resistance from some consumers during the special inspection drive. My strategy involved the formation of dedicated teams to scrutinise consumer premises, install new meters, and take legal action against those engaged in power theft. As positive results emerged over time, engineers began conducting raids on power theft hotspots. In areas where resistance was anticipated, I personally accompanied the special teams.

During one such incident, a raid aimed at disconnecting electricity at the private residence of a state minister in Imphal resulted in confrontation where bullets were fired at the officers.

Nevertheless, they persevered even in the face of gunfire from the minister's premises.

Close Encounter with Militants

One day, the finance department approved a proposal for constructing a grounding grid of a substation at Rs 36 lakh, a proposal I hadn't seen before. After I got it, I was pressurised to quickly convey government sanction to the chief engineer, power. Suspecting some mischief, I checked the market prices of the iron strips and pipes in Imphal and estimated the total cost of this work to be about Rs 12 lakh. With potential profits, it could reach only Rs 14 lakh, not the sanctioned Rs 36 lakh.

In the evening, two young boys (later identified as members of a militant organisation) visited my house. They urged me to immediately approve the proposal as they knew the contractor. With calculations in hand, I explained that the actual cost was not more than Rs 12 lakh. I expressed willingness to award the contract up to Rs 14 lakh but not at the inflated Rs 36 lakh. One of them noted down my calculation points, and they thanked me for clarifying. Before leaving, they advised me against approving the proposal at Rs 36 lakh. The next day, I heard that the contractor who was pursuing the work was beaten up for trying to defraud the government. They also warned the finance department officials and the minister to be careful in the future.

At the Power Ministers' Conference held in New Delhi in 1988-89, Manipur state garnered acclaim as the top performer in reducing power losses for the 1987-88 period, coinciding with my tenure as Secretary (Power). The state received an award comprising a shield, a Certificate of Distinguished Performance and a cash prize. Interestingly, at the time of the conference, I was pursuing the Master in Public Administration program at Harvard University. Subsequently, the president of the Manipur Electricity Department Employees' Union expressed gratitude in a letter to me, acknowledging my dedicated efforts towards enhancing the department's performance.

CHAPTER 17

Going to Harvard University

In October 1987, the Government of India, through the Manipur government, circulated a list of study programmes available to IAS officers for the upcoming year and invited applications from interested persons. I applied for the Master in Public Administration (MPA) programme in Public Policy and Management under the Edward S. Mason Program at Harvard University's John F. Kennedy School of Government. I was not hopeful that my application would be favourably considered, as there were many influential applicants for the programme.

To my pleasant surprise, on 6 January 1988, I received a letter from the Department of Personnel and Training (DoP&T), Government of India, to appear for an interview on 20 January in Delhi. The interview, conducted by a Board of Professors from Harvard, had six participants. Much to my delight, I was selected and placed on top of the list!

After the interview, I visited the DoP&T office in the North Block, where I met Jitesh Khosla, an IAS officer serving as an under-secretary in the Government of India. He was aware of my selection and enquired, 'How did you know Mrs P.P. Trivedi, the Secretary, DoP&T?' I told him that I met her in 1980-81 when she visited Ukhrul, where I was the DC. I also told him that she was very pleased with my work in the district.

During my visit to the DoP&T office, I learnt that more than 200 candidates from the IAS and other services had submitted applications for the Edward S. Mason Program at Harvard. To select persons for the programme, a Committee of Secretaries was formed under the DoP&T Secretary's purview. Additionally, I learnt that several recommendations had been made by certain Union ministers and governors. However, I had no one in higher places to put in a word for me.

It was only later that I discovered that my past work in Manipur had earned me a reward. The officer who appreciated and did not forget me was none other than Mrs P.P. Trivedi. Apparently, when the Committee of Secretaries met, Mrs Trivedi went through the list of applicants and personally selected me, placing me at the first position among the six chosen candidates. During this process, she reportedly commented on my excellent work in a remote district of Manipur during 1980-81. Mrs Trivedi still remembered her visits to Ukhrul district when she served as the Adviser in the Planning Commission.

To cover the full cost of study at Harvard, I was awarded the Ford Foundation Fellowship, as I had secured the top spot among the selected candidates. Four colleagues below me on the list received United Nations Development Programme (UNDP) Fellowships, though in slightly lesser amounts. In April 1988, I got a letter from Harvard University, admitting me into the MPA programme. I also got a letter from the Department of Economic Affairs, Ministry of Finance, offering me the Ford Foundation Fellowship to fund my studies. I could not have ever imagined in my wildest dreams that I would be selected for the Edward S. Mason Program and placed at number one in the list. My selection demonstrated that the government system works well, even though at some stage it could be manipulated. One just has to be patient and wait it out. I attributed my selection to the diligent efforts I invested while serving as the DC, as well as the innovative ideas I put forward for the implementation of water supply schemes in the hills, inspired by the dysfunctional water supply scheme in Ningchou village.

Study at Harvard University

In June 1988, I went to the USA and joined at Harvard University. Since there were adequate funds under the Ford Foundation Fellowship, my wife and sons, Paramjit Singh and Vikramjit Singh, accompanied me there. Harvard University, situated in the picturesque Cambridge town of Boston, Massachusetts, became our home. Notably, the renowned Massachusetts Institute of Technology (MIT) is also in Cambridge, about four kilometres from Harvard.

Our time in the USA proved to be an enriching experience. From June to August 1988, there was a refresher programme conducted by the Edward S. Mason Program office. During this period, the Mason Fellows were familiarised with the town and key locations in Massachusetts. We were also hosted by the family members of Robert F. Kennedy in Amherst. Harvard's MPA program is very flexible, allowing students to specialise in various areas such as energy, health, urban planning, etc. Furthermore, students had the option to take courses at MIT or any other school within Harvard, including the Harvard Business School.

Given my proficiency in mathematics and quantitative skills, I chose courses that aligned with my strengths. These courses included Applied Economic Analysis, Macroeconomic: Theory and Policy, Appraisal of Development Expenditure, Natural Resources Economics in Developing Countries, Analysis for Decision-Making, Financial Management, Budgeting and Control, International Development: Theory and Policy and Macroeconomic Policy in Developing Countries. I worked hard to excel at Harvard, prioritising my studies over personal comfort. This commitment paid off, as I got the highest scores in three courses: Applied Economic Analysis, Macroeconomic: Theory and Policy and Appraisal of Development Expenditure.

During the fall of 1988, I enrolled in the course M224 – Macroeconomic: Theory and Policy, taught by Professor Francis M. Bator, the distinguished Ford Foundation professor of political economy at the Kennedy School of Government. This course played a crucial role in enhancing my understanding of the impact of various fiscal and economic policies of the governments on economic development. I always approached every assignment with focused interest, meticulously presenting them in my best handwriting. A few times, Julia Monar, the Teaching Assistant (TA) of this course, advised me not to spend too much time on assignments, as these did not have any weightage in final grades. However, I continued doing them with the same zeal without bothering about their weightage in final grades. I fared extremely well in the final examination and was expecting to get the 'A' grade, the highest grade allotted to top rankers of the courses at the Kennedy School of Government. A few days after the final examination, I received a small note on a yellow slip (through my school mailbox) from the personal assistant of Professor Francis M. Bator, which read as follows:

'*Your grade in M224 Macroeconomic: Theory and Policy has been changed from A to +A. You may meet Prof. Francis Bator or me in office if you have any questions.*'

I was surprised and happy to get the note. The Kennedy School of Government adhered to the following grading system: A=4, -A=3.70, +B=3.30, B=3, -B=2.70, +C=2.3, C=2, D=1 and E=0. The highest grade 'A' carried four grade points. While I wasn't certain about the potential impact of a '+A' on upgrading grades in other courses from '-A' to 'A,' I decided to seek clarification from Professor Bator. During our meeting, I was thrilled to discover that I had achieved the top score, earning 97 out of 100 marks in the final examination for the course. What surprised me even more was that the marks of all the other students were less than 90.

The grading was determined through a probability distribution, and I learnt that if I were included in this distribution, I would be the only one to receive an 'A' grade. This led to the realisation that it would be unfair for the student just below me to receive a '-A,' as a certain percentage of students were to be assigned 'A,' '-A,' '+B,' 'B,' '-B' grades.

To rectify this, I was removed from the probability distribution, given '+A' grade, and the distribution was applied to the remaining class, excluding me. This unexpected turn of events not only resulted in me receiving a '+A' grade but also meant that some students below me were awarded 'A' grades. This was a pleasant surprise and boosted my confidence.

In February 1989, the Mason Program office arranged a tour of Nicaragua and Costa Rica for all Mason Fellows. We had the opportunity to meet the then President of Nicaragua Daniel Ortega, who expressed his discontent with the US administration. In his address, he highlighted the financial strain his government faced, citing the cost of US$1.37 for each bullet fired at the 'Contras' who were rebelling against his regime. The poor financial position had affected the infrastructure in Nicaragua. The roads were in a bad shape, with no signs of repair. We were also taken to a government-run fruit processing factory, where we observed inefficiencies in its operation. We also visited Lake Nicaragua, the largest lake in Central America, spanning 8,264 square kilometres.

In Costa Rica, we met President Oscar Arias and his cabinet ministers. A surprising revelation was that Costa Rica maintains peace with both its neighbours, Nicaragua and Panama, without having a standing army. The country showcased robust development, attracting numerous private investments.

During our meeting with President Arias, one of the Costa Rican ministers informed me about an Indian named Dharma Teja of the Jayanti Shipping Corporation who had become a resident of Costa Rica by investing the required funds in Costa Rica. I recalled reading Teja's name in Indian newspapers many years ago when he left India after defrauding the banks.

In mid-April 1989, a team from the World Bank visited the Kennedy School to interview prospective candidates interested in joining the organisation or undertaking assignments in various countries after their graduation. Despite not having initially applied for a position due to a different visa, I was approached by a member of the World Bank team during lunch in the school cafeteria. The team member enquired about my interest in interview for a World Bank assignment, to which I responded in the negative, explaining that I intended to return to India.

Intrigued, I questioned the reason behind the enquiry. The team member revealed that he had spoken with my professor, Glenn Jenkins, who taught 'Appraisal of Development Expenditure' course. Professor Jenkins had recommended me, the gentleman from India wearing a turban, as the best candidate for selection by the World Bank. While I was grateful to Professor Jenkins's endorsement, I remained committed to my desire to return to India and contribute to development work in Manipur.

A Touching Incident

During my time at Harvard, my family and I lived at Peabody Terrace, a housing complex of Harvard University near the Charles River. The area had recreational facilities, including a tennis court and park. My daily commute to the Kennedy School and back involved walking through this park. It was during these walks that I frequently came across an elderly couple seated on a bench.

One day, the gentleman spoke to me in Punjabi, inquiring about my background. He spoke Punjabi similar to that of the Malwa region in Indian Punjab, to which I belong. His fondness for conversing with me soon became apparent. He often mentioned that encountering a Sikh student at Harvard was a rare occurrence. He expressed joy when I wore turbans of different colours, as it reminded him of Punjab. Quite often, the old man would invite me to join him for a brief chat.

Despite my busy schedule, I sometimes yielded to his persistence and joined him on the bench for a conversation. He recounted stories of Punjab's renowned wrestlers, including Gamma Pehalwan (Gulam Mohammed Baksh Butt), Kikkar Singh, and Rohi Ram. He fondly reminisced about the vibrant yellow mustard and gold-coloured wheat fields, the cotton harvesting season, *desi* ghee and butter milk in Punjab. He even advised me to buy a jacket insulated with duck feathers to endure Boston's harsh winter.

Through our conversations, I learnt that he was a Muslim from a village near Patiala. He had migrated to Sakargarh in Pakistan, where he was allotted around 50 acres of agriculture land. He had four sons and two daughters. His three sons had migrated to the USA, and he followed with his wife and one unmarried son. While his married sons lived separately, he and his wife resided in a one-room apartment in a complex meant for the elderly near Peabody Terrace.

He often told me how content he was living in his village in Pakistan Punjab, cultivating his 50 acres of land. He had engaged a number of labourers who would work in his fields daily. In the USA, the cold Boston weather and a lonely life took a toll on him. To combat loneliness, he would sit in the park, eagerly waiting for someone to talk, often with little success.

Despite his desperate desire to talk to me, his sons, daughters-in-law and grandchildren seemed to have shown little interest in his stories of Punjab and Punjabi culture. He once invited us to his apartment and served *Kheer*, a Punjabi sweet dish.

On numerous occasions, I found tears welling in his eyes as he narrated memories of Punjab and lamented leaving his 50 acres in Sakargarh to live as a homeless person in the USA. Once, he sobbed so intensely in the park that I felt uncomfortable and gently wiped away his tears.

In December 1988, he suffered from heart problems and was hospitalised at Massachusetts General Hospital. He sent a message for me to visit him, but his younger son, concerned about my bad cold, advised against it. Unfortunately, he passed away a few days later. After his death, I often saw his wife, Rashida Begum, near Charles River Bridge, feeding the ducks.

Even today, I am deeply affected by the profound sense of loneliness felt by an elderly person who was uprooted in his later years and thrust into a completely new and unfamiliar environment. Sometimes, younger generations fail to understand the emotional attachment the elderly have to their roots and take arbitrary decisions.

An Amusing and Embarrassing Incident in Class

As part of my MPA program, I enrolled in the course 'Analysis for Decision Making', taught by Professor Michael O'Hare. The course focused on quantitative techniques applicable to public policy analysis—a skill set I deemed essential for civil servants dealing with real-life public issues in India's public administration.

While Professor O'Hare led the class, three Teaching Assistants (TAs) played a vital role in supplementing the teachings and guiding the students. The course comprised 10 case studies and assignments, which helped students in understanding various quantitative techniques. These exercises also illustrated the practical applications of these techniques in diverse field cases related to public policy issues. Given that these assignments carried significant weightage, accounting for 40 per cent of the final grades, completing them properly was paramount for students. Personally, I devoted my full attention to these assignments, not only striving for a higher score but also to understand and apply quantitative techniques to public policy issues upon my return to India.

Every Friday, one of the TAs would review the key concepts taught that week. On some Fridays, the TAs provided subtle hints about upcoming assignments and clarified doubts students had regarding the assignments. One particular incident during a TA session stands out in my memory.

One day, Professor O'Hare assigned a 15-page project centred on the 'Valuation of an Amusement and Wildlife Park' in the northwest USA. The assignment included intricate data, algorithms and considerations about various groups and communities, transportation costs, time spent in reaching the park, and wildlife valuation. Determined to approach the assignment strategically, I devoted significant time daily to understand the intricacies of data.

After a week, I attended the TA's class seeking subtle hints and clarifications. This assignment required the application of Laplace's Theorem, multi-criteria decision analysis, discounting and integral calculus. The TA, a PhD student from Harvard, guided the class through the assignment, occasionally asking questions to ensure we grasped the subject. About 10 minutes into the class, she asked if anyone could contribute to the next step. I eagerly raised my hand and was invited to the front to write the next step on the board.

I had practiced this assignment at home a few times. In my enthusiasm, I forgot the TA's instruction to write only one step and began solving the entire assignment. The class observed in complete silence as I continued writing the solution at a fast pace, completing the entire assignment in about 10 minutes.

After finishing, I looked back at the TA and the students. A moment of silence ensued, followed by uproarious laughter from all of them. Initially, I wondered if I had made any serious mistakes. The TA approached me and clarified that I had indeed solved the problem correctly but had misunderstood her instruction.

The TA then dismissed the class, acknowledging the completion of the assignment. I felt a little embarrassed and also happy. Later on, whenever I met that TA again, whether in the corridors of Kennedy School or elsewhere, she would often smile and jest about the incident, turning the amusing mishap into a memorable classroom tale.

Redesigning IAS Training Modules at LBSNAA

While at Harvard, on most holidays, I used to go for long morning runs along the Charles River, situated on the boundary of Cambridge and Boston. These were very refreshing. Throughout my studies at Harvard, my primary focus was on acquiring skills related to public policy analysis and decision-making. I frequently compared Harvard's educational approach with the training modules, exercises and methodologies employed at the LBSNAA for IAS officers. Harvard provided an environment where one could learn all policy analysis techniques and stay updated on the latest advancements in management science.

Motivated by a strong conviction of the need to improve the training modules for IAS officers at the LBSNAA, I wrote letters to the Secretary, DoP&T, Government of India, and the Director of LBSNAA, outlining my ideas for improvement. When I returned to Manipur, I received a letter from B.N. Yugandhar, an IAS officer who served as the joint director of the LBSNAA, inviting me to visit the IAS Academy and discuss my proposals for amending the training modules.

During my visits to LBSNAA, I advocated for a more hands-on approach and the inclusion of case exercises to enrich the officers' learning experience. I prepared a comprehensive brochure titled 'Public Policy Analysis Techniques', covering policy analysis techniques. The LBSNAA also issued an order appointing me as professor with the grade of a deputy director in the Academy. However, I could not join the LBSNAA as I was also the Chief Electoral Officer of Manipur. The Election Commission of India did not grant permission for my deputation to Mussoorie or for teaching a short module at the Academy.

Again to Harvard

In the academic year 1992-93, I returned to Harvard University for a year-long stint, enrolling as a regular student in the Graduate School of Arts and Sciences during both the fall of 1992 and the spring of 1993. Over these two semesters, I studied eight subjects relating to finance, economics and urban planning. I also worked as a TA for three graduate courses, when I got the opportunity to design case exercises for the students in these subjects.

During the winter break, from December 1992 to February 1993, I dedicated my time to preparing a manual titled 'Public Finance in Opening Economies', tailored for graduate students. Subsequently, from June to August 1993, I became a member of the then Harvard Institute for International Development (HIID) team which conducted a six-week program for international professionals focused on 'Project Investment Appraisal and Management' (PIAM).

This additional year of further study, coupled with my role as a TA and involvement with HIID in teaching PIAM to international professionals, bolstered my confidence and honed my skills in public policy analysis and decision-making.

CHAPTER 18

Significant Assignments

Joining the Prime Minister's Office

My time at Harvard University from 1988 to 1989 and again from 1992 to 1993, along with my field experiences in Manipur, played important roles in shaping my career and instilling the confidence in me to introduce innovations in public administration. In fact, this background facilitated my induction into the Prime Minister's Office (PMO) as joint secretary to the prime minister in 1996. Normally, the PMO does not invite applications; individuals are selected based on their records or personal acquaintances with senior officers. I had known B.N. Yugandhar since 1989, during his tenure as joint director at the LBSNAA in Mussoorie, where I had suggested improvements in the training modules for IAS officers. This seemed to have worked in my favour with Yugandhar who, by August 1996, became secretary to the prime minister and in charge of the selection of joint secretaries in the PMO.

My appointment in the PMO happened all of a sudden. On 9 August 1996, around 11 a.m., while serving as the commissioner of the PWD in the Government of Manipur, I was seated in my office in the North Block of the Manipur Secretariat when I heard a loud bomb blast. A bomb had been thrown on the road in front of the Secretariat Building and accountant general's office. From my office window, I saw an injured rickshaw driver on the ground. Onlookers were hesitant to approach him, fearing the presence of more live bombs.

After a few minutes, my focus was diverted when my private secretary, M.A. Khalique, informed me of a telephone call from the PMO. Initially, I presumed it might pertain to the frequent bomb blasts in Imphal, so I instructed Khalique to provide the contact details of the Manipur chief secretary. However, he conveyed that the PMO official specifically requested to speak with me directly.

When I answered the call, I was told that Yugandhar urgently wished to talk to me. After a few seconds, he was on the line and informed me that, after careful scrutiny of the biodatas of eligible joint secretary-level officers for appointment, I had been shortlisted for a posting as joint secretary to the prime minister. He enquired whether I was willing to join the PMO, to which I enthusiastically responded in affirmative. 'What incredible luck,' I thought, as joy overcame me and I practically jumped with excitement!

It appeared that my professional record had indeed spoken favourably for me. I considered myself lucky to secure a position in the highest office of India. Within a day, I received the official order from the establishment officer, DoP&T, Government of India, to assume the charge of joint secretary to the prime minister. It was a dream posting that filled me with immense happiness. It was not just a dream but a reality!

After spending a few days in Manipur, I joined the PMO, where I served for eight years (August 1996 to July 2004), setting a record for any joint secretary in the PMO at that time. During this period, I also had the privilege of working with four prime ministers—H.D. Deve Gowda, Inder Kumar Gujral, Atal Bihari Vajpayee and Dr Manmohan Singh.

On my very first day at the PMO, I received a firm advisory from Yugandhar stressing the zero-error standard of the office. I was cautioned not to make any mistakes or provide inaccurate data or figures while preparing notes and submitting files to the prime minister, as these could be referenced by him in public speeches or meetings. If there were uncertainties, I was instructed not to quote them and also not to present the matter for the prime minister's consideration.

In the PMO, I handled ministries and departments related to economic and infrastructure sectors, as well as issues pertaining to the North-eastern and southern states, and Jammu and Kashmir. It was in the PMO that I acquired insights into policy formulation and decision-making process at the highest levels in India. I used the skills that I had learnt at Harvard to the best of my abilities. It was during these eight years that the country witnessed substantial economic development initiatives across various sectors, including telecommunications, roads and highways, civil aviation, petroleum and natural gas, power, and ports, and an increased focus on the development of the North-eastern region. In fact, the tenure of Prime Minister Vajpayee, from March 1998 to May 2004, stands out as a 'Golden Era' for infrastructure and economic development in the history of India. I feel satisfied that I was associated with some important initiatives taken during that period, which I have described in my book, *With Four Prime Ministers—My PMO Journey*.

While working with each of the four prime ministers, what stood out the most to me was their remarkable listening skills. Whether in meetings or conferences, they listened attentively without interruptions. Throughout my eight years, not even once did I observe any prime minister interrupting or undermining a speaker. They had great respect for the viewpoints of those they engaged with. This experience led me to appreciate that listening is indeed an art. Those who lack the patience to listen to others may struggle to understand diverse perspectives and present balanced arguments. To be a true statesman, one must cultivate virtues such as patience, active listening, and an openness to appreciate differing viewpoints. In this aspect, I found all four prime ministers to be exemplary role models.

Back in Manipur as Chief Secretary

In the last week of July 2004, Manipur was shaken by serious violence following the alleged killing of Th. Manorama Devi by security forces. With the situation spiralling out of control, a high-level meeting was convened at the PMO on 5 August 2004, chaired by the prime minister, to deliberate on restoring normalcy in Manipur. In this meeting, it was agreed upon that major administrative changes, including the replacement of the Governor and chief secretary, were necessary. As a result, it was decided that I should return to Manipur and be posted as chief secretary.

I was promptly released from my duties at the PMO. I took over as the chief secretary of Manipur on 9 August 2004. At that time, the southern part of the state, comprising nine subdivisions and spanning around 8,900 square kilometres, resembled a 'liberated area', where militants held sway, influencing and dictating terms to the civil administration. The Governor of Manipur had even mentioned about these 'liberated areas' in his monthly reports to the Government of India.

To reclaim control over these 8,900 square kilometres and bring stability to the state, a unified command was established under the chief minister of Manipur. This unified command coordinated the efforts of the army, Central Reserve Police Force (CRPF), Assam Rifles, state police force, Border Security Force (BSF), and Intelligence Bureau (IB). I was made the chairman of the Special Operations Group (SOG), responsible for guiding and coordinating the day-to-day operations of various security agencies operating in the state. It took about three and a half years of concerted efforts to liberate these areas from the influence of militants.

Apart from addressing the law and order situation, I spearheaded initiatives to advance crucial infrastructure projects such as roads, power projects, and state capital projects. This included overseeing the construction of key structures such as the Manipur Legislative Assembly and the High Court of Manipur, as well as taking over and beautification of Kangla Fort complex and the construction of a state convention centre, among other endeavours. My education at Harvard had honed my skills and bolstered my self-confidence, motivating me to introduce several innovative measures in public administration in Manipur. In recognition of these initiatives, I was honoured with the 'Prime Minister's Award for Excellence in Public Administration for the Year 2007-08' on the Civil Services Day, 21 April 2009. I have chronicled my experiences, initiatives, and the challenges faced during my tenure in Manipur in my book *My Tryst With Manipur*.

In July 2008, when I handed over the charge of the chief secretary, I took pride in the restoration of normalcy in the state. Several important infrastructure projects were underway, the state's financial situation had stabilised, and the recruitment of state civil service officers (modelled after the UPSC) had been successfully initiated and completed. All newly recruited civil servants underwent training in national-level institutions. The implementation of a 'Computerised Personnel Information System' ensured that government employees were stationed in their designated posts which, in turn, enhanced the delivery of public services in remote hilly and rural areas.

Challenging Assignments Post-IAS Retirement

Averting Commonwealth Games Crisis

Just immediately after retiring from government service, I was appointed as the Chief Executive Officer (CEO) of the Organising Committee Commonwealth Games 2010 Delhi (OC CWG) in October 2009, with less than 11 months remaining before the Games commenced. This was my second assignment managing a crisis situation, the first being in August 2004 when I was appointed chief secretary of Manipur amid violent agitations in the state following the brutal killing of Th. Manorama Devi.

Despite India being awarded the Games in 2003, with the event scheduled for October 2010, the progress in preparation during the six years following the allotment was regrettably sluggish.

By October 2009, serious doubts had arisen about India's ability to successfully host the Games, with preparations way behind schedule and discussions even circulating about shifting the Games outside India. I used my expertise in contract management to efficiently address the impending tasks, working tirelessly under tremendous pressure throughout the 11 months till October 2010 to ensure the timely completion of the Games.

Restoring Normalcy in Manipur University

My third experience addressing a crisis situation occurred when I was appointed as the administrator of Manipur University (MU). The turmoil began in May 2018 when students, faculty and staff started a series of protests, demanding the removal of the university's vice-chancellor over allegations of maladministration. With both the Government of India and the state government unable to resolve the deadlock, MU was eventually closed on 31 May 2018. Tension escalated to the extent that in the midnight of 20/21 September 2018, the police raided the university to arrest students and teachers, pushing the situation beyond the possibility of returning to the negotiation table.

Concerned about the potential loss of an academic year of students and responding to Public Interest Litigations (PILs), the High Court of Manipur on 11 October 2018 appointed me as the administrator of MU with full powers of the vice-chancellor under all relevant statutes. The primary objective was to restore normalcy and resume academic activities.

I took charge as administrator of MU on 12 October 2018, and successfully started the academic activities within a week. During my 25-month tenure, I not only reinstated the institution's academic credibility but also opened six new departments, recruited the necessary faculty, and streamlined the university's financial management. These accomplishments have been documented in my book titled *Manipur University: Restoring Normalcy.*

CHAPTER 19

Reflections: Bitter and Sweet

My journey from a *jand* tree school in a remote village of Punjab to Harvard University involved hard work, perseverance and determination. Throughout this period, I was helped, encouraged and supported by numerous people, which included my maternal grandmother, parents, colleagues, friends, superiors as well as those I did not know well. Reflecting on these years, I feel satisfied with what I did, learnt and achieved. During this remarkable journey, there were ups and downs, moments of both sadness and joy, and instances of failure and success. Yet, I took all these in my stride and kept my aim straight and objective in clear focus. I did not sway from the path I had chosen.

When I started staying with my maternal grandmother in Kanjla, I was around five years old, while she was over 65. Throughout this period, I assisted her with household chores, many of which were not very easy to do, as detailed in earlier chapters. The period from 1954 to 1961 was tough, yet I never thought of it that way. In the company of my maternal grandmother, I was carefree and did not realise her financial struggles and helplessness. She provided me with whatever I requested, and I had my own circle of friends. Immersed in my studies at that time, I neither had the time nor the awareness to recognise my grandmother's relative poverty. I believed that our neighbours were friendly, and they never made me feel any sense of inequality, appreciating the way she looked after me. It was her nurturing support that allowed me to dedicate myself to my studies.

In those days, the rural communities of Punjab thrived on the camaraderie among neighbours. It was common for families to freely share agriculture implements and food, work together in each other's fields and offer help to one another. As my grandmother did not prepare vegetables every day for our meals, we relied on our neighbours. Not once did any of them refuse to help us.

In contrast to the present-day urban and rural lifestyle, where indifference and selfishness prevail, the past reflected a spirit of genuine cooperation, with neighbours coming forward to help those in need. My grandmother lived among well-off families, with their substantial landholdings and *pucca* houses, without having any feeling of inequality. The neighbours and most of the villagers empathised with her and supported her.

In my early years of schooling, my teachers emphasised the importance of having neat handwriting. It wasn't until later that I realised the usefulness of this lesson in my career in the IAS. Even during my time at Harvard University, numerous professors complimented me on my handwriting. From 1996 to 2004, when I served as joint secretary to the prime minister, my clear and legible handwriting garnered appreciation from the officials in the PMO and various ministries. I owe this achievement to my teachers, particularly Gurbachan Singh.

Hard Work, Sincerity and Resolve Reap Rewards

Hard work, sincerity and determination are crucial in any endeavour, including one's professional pursuits. I worked hard during my school years and throughout my time at the engineering college. At PEC, Chandigarh, I consistently ranked among the top achievers mainly because of my perseverance. These efforts resulted in high scores, fostering a sense of confidence in me. When I resigned from my permanent job as a Sub-Divisional Engineer on 5 May 1973, just after 20 days of joining, and returned to Chandigarh to prepare for the Combined Competitive Examination (CCE) of 1973, it was only because of the confidence I had in myself. My never-say-die spirit helped me to strive. Even during my tenure in the IAS, I worked with equal zeal and dedication, and was always rewarded for my hard work.

Turning Points

There were some incidents and circumstances that significantly altered the course of my life. The first occurred in 1954 when I insisted on accompanying my maternal grandmother to Kanjla and staying with her. Luckily, the local school there provided me with a strong educational foundation. The second turning point transpired with the delayed declaration of my pre-engineering (Class XII) examination result because of which, as a late applicant, I could not join the MSc Physics programme and instead joined the engineering college. However, later developments proved that pursuing an engineering degree better aligned with my career growth. The third pivotal moment unfolded in 1972 when Professor K.K. Suri of PEC called me to his room, where the external examiner of the nuclear physics paper advised me to prepare for the CCE. The fourth and perhaps the most crucial turning point was the allotment of the Manipur cadre to me for serving in the IAS, where I got excellent treatment, cooperation and ample opportunities to grow as well as innovate.

As mentioned earlier, in 1980-81, during Mrs P.P. Trivedi's visit to Ukhrul, she was impressed by my sincerity and the successful implementation of development schemes that I undertook as the DC. Later on in 1987-88, when she was secretary, DoP&T, she chaired a meeting of the Committee of Secretaries for selecting candidates for the Edward S. Mason Program at Harvard University. It was because of her appreciation of my work in Ukhrul that she placed me at number one in the list of five selected persons out of over 200 applicants. I owe my selection to her, and I cherish the fact that she remembered and acknowledged my contributions even after seven years of her visit to Ukhrul.

It is truly heartening to find supportive and appreciative people in every corner and in every system. A sincere and hardworking person is bound to receive encouragement from such people. Right from my childhood till I retired from the IAS, I got motivation and help from numerous persons, often from unexpected quarters. Among those who played important roles in my life were Durga Parshad, the headmaster of the Kanjla school, Professors M.S. Ghumman and K.K. Suri of the Punjab Engineering College, Chandigarh, who encouraged me to appear in the CCE, and S. Venkitaramanan, the then Secretary (Power), for encouraging me to enhance my skills in public policy analysis and decision-making.

Believing in Oneself

At the midpoint of my engineering degree programme, I had emerged as one of the top-ranked students in the college. This accomplishment was primarily attributed to my punctuality in attending classes and completion of assigned work within deadlines. This not only bolstered my confidence but also fostered a growing belief in my capabilities. It was only because of my self-belief that I did not apply for jobs after completing my Bachelor's degree in engineering whereas most of my colleagues had started working. I completed my Master's degree, further enhancing my qualifications, and gave my best shot at the CCE. Later on, the study at Harvard University, significantly increased my self-confidence, empowering me to introduce innovative practices in public administration and leave a lasting impact.

When I was allotted the Manipur-Tripura cadre of the IAS in November 1974, I was disappointed. During those days, being alloted to any North-eastern state or cadre in an All India Service was viewed as a punishment. Since there was no alternative, I came to Manipur. I got the opportunity to work in the remote hill areas of the state. I undertook extensive journeys on foot, sometimes spanning weeks, through the interior regions of Senapati, Ukhrul and Chandel districts, where I stayed in villages. These travels allowed me to witness firsthand the difficulties faced by villagers and recognise the untapped potential for development. Later on, this knowledge and insights gained during these travels became invaluable in the strategic planning of infrastructure projects such as roads, power stations and water supply schemes for these areas. It was my visit to the remote Ningchou village (now part of Kamjong district) in 1980 which brought good luck for me. It was in Ningchou village that I decided to use hydrams to provide drinking water to villages as the diesel engine-operated schemes used to be out of action for months together. Later on, the idea of the use of hydrams for drinking water supply schemes and the preparation of better village development plans helped in my selection in the Edward S. Mason Program for MPA at the John F. Kennedy School of Government of Harvard University. I attribute my selection to the hard work and dedication I demonstrated from 1979 to 1981.

Good times are fleeting, not permanently bestowed upon any person, society or country. Life consists of both highs and lows in a cyclic fashion. Just as societies degenerate and create their own downfall during prosperous times, bad times have the power to shake established systems, compelling people to summon courage, innovate and overcome adversity. This cyclic law of nature is inevitable and visible globally. The duration of these cycles varies—some enduring for years, decades or even centuries, while others could be relatively short-lived. It is one's determination, perseverance, hard work and sincerity in pursuing goals that shape their ultimate destiny.

Benefits from Studying at Harvard

During my study at Harvard, I acquired valuable skills in public policy analysis and decision-making. These skills significantly enhanced my performance at both the state and national levels. It was only because of my expertise in these areas that I got the opportunity to serve in the PMO for eight years with four prime ministers of different political ideologies—two prime ministers belonged to the United Front, one to the Bharatiya Janata Party and one to the Indian National Congress. My political neutrality and focus on work enabled me to function impartially and deliver my best. During this period, I was associated with policymaking at the national level when decisions were taken to open up important sectors of the Indian economy. Reflecting on this experience, I derive a sense of fulfillment from knowing that my contributions played a role in the development of crucial sectors of the economy.

Qualities Needed in Public Service

I have had a long career in public service. I equipped myself with public policy analysis and decision-making skills during my time at Harvard, and applied these skills in various capacities throughout my service. Recognising the potential impact of utilising these skills to address real-life public policy issues, I strived to make more informed and effective decisions. Even in situations where risks were present, these skills have proven instrumental in reducing and managing risks for all stakeholders involved.

Beyond the significance of policy analysis and decision-making skills, a civil servant should possess other equally essential qualities of both intellect and empathy. Throughout my career, I have remained mindful of these attributes while diligently performing my duties and responsibilities. The important qualities are:

A: Quick Decision-Making: Those in the know understand that prompt and timely decisions are the essence of public administration. I firmly believe that delayed decision-making fosters corruption. When decisions are postponed, people often impute motives to the delays. Some may even be tempted to intentionally prolong the process for personal gain. To curb such tendencies, I made it a practice to address files and papers requiring decisions or information-sharing within minutes. This commitment has ensured that my workspace remains free of pending files, as I consider each file a representation of lives of individuals and families that deserve swift attention.

B: **Attentive Listening:** When people approach a public office, they usually seek assistance in resolving their problems or addressing specific issues. It's uncommon for a person to visit a public office without a legitimate reason. By attentively listening to these individuals within the welcoming atmosphere of the office, they can share their burdens and find some solace. Keeping this in mind, I always made myself available to meet with anyone seeking my attention, ensuring careful listening. Even if I couldn't address their issues within the existing rules, it allowed me to identify issues that might require alternative approaches or solutions.

C: Composure in all Situations: As a figure of authority, people often turn to you for assistance or guidance, and it is a privilege to hold such a position. Maintaining composure is crucial, especially when people may not be fully familiar with rules and procedures. It's important to avoid becoming upset when someone repeatedly seeks your help. Throughout my 45 years of service, I never allowed myself to lose my temper with anyone in my office. I patiently listened to those who approached me with their concerns. Even if my colleagues or public figures became upset during meetings and left after uttering unpleasant words, I chose not to react. In every instance, they returned to apologise for their behaviour. Maintaining a calm demeanour and never losing your temper puts you on a higher pedestal than others.

D: Take Pride in Your Knowledge, But Remain Humble: Always seek opportunities to learn and generously share your knowledge with others. The world is vast, and there will always be individuals with greater knowledge than you. Our commitment to learning allows us to glean valuable information from seasoned individuals, regardless of their hierarchical positions. Many persons in lower-level positions have amassed years of valuable experience. Embrace the chance to learn from both experienced colleagues and academic institutions, as this will make you an invaluable asset of any organisation. Always be proud of your knowledge, but steer clear of arrogance, as arrogance and knowledge cannot go side by side.

E: Foster a Culture of Helpfulness and Kindness: Serving as a civil servant is a privilege, and it is our responsibility to demonstrate our worthiness of that honour. Extend assistance within the confines of established rules and procedures. The support from authorities goes a long way in building goodwill. Displaying kindness is a key quality that the public, in general, values in bureaucrats. A civil servant should have interactions with the public or colleagues with patience and handle their matters with empathy. This conduct will not only enhance public confidence in civil services but also contribute to the efficiency of overall delivery system.

F: Innovate Wherever You Can: The routine of a civil servant's life can become monotonous within the confines of the office. A plethora of rules and regulations, some dating back 30 to 40 years, shapes the administrative landscape. Meanwhile, there have been major technological advancements in the work environment, leading to evolving public expectations from the government, shifts in methodologies for project proposal formation, implementation of projects and programmes, and the flow of information, among other aspects. A civil servant's career spans around 35 years, during which they observe and participate in significant transformations. It is crucial for them to take a proactive approach in introducing innovations that improve the work environment, accountability mechanisms, and methods for delivering public services. Instead of adhering to the administrative status quo from their initial days of service, they should actively contribute to improving the system through changes and innovations, fostering a more effective work environment, before retirement.

A Pleasant Incident

I am narrating a small incident relating to the time when I served as the chief secretary of Manipur. This incident highlights the significance of patiently listening to individuals seeking to meet a civil servant and making quick decisions. Such actions not only help in gaining the confidence of the people but also contribute to bolstering the administration's credibility.

One day, an MLA came to meet me and shared a pleasant experience he had while waiting in the chief secretary's reception area. Alongside him, there were about half a dozen other people also waiting to meet me. When it was finally his turn, the MLA entered my office and asked me about the conversations that I had with those who visited me. Before I could respond, he revealed that he had been discreetly observing those entering and exiting my office. To his surprise, he noted that visitors who, while entering my office appeared serious or concerned, left with smiles on their faces. Intrigued, he sought to understand the nature of my interactions with them.

I told the MLA that when visitors entered my office, I warmly welcomed them, offered them seats, and listened carefully to their concerns. I helped them immediately if their requests fell within the purview of the rules. However, for those beyond the rules or seemingly impractical, I explained the reasons for my inability to help them. By engaging with visitors in this manner, the majority left my office reasonably satisfied.

Continuing Sharing My Knowledge

I served in the IAS for over 35 years, and after retiring in September 2009, I held prominent positions in a couple of organisations for about a decade. Whether within the government or beyond, I always tried to give my best, be it in the remote hilly areas of Manipur or at the highest office in the country, such as the PMO. I faced challenges head-on, such as handling the crisis during the Commonwealth Games in October 2010 or restoring normalcy in Manipur University in October 2018.

Throughout my career, I integrated administrative prowess with compassion and integrity, which delivered results. My approach involved attentive listening to others, quick resolution of matters, maintaining composure even in provocative situations, fearlessly operating within the rules, remaining politically neutral, and introducing innovative practices in public administration. These characteristics have been the defining features of my career. My administrative style has not only garnered appreciation but also instilled credibility in the organisations I have been part of.

During my time at Harvard, I focused on and excelled in the study of Appraisal of Development Expenditure. Additionally, I also actively contributed to the team of the then Harvard Institute for International Development, which conducted programmes for professionals from different countries on Project Investment Appraisal and Management.

Recognising the need to enhance capacity building in project appraisal in India, I established my own company called Project Appraisal Consultants LLP (LLP stands for Limited Liability Partnership). Since August 2012, I have been conducting programmes for professionals in Project Appraisal, Risk Analysis and Risk Management. Furthermore, in collaboration with my colleague, Dr Deo Narayan Sharma Dhakal, I co-authored a book titled *Project Appraisal, Risk Analysis and Risk Management Techniques* in December 2022, which addresses crucial gaps in decision-making in this field.

My area of specialisation lies in 'Project Appraisal', and I consistently update my knowledge in this domain while developing new case exercises for my programmes. Given my expertise, I am often invited to speak at institutes conducting programmes related to this subject. I find great satisfaction and fulfillment in sharing my insights on project appraisal with both students and professionals, and it keeps me actively engaged.

Looking forward, I hope to continue this endeavour for as long as I can, reflecting on a life that I have lived to the fullest.

Index